THE CHALLENGE OF TOURISM CARRYING CAPACITY ASSESSMENT

New Directions in Tourism Analysis

Series Editors: Kevin Meethan, University of Plymouth
Dimitri Ioannides, Southwest Missouri State University

Although tourism is becoming increasingly popular as both a taught subject and an area for empirical investigation, the theoretical underpinnings of many approaches have tended to be eclectic and somewhat underdeveloped. However, recent developments indicate that the field of tourism studies is beginning to develop in a more theoretically informed manner, but this has not yet been matched by current publications.

The aim of this series is to fill this gap with high quality monographs or edited collections that seek to develop tourism analysis at both theoretical and substantive levels using approaches which are broadly derived from allied social science disciplines such as Sociology, Social Anthropology, Human and Social Geography, and Cultural Studies. As tourism studies covers a wide range of activities and sub fields, certain areas such as Hospitality Management and Business, which are already well provided for, would be excluded. The series will therefore fill a gap in the current overall pattern of publication.

Suggested themes to be covered by the series, either singly or in combination, include – consumption; cultural change; development; gender; globalisation; political economy; social theory; sustainability.

Also in the series

New Directions in Rural Tourism
Edited by Derek Hall, Lesley Roberts and Morag Mitchell
ISBN 0 7546 3633 X

Tasting Tourism: Travelling for Food and Drink
Priscilla Boniface
ISBN 0 7546 3514 7

Tourism and Economic Development
Case Studies from the Indian Ocean Region
Edited by R.N. Ghosh, M.A.B. Siddique and R. Gabbay
ISBN 0 7546 3053 6

The Challenge of Tourism Carrying Capacity Assessment

Theory and Practice

Edited by
HARRY COCCOSSIS and ALEXANDRA MEXA

ASHGATE

Published by
Ashgate Publishing Limited
Gower House
Croft Road
Aldershot
Hants GU11 3HR
England

Ashgate Publishing Company
Suite 420
101 Cherry Street
Burlington, VT 05401-4405
USA

Ashgate website: http://www.ashgate.com

British Library Cataloguing in Publication Data
The challenge of tourism carrying capacity assessment :
    theory and practice. - (New directions in tourism analysis)
    1. Ecotourism 2. Tourism - Social aspects 3. Tourism -
    Economic aspects
    I. Coccossis, Harry, 1950- II. Mexa, Alexandra
    338.4'791

Library of Congress Cataloging-in-Publication Data
The challenge of tourism carrying capacity assessment : theory and practice / [edited by]
    Harry Coccossis and Alexandra Mexa.
        p. cm. -- (New directions in tourism analysis)
    Includes bibliographical references and indexes.
    ISBN 0-7546-3569-4
        1. Tourism--Economic aspects--Europe. 2. Tourism--Europe--Management. I.
Coccossis, Harry, 1950- II. Mexa, Alexandra. III. Series.

G155.E8C495 2004
338.4'79140456--dc22

2003064706

ISBN 0 7546 3569 4

Printed and bound in Great Britain by MPG Books Ltd, Bodmin, Cornwall

Contents

PART II: DEFINING AND IMPLEMENTING TOURISM CARRYING CAPACITY IN SELECTED TYPES OF TOURIST DESTINATIONS

List of Figures

List of Tables

List of Contributors

Prof. Jan van der Borg: Department of Economics, University of Venice and EURICUR, Erasmus University Rotterdam, San Giobbe 873, 30 121 Venice, Italy.

Prof. Richard W. Butler: School of Management, University of Surrey, Guildford, Surrey, GU2 7XH, United Kingdom.

Prof. Harry Coccossis: Department of Planning and Regional Development, University of Thessaly, Argonafton and Filellinon, 38 334, Volos, Greece.

Anna Collovini: Department of Planning and Regional Development, Environment and Spatial Planning Laboratory, University of Thessaly, Argonafton and Filellinon, 38 334, Volos, Greece.

Dr. Giorgos Kallis: Department of Planning and Regional Development, Environment and Spatial Planning Laboratory, University of Thessaly, Argonafton and Filellinon, 38 334, Volos, Greece.

Dr. Alexandra Mexa: Department of Marine Sciences, University of the Aegean, University Hill, 81 100 Mytilene, Lesvos, Greece.

Thymio Papayannis: Senior Consultant, Mediterranean Institute for Nature and Anthropos, 23 Voucourestiou Street, 10 671 Athens, Greece.

Dr. Apostolos Parpairis: Department of Planning and Regional Development, University of Thessaly, Argonafton and Filellinon, 38 334 Volos, Greece.

Prof. Michael Scoullos: Department of Chemistry, DIV III, Environmental and Marine Chemistry, University of Athens, Panepistimioupolis, 157 71 Athens, Greece.
Mediterranean Information Office for Environment, Culture and Sustainable Development (MIO-ECSDE), Chairman, 28, Tripodon str., 105 58 Athens, Greece.

Prof. Jan van der Straaten: Saxifraga Foundation, Bredaseweg 335, 5037 LC Tilburg, The Netherlands.

Ivica Trumbic: Director, Priority Actions Programme Regional Activity Centre, Mediterranean Action Plan, United Nations Environment Programme, Kraj Sv. Ivana 11, 21 000 Split, Croatia.

Introduction

Tourism is incontestably a key economic activity for many European countries and regions. Europe has long been a leading world destination benefiting from a rich cultural heritage and environmental diversity, but also from a longstanding tradition in high quality services and infrastructure (for example hotels, airports). Tourism provides opportunities for local and regional development but as it grows it exerts pressures on environmental and cultural resources and often alters the social and economic structures, the characteristics and functioning of resorts, towns and villages and in general affects the quality of life in tourist destinations. Seasonal peaks, either in the winter, summer or in national holidays accentuate such problems. In addition, these negative impacts may affect the very basis for tourist attraction and the tourist activity itself.

Many European destinations are facing such problems already and the pressures are likely to increase in view of the anticipated growth of tourism in Europe. The emergence of new tourist destinations, in Europe and further afield, is likely to intensify pressures on existing destinations to keep their position in a competitive market by facing their problems caused by tourism growth. Already several mature destinations (cities, coastal or mountain resorts) are taking action to diversify their tourist product in an effort to keep or even expand their clientele. Opportunities for further development are sought since tourism remains a vital factor for local employment and income. Evidence from practice indicates that in most cases the response to the problems and impacts from tourism (for example environmental) has been reactive and remedial. Pro-growth attitudes still prevail even when, due to the increasing numbers of visitors and their activities, the area is facing problems. In the very few cases where active policies are pursued to control the growth of tourism the emphasis is still on short-term management of pressing and urgent critical problems, with a priority on costly infrastructure investments and less on managing the causes of these problems often rooted in growth patterns.

It is evident however that tourism needs to be developed in accordance with certain principles, which focus on managing and controlling tourism growth respecting the capacity of local systems to sustain such growth. This orientation is also dictated by contemporary general concerns about the ways communities develop and grow, seeking a balanced way among economic efficiency, social equity and environmental conservation, a broader strategy towards sustainable development.

Controlling tourism growth becomes a central policy issue in this context bringing forward the issue of tourist carrying capacity or 'how much tourism can be acceptable' in a tourist destination. Tourism Carrying Capacity Assessment

(TCCA), with the aim to identify and impose limits, can be valuable in planning for sustainable tourism.

TCCA is not a new concept. It appeared in scientific literature in the sixties with an emphasis on the ecological limits, and it gradually evolved so as to include socio-cultural and economic aspects. This evolution has been accompanied by significant criticism, which gave birth to alternative approaches, implicitly or explicitly alluding to the need of imposing some kind of limits on the number of tourists, or on their activities. Most of the conventional analyses are based on the predominant model of mass tourism, probably because in the last thirty years or so this model was responsible for many of the problems encountered. However recent tourism demand and supply changes suggest a diversification of tourist products and the need to change the way we conceive tourism policy interventions. TCCA needs to be regarded more as a management tool and less as a rigid technique which could lead to the definition of a unique numeric value. Furthermore defining tourism carrying capacity needs to take into account the particularities of the tourist destination and the characteristics of tourism demand. So, from a policy perspective it is inevitable to distinguish tourism carrying capacity assessment among various types of tourist destinations, such as *coastal areas, islands, mountain resorts, cultural sites and cities and areas of significant ecological significance.* This *typology* is based on similarities (demonstrated for example among cultural cities throughout Europe) and in terms of characteristics (of both the area and the type of tourism development), problems, policy issues, etc., facilitating not only the assessment of limits but furthermore their implementation. In practice, the implementation of tourism carrying capacity assessment has been easier in the case of areas of ecological value, since they conform to the prevailing concerns for conservation of natural and cultural heritage.

The purpose of this volume is to review the concept of tourism carrying capacity assessment, highlight the methodological aspects in respect to defining, measuring and evaluating tourism carrying capacity for various types of tourist destinations and seek its relation to a comprehensive methodological framework for tourism carrying capacity assessment. Furthermore the book aims at presenting the experience from implementing TCCA mainly in *European* tourist destinations – with special reference to the Mediterranean region – and, on the basis of the lessons learnt, at drawing some conclusions regarding measurement and implementation of TCCA.

Many of the contributions are developed in the context of a special research project on 'Defining, Measuring and Evaluating Carrying Capacity in European Tourist Destinations' financed by the European Commission (DG Environment) (http://europa.eu.int/comm./environment/iczm/tcca_material.pdf).

The project involved the analysis of various scientific approaches and methodologies developed to define TCC, a review of indicators developed to assess and implement carrying capacity, the analysis of key limiting factors for tourism development for different types of tourist destinations in European countries in respect to carrying capacity components, based on review of case studies, the elaboration of a methodology for defining and implementing TCC, the formulation of policy guidelines for implementation and finally the selection on the basis of certain criteria (types of tourist destinations, types of environmental problems, etc.) of case studies (either sites where tourism carrying capacity could be appropriate as a tool for managing pressures from tourism development or sites where TCCA has been already implemented) and detailed descriptions of them.

A Workshop with invited international experts (many of whom are authors of chapters in this book) was organized in Athens in September 2001 to discuss the problems related to tourism flows, the limiting factors for tourism development and the environmental thresholds and the experience from managing tourism and in particular from implementing carrying capacity in various types of tourist destinations (rural areas, natural areas, cultural cities, etc.).

The book is addressed to academics, researchers, planning and tourism practitioners, policy-makers, scientists and public administrators dealing with environment, tourism development and planning issues, who wish to learn more about the TCCA approach, from both a theoretical and a practical point of view.

The book consists of two parts. The first, under the title 'Methodological Issues in Respect to Defining, Measuring and Evaluating Tourism Carrying Capacity', includes six chapters and the second, under the title 'Defining and Implementing Tourism Carrying Capacity in Selected Types of Tourist Destinations', eight chapters. The first part focuses, as suggested by the title, on the methodological aspects in respect to defining, measuring and evaluating carrying capacity as well as on the implementation of TCCA.

The *first chapter* highlights some of the major changes in the tourism industry, revealing both quantitative and qualitative aspects (for example growth prospects, new forms of tourism). These changes often reflect broader socio-economic changes on the demand and supply side (for example preference for high quality services and products). Changes are also evidenced in the policy and institutional field and in the responses of the tourism industry. All these suggest the need to look at carrying capacity in the context of broader policies and priorities. The *second chapter* discusses the concept of limits and compares it with alternative views of sustainability. New elements that need to be introduced in capacity assessment are revealed, reflecting the so-called co-evolutionary perspective of society and nature. Both chapters (first and second) provide a broader perspective on the issue of carrying capacity enriching in this respect the analysis that follows. *Chapter three* highlights some of the main issues that have been subject of criticism and the limitations of tourism carrying capacity assessment as identified by various researchers. The authors suggest another perspective at looking at these limitations (mentioned as inherent characteristics) supporting the idea that TCCA remains still a useful concept that can be valuable in managing tourism development. *Chapter four* attempts to provide a methodological framework for measuring tourism carrying capacity following a process similar to a planning process for tourism development; the integration of these two processes – of TCCA and of planning for tourism development – is suggested by the authors. The framework although rather analytical should be considered as indicative of how TCCA may be approached; it does not intend to appear as the 'proper' or the only way of identifying limits on tourism development. *Chapter five* provides insight on the implementation issues of TCCA. In the first part a short overview of the various tools that have been applied for TCCA is included with the note that several of them have been developed and used for natural conservation, tourism and environmental management; they can however provide good services in applying TCCA. In the second part of this chapter some factors to be considered in implementing tourism carrying capacity are discussed (the changing role of the state, the increasing role of the private sector and so on) suggesting that all these changes or factors need to be considered before deciding on the tools to be utilised, since this selection will affect the implementation of tourism carrying capacity and eventually tourism development. *Chapter six* provides a 'bridge' between the first more 'theoretical part' and the second part of this book which focuses more on the experience regarding the implementation of tourism carrying capacity. Some theoretical aspects are discussed in respect to the debate of environmental economists over environmental externalities, which provide the basis for arguing about capacity limits. Reference is made to several cases, which demonstrate the way that the basic principle of TCCA, that of identifying some kinds of limits, has influenced several policy decisions throughout Europe. Carrying capacity can serve as a framework for taking some critical policy decisions even though capacity limits are not always clearly set in advance.

The second part of this book discusses some of the experiences regarding the application of Tourism Carrying Capacity Assessment. Traditionally second 'parts' host experience from practice, allowing readers to learn more on particular problems, approaches, models, etc. In this case although specific cases are described the various contributions continue to build on the theoretical aspects discussed in the first part of this volume. The discussion concerns various types of tourist destinations, mainly areas with ecological value and rural areas, heritage cities and sites, coastal areas and islands. Mountain tourism is partially presented in *chapter six* and *chapter thirteen*. The main argument that emerges is that different types of destinations may require a different or a differentiated approach in applying tourism carrying capacity. In *chapter seven* the experience notably from the development of recreational activities in the United Kingdom is presented. Reference to various cases (for example National Parks) with a description of the particular problems confronted and the management responses to them are made. In spite of all limitations related to tourism carrying capacity assessment the need to continue studying carrying capacity and searching for acceptable maximum levels of use is confirmed. *Chapter eight* focuses on the case of areas with ecological importance (for example wetlands), highlighting the experience from the Mediterranean basin. The experience from these cases is greater, as the attempts to limit human intervention and preserve ecosystems have multiplied at least during the past decades. A description of an 'appropriate approach' of managing tourism in areas with ecological value is provided while the idea of a more 'operational' determination of TCCA based on a careful and on-going monitoring is supported. In *chapter nine* the various issues regarding tourism development in heritage cities (providing evidence from seven European art cities) are discussed. A quantitative methodology for measuring carrying capacity is presented along with the implications of limits. Special reference to Venice and the use of some management tools such as the Venice Card is made. Chapters ten and eleven refer to two types of particularly popular destinations, that of coastal areas and islands. *Chapter ten* provides an overview of the long experience of the Priority Actions Programme in implementing tourism carrying capacity assessment in the Mediterranean region. Some case studies are described. Emphasis is placed on the integration of TCCA into the process of Integrated Management of Coastal Areas. In *chapter eleven* the particular case of the island of Myconos, a rather famous tourist resort located in the central Aegean, is used as an example so as to make reference to island particularities and to the need to adopt some limits to tourism growth so as to safeguard their unique ecological and cultural heritage. In *chapter twelve* the case of another Greek island, that of Rhodes, is used so as to discuss a significant issue in implementing tourism carrying capacity, that of actors, participation and of the integration of TCCA into a participatory process for shaping a strategic vision for tourism development. In *chapter thirteen* an overview of the characteristics of tourism development in Europe is provided, with a special emphasis on the impacts provoked by tourism development The presentation of these impacts is organized in two ways: presentation of ecological, socio-cultural and economic impacts and presentation of impacts for each type of tourist destination (coastal, rural, etc.). In the second part of this contribution reference to selected case studies, which have either applied TCCA in an explicit or in an implicit manner (adoption of measures, which reflect the major concerns of the carrying capacity concept), is made. Evidence from actual implementation of TCCA is rather limited, 'uneven' with the attention that the approach has gained. *Chapter fourteen* hosts some reflections in respect to the future implications of some major policy development (regarding for example new forms of governance for tourism carrying capacity assessment).

This volume intends to contribute to the scientific and policy debate on Tourism Carrying Capacity in the context of tourism policy. It reflects international thinking and practice, focusing on already developed tourist destinations in the European context, representing already developed policy contexts at a national/regional level and developed decentralized administration systems at a local/regional level. In that sense it is not intended to become a book of Guidelines or Good Practice for developing countries or areas. The European experience however can be used as a benchmark in such cases as well. This volumes wishes to support the use of tourism carrying capacity, suggesting that there is a need to re-approach the concept taking into account broader policy developments, for example planning for sustainable development. It discusses methodological issues in the light of this new evidence and suggests that there is a need to encourage further implementation of TCCA in an effort to promote sustainable tourism development.

The editors would wish to thank many individuals and institutions who provided assistance and support for this book and particularly Ms Theoni Dede for her valuable contribution in putting this volume together.

Harry Coccossis and Alexandra Mexa
Athens

PART I
METHODOLOGICAL ISSUES IN RESPECT TO DEFINING, MEASURING AND EVALUATING TOURISM CARRYING CAPACITY

PART I

Chapter 1

Sustainable Tourism and Carrying Capacity: A New Context

Harry Coccossis

Tourism, Impacts of Tourism and Tourism Carrying Capacity

Tourism is a complex socioeconomic phenomenon based on the growing needs of modern societies for recreation and leisure and has become a major economic activity worldwide and a priority field in policy making at local, regional, national, supranational and international level. It is the result – and a cause – of wide sweeping changes in modern societies with far-reaching consequences for both developed and developing economies (Vellas, 2002). Its spatial extent, in the past involving a few world regions, is becoming increasingly global reaching even far distant places.

International tourism has tripled in 25 years (1975-2000) and according to recent forecasts (WTO, 2001) it will continue to grow, more than doubling in the next twenty years (around 2020). Europe is a primary destination for tourists as it concentrates about 60 per cent of international arrivals (403.3 million in 2000) at global scale and in spite of new destinations emerging around the world it is likely to continue to represent the largest tourist market. Contemporary estimates foresee a doubling of tourist arrivals in European destinations in the next twenty years or so (WTO, 2001).

The spectacular growth of tourism has brought its potential to the attention of policy makers, but also the problems it generates. Tourism as a complex of economic activities has the advantage of having multiple linkages to a wide range of other economic sectors and activities, thus having the potential to act as a catalyst for economic development due to its eventual multiplier effects. At national level it contributes to the balance of payments, but also provides employment and investments. At a local and regional level it offers opportunities for employment and income spurring regional and local economic development, which might be unique for many small and distant places.

An ever-growing number of countries, regions and local communities around the world compete to attract tourism and secure its multiple benefits. The last few decades have brought ample evidence of a proliferation of policies to develop tourism. In the majority of cases such efforts are sectorally driven in the sense that they focus on a single economic activity perspective with little if any concern over cross-sectoral issues, which in the case of tourism are important (for example in relation to agriculture and fishing, transport, construction, finance and banking services, etc.). Public policies for tourism often focus on stimulating tourism by also providing the essential conditions for tourism growth (such as infrastructure, training, promotion, regulation of services, etc.). To a large extent this orientation reflects the early developing stage of tourism. As tourism destinations grow and mature there is increasing concern with managing the impacts of tourism.

Tourism often has significant impacts on the environment, social and economic structures and dynamics, as well as on culture and lifestyles. However not all of tourism's impacts are always beneficial. There can be negative effects on demographic characteristics, social structures and relations, economic activity structures and sectoral dynamics, societal values and attitudes, culture, built environment and land use, natural and cultural heritage, environmental resources, and so on. Not all of the impacts attributed to tourism are due to tourism alone as there are often indirect effects (through the other activities and sectors influencing society, economy and the environment) which might be more important or other broader transformations and processes (such as globalization, mass culture, modernization, etc.), which may be triggered by tourism, as a fast-growing activity with multiple linkages. Tourism, as a dynamic and growing activity, competes with other activities and sectors for labour, investments, infrastructure, land, water, energy and other resources. Growth and competition often lead to displacement and dominance, sometimes leading to 'monoculture', abandonment and risks. The negative impacts of tourism might be quite significant for some areas depending on their size and tourism's relative importance and growth. Sometimes the negative impacts from tourism might have negative feedback effects on the tourist activity itself, particularly when it affects the very basis of its growth and existence, the tourist assets and tourist experience. Tourism depends on the quality of the sociocultural and natural environment as well as on the quality of services provided, both essential components of tourism attraction, particularly in an increasingly competitive world economy.

As a consequence it is not surprising that a growing number of countries, regions and local communities are increasingly concerned about the impacts of tourism and adopt policies to confront the problems which tourism generates. While early attempts at policy making focused on establishing the basic conditions for tourism development (i.e. infrastructure, services, etc.) relying on traditional instruments (i.e. economic incentives, regulatory controls over land development and land use, etc.), it became apparent that a broader perspective was needed to incorporate cross-sectoral and 'system-wide' issues. It also became apparent that a pro-active policy was necessary to take into consideration the social, economic and environmental aspects of tourism development and their interactions, evidenced in terms of spatial development patterns. Anticipating and managing the impacts of tourism and its growth became a central issue in national, regional and local policy making.

Any type of activity usually has impacts of varying kinds on a system. The key question is whether these impacts are significant or not, in order to take remedial action or act early in anticipation of impacts. Significance is a matter of relative assessment and this brings up two kinds of questions: 'in relation to what?' and 'how much is enough?', reflecting on the types of impacts and their relative magnitude. Both of these issues have been central to the concept of 'tourism carrying capacity' in tourism planning and management. Assessing the impacts of tourism became a central policy issue, as well as establishing the mechanisms and tools to cope with such impacts.

The concept of tourism carrying capacity has been under consideration for at least as long as there has been increasing concern about the impacts of tourism. It stems from a perception that tourism cannot grow forever in a place without causing irreversible damage to the local system, whether expressed in social, economic or environmental terms (in the wide sense, including the built environment). Therefore there should be limits on tourism development in a place (size, intensity, etc.). The concept can be interpreted and used in many ways. For some types of destinations, such as protected areas, natural parks, archaeological sites, small beaches, etc., the interpretation of capacity can be related to crowding, that is the number of people present at a given period of time. So, tourism carrying capacity can be the maximum number of people who can use a site without causing an unacceptable alteration to the physical environment (natural and man-made) and without an unacceptable decline in the quality of the experience gained by visitors. If applied to a large geographical area (such as an island, a historic settlement or town, a region, etc.) the concept may acquire a broader significance so as to express a maximum acceptable tourist development (number of beds, hotels, mooring places, etc.) on the basis of the capacity of key resources (such as beaches, land area, energy, water, etc.) or infrastructure (such as ski lifts, etc.).

There are basically three dimensions (*environmental*, social and economic) in tourism carrying capacity assessment: environmental limits can be assessed in terms of ecological or physical parameters (the capacity of natural resources, ecosystems and infrastructure), *social* in terms of psychological and sociocultural aspects (visitor enjoyment, resident population tolerance, crime, etc.) and *economic*, in terms of the losses in the diversity of activities in a place and monoculture, but also unemployment, etc. In practice, there is a broad range of factors and issues which shape capacity levels reflecting the characteristics of the place, the type(s) of tourism and the tourism/local system interface (Coccossis, 2002). In reality there is a complex pattern of interaction among limits or capacity thresholds (Pearce, 1989). Capacity levels, expressed as a function of limits or thresholds can be real or perceived, and may change as a result of functional adaptation, or social intervention through organizational or technological measures.

The particular value of tourism carrying capacity as a concept is that it can be used in policy making as well, as a basis for making decisions about measures to control tourism development and growth. For example, in visitor management inside a protected and managed area it can be a basis for making decisions about taking control measures (such as entrance fees, restrictions of access and use, etc.). In tourism development planning, carrying capacity can be used as a planning standard, benchmark or planning scenario, as the maximum acceptable level of tourist development in an area, measured in terms of number of beds and desirable densities. On the basis of that number, associated infrastructure and related urban development can then be projected. In development planning, tourism carrying capacity can be a central concept in a process of seeking (and selecting) 'appropriate' (desirable, acceptable, feasible, and so forth) types of development, measured in terms of size of tourist activity, linkages to other sectors, tourist/inhabitant relations, and so on. In environmental management, carrying capacity is a central concept in environmental impact assessment, therefore tourism carrying capacity can be linked to environmental degradation, measured in terms of loss of biodiversity, degradation of natural resources, threats to species, and so on. It can guide decisions on land use and activity restrictions, environmental standards, appropriate technology and other policy measures.

Tourism carrying capacity is a versatile concept and as such it can be used in a variety of functions in planning and policy making (assessment, goal identification, alternative strategy formulation, raising awareness, consensus building, and so on). In spite of its versatility though, its application in practice is limited, probably reflecting a number of reasons: methodological difficulties in measuring and assessing multi-dimensional and complex issues, political difficulties in accepting limits to development (particularly for a dynamic and growing activity such as tourism), societal difficulties to arrive at common 'visions', administrative inertia in adopting innovative concepts in policy making, fragmentation of decision making and difficulties in policy coordination and integration and many more. Of course many of these reasons reflect broader deficiencies of modern societies in policy making. However, there are positive signs that the policy context is changing to encompass sustainability, policy integration and governance, concepts which are compatible with the basic assumptions of considering multiple dimensions in integrated assessment, goal setting, policy development and policy evaluation. Such changes are likely to support the adoption and application (measuring, assessment and policy decisions) of integrative concepts such as tourism carrying capacity.

A Changing Policy Context

The compiling environmental problems have led modern societies to reconsider their development paths and options. To face such problems in earlier periods such as the seventies, basic environmental legislation was gradually developed and adopted addressing specific thematic problems (as for example, species protection, sea pollution, water waste treatment, etc.). Subsequently environmental policy was enriched to reflect improvements in understanding the complexity of environmental issues leading to the adoption of broader concepts such as ecosystem protection, environmental impact assessment, etc. Environmental policy was linked to development policy in the sense of mitigating impacts. Environmental problems were perceived as unwanted outcomes of human activities and the development of economic sectors. The environment was considered by many as antithetical to development. It soon became apparent though that to a great extent development prospects depend on environmental quality, that nature protection is essential not only on ethical grounds but because natural systems support human activities, resource protection is essential for the long-term support of human activity and the quality of life in cities and rural areas is directly linked to environmental quality. Protecting the environment was conceived as intricately linked to social and economic development. To symbolize such a shift in thinking the international community adopted a new term: sustainable development (WCED, 1987), officially endorsed at the World Conference on Environment and Development at Rio de Janeiro (1992). Sustainable development recognizes the need to balance the three basic goals: economic efficiency, social equity and environmental conservation. So, it became apparent that environmental policy was as important as social and economic policy. The concept of sustainable development in the past decade or so has influenced the way sectoral policies are pursued, as in the case of tourism.

There is still no wide agreement on sustainable development. There are various interpretations of sustainability (soft vs. hard, etc.), depending on the determinism attributed to ecological issues, as there are also varying interpretations of sustainable development, depending on the relative weight in balancing the three basic goals. Consequently there can be various interpretations of sustainable tourism whether the priority is on sustaining growth of the activity or protecting the environment. However it seems that in the end there is a convergence towards an interpretation which bases sustainable tourism on the capacity to integrate tourism policy in a broader strategy for sustainable development. This means that tourism related goals, objectives and measures are defined in relation to their impacts and interaction (complementarities, conflicts and synergies) to other sectors and dimensions (social, economic, environmental) looking at the system as a whole (Coccossis, 1996). Sustainable tourism seems to be moving beyond greening of tourism products towards integrating environmental concerns in tourism management and planning (Godfrey, 1998).

Although the environmental impacts of tourism have been an area of policy concern at an international level since the early eighties (UNEP, 1986), it was in the nineties that there was a special focus on sustainable tourism as evidenced by a proliferation of activities, initiatives and political declarations (such as the Charter for Tourism and Sustainable Development in Lanzarote in 1995, the Agenda 21 for the Travel and Tourism Industry in 1996, the Global Code of Ethics for Tourism in 1999, etc.). This was in some ways a direct outcome of the Earth Summit at Rio (1992) where the focus was placed on prioritizing the environmental dimension of tourism impacts. This led towards strengthening environmental action within the sector and strengthening environmental legislation to take account of tourism impacts. In the process, the tourist industry and environmental NGOs, countries, regions and communities undertook various initiatives towards making tourism more sensitive to environmental issues. Ten years later, the World Summit for Sustainable Development (held in Johannesburg in 2002) reinstated sustainable tourism development as a primary concern in the Plan of Implementation but the significance of WSSD was that social and economic development issues were brought forward, as environmental issues were in 1992. Sustainable tourism development is directly linked to protecting and managing the environment as a basis for social and economic development. This shift probably reflects a growing concern with the side effects of economic development policies adding social issues to the agenda (such as poverty and tourism development), linking social issues to environmental management (such as resource conservation and poverty). Such a shift also underlines a receding priority on efforts towards environmental policy as an increasingly complex system of international agreements (Conventions, Protocols, etc.) is gradually put in place and national legislation on environmental policy is expanding. Although sustainable tourism is an issue in the agenda it is probably seen through a slightly different perspective highlighting some horizontal issues such as poverty and sustainable production and consumption patterns. The latter refers to the need for fundamental changes in the ways societies produce and consume in achieving global sustainable development. This brings a new perspective on sustainable tourism as it touches on some of its key characteristics: seasonality, saturation and carrying capacity.

At a European level (EU) sustainable development of tourism has become a priority at least from an environmental policy perspective since the mid-nineties (for example in the Fifth Action Programme for the Environment) in spite of the lack of specific European policy for tourism. Recently, the European Sustainable Development Strategy (adopted in Gothenburg in 2001) highlights as basic orientation the integration of environmental concerns in sectoral policies, which is a more radical stance compared to adopting environmental policies in response to the impacts from economic development. This shift is also likely to affect the way sustainable tourism is interpreted. Already, the basic orientations for the sustainability of European tourism (EC, 2003) – which are still in a consultation process – consider the sustainability of tourism as concerning corporate responsibility, opportunities for all citizens to participate in tourism, employment opportunities in the sector and benefits from tourism for local communities, integration of environmental concerns in tourism policies, participation of all the stakeholders in the context of good governance, etc. The major challenge for European tourism is how to manage tourism growth in respect of the limits of the resource base and the capacity of resources to regenerate while maintaining the activity's competitiveness (EC, 2003). So, carrying capacity is central to European tourism policy. It actually explicitly features in one of the measures to be considered by the Commission in the sense of refining carrying capacity analysis and implementing the concept in European tourist destinations (ibid, p.19).

Another shift in policy orientation which is also relevant for sustainable tourism is an increasing reliance and interest at the tourist destination level. This is the outcome of general trends and specificities relating to tourism. Overall modern societies, particularly on the European continent, are moving towards decentralized decision-making systems where the local and regional level become increasingly strengthened by transferring to them a widening range of responsibilities. Within the EU this is based also through the subsidiarity principle. In the case of tourism, although it is a global phenomenon and the industry is increasingly responding to economic globalization forces, the impacts of tourism are mostly evident at the local/regional level. Managing these impacts falls within the competencies of local/regional authorities (for example infrastructure development, land use regulation, environmental impact assessment, etc.) and tourism becomes increasingly integrated in local area (community) management (Haywood, 1989). Even from a sectoral point of view a lot of interest in recent tourism management literature focuses on 'destination management' (Dredge, 1999). Therefore it is at this level that a lot of attention is focusing on sustainable tourism (Westlake, 1995, WTO, 1998) as evidenced by a growing number of initiatives (for example through Local Agenda 21). Tourism growth, saturation and carrying capacity become central issues in this context particularly for mature destinations. However, many of the problems of tourism and certainly seeking a sustainable tourism strategy surpass the capacities of local/regional authorities alone to confront them as several other actors are still important, many outside the area.

Contemporary international thinking and European policy (EC, 2001) introduce another dimension which is also relevant for sustainable tourism: governance. It is a new way of shaping policies following the basic principles of openness, participation, accountability, effectiveness and coherence. Tourism has multiple linkages and impacts, therefore there is a wide variety of stakeholders that may need to be involved in sustainable tourism. Inevitably managing a complex process of sustainable tourism policy has to follow certain basic principles and rules and governance offers a reasonable platform. Sustainable tourism is not an automatic outcome of governmental regulation concerning environmental protection (performance standards, environmental management infrastructure, EIA, etc.) and the private sector initiatives towards environmentally friendly practices (EMAS, etc.). It is a matter of bringing in a dialogue towards concerted action, all stakeholders ensuring that cross-sectoral issues are taken into consideration in a long-term perspective about sustainable tourism. This highlights a shift from reliance on the public sector to provide the basic framework for sustainable tourism to realizing its limitations in capturing and implementing a holistic perspective towards mobilizing all possible actors in a puzzle of concerted actions. If carrying capacity is conceived as a means to formulate 'visions' and strategies about the future for tourism taking into consideration the basic sustainable development principles (such as respect to capacity of natural resources, and so on) then it can be useful as a means towards good governance, leading to sustainable tourism.

Changes in Tourism Activity

The changing policy context for tourism towards sustainable development is in many respects reflecting changes in tourism. The tourist demand is changing. A number of such changes are expected to have a major impact on sustainable tourism (EC, 2003). So far, the dominant model has been mass tourism, which in many ways reflects the needs and organizational structures of the early phases of tourism. In spite of the tremendous growth observed and the long period passed since then, the organized movements of tourists for leisure on the basis of low prices represent the bulk of tourism. Although this type of tourism is likely to represent the largest share even in the future it would be worth examining some qualitative changes which are of interest in a perspective of sustainable tourism, particularly in discussing tourism carrying capacity.

Contemporary societies are characterized by increasing individualism and priority on freedom of choice. Mass media, travel, the Internet (e-commerce) and other organizational and technological improvements have rapidly expanded the amount of information available on places, activities and lifestyles, so choices have expanded. The perception of the needs for leisure is not constrained anymore to the basics: a place in the sun on the seaside, vacations once a year, etc. Contemporary tourists have multiple needs (relaxation plus culture, health, and so on) nowadays and increasing demands. Many are not first time visitors and as experienced tourists they can compare places, look for better options which satisfy multiple needs and new preferences. There will be further growth of special types of tourism. There would be pressures for the tourism product to become increasingly complex, diversified and of high quality. This would require careful management of tourism destinations.

The travel intensity will increase further as a larger part of the population will be able to travel and the trips are expected to become shorter and more frequent. As a consequence it is expected that pressures (concentration, congestion, etc.) on destinations are likely to become more intensive and recurrent. The increased mobility and the special interests are likely to increase the social-economic and ecological 'footprint' of tourism, linking tourist destinations with their hinterland, spreading the spatial patterns of the activity and strengthening the 'gate' role of some destinations, therefore further increasing the flows and the pressures.

Choices would have to be made on local capacities to cope with the growth of tourism. Carrying capacity is likely to become a central concern in tourism management particularly for several types of destinations (historic towns, small islands, natural parks, etc.). Selective tourism is likely to grow faster particularly oriented towards places with rich natural and cultural heritage. Places which should be protected are likely to face increasing pressures. These are probably the destinations which most need a strategy which will base tourism growth on carrying capacity assessment. Pressures on existing tourist destinations which can remain competitive are likely to intensify further, requiring putting together effective tourism management to cope with increasing pressures. In parallel, new destinations are likely to emerge, not always ready to cope with the pressures of tourism.

This would require careful assessment of strengths, weaknesses, opportunities and threats from tourism growth and development in the context of sustainable development. Destinations would have to become competitive, putting together a coherent strategy. A central element of such a strategy could be tourism carrying capacity assessment. It would assist in maintaining the level of development and use without serious environmental deterioration, social and economic problems or decreasing the perceived tourist enjoyment of the area (WTO, 1998).

Carrying Capacity Revisited

The changes in tourism and anticipated tourism growth suggest that the impacts on destinations are likely to become complex, more intensive but also more widespread in geographic space. In addition, increasing competition and progressively more complex policy framework affect tourism policy in the context of sustainable development strategies. Across Europe pressures on tourism destinations are expected to increase to develop their own mechanisms and strategies towards sustainable development. Within this context tourism carrying capacity assessment can be a useful concept in tourism destination planning and management. However, the changing policy context and the qualitative changes in tourism activity suggest also that perhaps the way we look at tourism carrying capacity assessment should change as well.

Traditional approaches to tourism carrying capacity are based on some key assumptions which need to be revisited and revised:

- *Mass tourism as a basic model*, meaning relative homogeneous tourist behaviour and tourist development patterns which lead to certain specific types of pressures (seasonality, spatial concentration, etc.) on land and natural resources, therefore to specific types of impacts (crowding, large visitor flows, etc.). The emerging specific types (special interest) of tourists have different values and expectations, a wide range of varying patterns of use of facilities, space and time, and very different types of impacts from mass tourism. Environmental quality and quality of services are valued higher, influencing also the perception of impacts and stance over eventual limits to growth.
- *Impacts* are often perceived in terms of utilization of resources (including land as space for development) in a simple PSI (Pressure-State-Impact) model (using part of the widely used model) which is a-spatial and a-temporal in the sense that there is no recognition of the spatio-temporal dynamics involved. Furthermore, the perception of impacts (positive or negative) might be different for, and by, different types of tourists, therefore a range of impacts have to be taken into consideration for a range of user groups with differences in values.

- *Limits* or thresholds as expressions of 'capacity' are conceived in static quantitative terms – on the basis of peaks and maximum loads – and do not reflect necessarily the particularities of the life-cycle of tourist destinations (i.e. the cumulative effects) nor the qualitative characteristics of tourism or processes (i.e. social adaptation). Limits, or capacities, may be of different type from season to season as the types of tourists (or their activity patterns) might be different.

Capacity has to be seen as a dynamic concept with spatio-temporal characteristics, expressed in various ways over time and from place to place within a destination. As destinations cater to a widening range of types of tourism – to broaden their tourist base, season, etc. – it is more and more difficult to identify single thresholds and express them in a concise and simple manner. For example, while in the past (mass) tourists were moving in an organized manner (i.e. bus) when visiting places, modern tourists, using mainly their private cars, have more diffuse (and less spatially focused) patterns. Therefore, thresholds and capacities can be expressed in a number of different ways at different periods of time. The conception of capacity has to be broadened from 'numbers of tourists' to incorporate the types of tourism and their activity patterns. Dealing with 'peak' conditions in 'points in space' does not necessarily provide a good guidance to the capacity issue. It could be that the duration of impacts might be as important as well as their timing in relation to critical periods or conditions, particularly in protected areas. As the impacts of tourism become increasingly indirect diffuse and less distinct, therefore policies for tourism become more and more enmeshed with local and regional development policies.

The role of carrying capacity is changing. It has been developed as a concept around the issue of limits as a central concern leading to regulation and control of the growth of tourism. Often 'limits' may not act as predicted, in other words as deterring or controlling growth. In many tourist places, a higher level of regulatory control (for example on the basis of carrying capacity) instead of limiting growth as intended it has led to an opposite effect of attracting further growth, perceived as guaranteeing high quality environments, as in the case of many Mediterranean islands, historic cities, etc. Sometimes capacity constraints, for example, 'crowding' might become a tourist 'asset' – and attraction – for some types of tourists (for example the young and active, cosmopolitan, etc.) as is the case with Mykonos, Ibiza, etc., where people go, just 'to be there'. So there are important feedback effects which suggest revisiting the way that tourism carrying capacity is used in tourism management and planning. Whether real or perceived, limits can stimulate communities to take action at a destination level in terms of considering future options and developing local strategies for sustainable development. Decisions on limits are increasingly to be sought in terms of complex processes of pressures, impacts, responses and feedbacks. In this context carrying capacity has to be sought intricately woven in a mechanism of monitoring and evaluation in a cyclical process of management and planning.

The above are just some of the issues which need to be addressed in adapting tourism carrying capacity assessment to a changing tourism activity and policy environment. However, as a conceptual tool carrying capacity cannot overcome many of the inherent open policy issues in tourism management and planning as for example, the issue of identifying and assessing impacts. Many of the impacts attributed to tourism stem from broader forces of change, as already noted, therefore to a great extent 'carrying capacity' has to reflect concerns about wider development/society-economy-environment issues and be integrated in a context of 'sustainable development'. Carrying capacity has been used in tourism management and planning but in a contemporary perspective it has a much broader significance which is at the center of the search for sustainable development strategies.

Whether it is worth the ambiguity and the trouble remains to be seen in practice.

References

Coccossis, H. (1996), 'Tourism and Sustainability: Perspectives and Implications' in Priestley, G.K., Edwards, J.A., Coccossis, H. (eds), *Sustainable Tourism? European Experience*, CAB International, Wallingford, UK, pp. 1-21.

Coccossis, H. (2002), 'Tourism Development and Carrying Capacity', in Apostolopoulos G. and Gayle D. (eds), *Island Tourism and Sustainable Development: Caribbean, Pacific and Mediterranean Experiences*, Praeger, Westport, Connecticut, pp. 131-144.

Dredge, D. (1999), 'Destination Place Planning and Design', *Annals of Tourism Research*, 26(4), pp. 772-791.

European Commission (EC) (2001), *European Governance: A White Paper*, COM 428 final, Brussels, p. 35.

European Commission (EC) (2003), *Basic Orientations for the Sustainability of European Tourism*, Consultation Document Brussels.

Godfrey, K. (1998), 'Attitudes Torwards "Sustainable Tourism" in the UK: A View from Local Government', *Tourism Management*, Vol 19 (3), pp. 213- 224.

Haywood, K.M. (1989), 'Responsible and Responsive Approach to Tourism Planning in the Community', *Tourism Management* 9(2), pp. 105-18.

Pearce, D. (1989), *Tourist Development*, Longman Scientific and Technical, Essex.

Vellas, F. (2002), *Economie et Politique du Tourisme International*, Economica, Paris.

Westlake, J. (1995) 'Planning for Tourism at Local Level: Maintaining the Balance with the Environment' in Coccossis, H. and Nijkamp, P. (eds), *Sustainable Tourism Development* Avebury, Aldershot, UK, pp. 85-90.

World Commission on Environment and Development (WCED) (1987), *Our Common Future*, Oxford University Press, Oxford.

World Tourism Organization (WTO) (1998), *Guide for Local Authorities on Developing Sustainable Tourism*, WTO, Madrid.

World Tourism Organization (WTO) (2001), *Global Forecasts and Profiles of Market Segments*, Tourism 2020 Vision, Vol. 7, WTO, Madrid.

Chapter 2

Theoretical Reflections on Limits, Efficiency and Sustainability: Implications for Tourism Carrying Capacity

Giorgos Kallis and Harry Coccossis

Introduction

The concept of carrying capacity is rooted in a notion of 'limits to growth'. The discussion for and against limits has been going on for over three decades and has been central in the debate for the interpretation and implementation of the concept of 'sustainability'. This chapter turns to a more fundamental, theoretical examination of the concept of limits and compares it with alternative views of sustainability attempting to relate it to issues of tourism carrying capacity. This debate on sustainability is caught in what Norgaard (1994) has called the confrontation between the two mal-adaptive determinisms of 'ecologism' (limits) versus 'economism' (efficiency). Our argument is that moving towards sustainability is neither about staying passively within 'objectively defined' limits nor is it about doing what the markets dictate; it is about a dynamic, integrated and, most importantly, democratic and participatory process of managing socio-environmental change. This provides a new perspective on the concept and application of tourism carrying capacity.

Limits to Growth and Carrying Capacity

Several writers in the 1960s and 1970s warned that human population growth and the accelerating rate of economic growth stressed the natural ecosystem beyond its ability to absorb such stresses. Most prominent among these were Boulding (1966) with his 'spaceship earth' metaphor and Meadows et al. (1972) with the 'limits to growth' thesis. Well known contemporary scientists insist that we are reaching if not already exceeding the limits of global and local ecosystems (Arrow et al., 1995; Costanza et al., 1997).

Implicit in most of these perspectives is a notion of carrying capacity or sustained yield as the basic criterion of sustainability. Ecosystems and populations, it is assumed, have a limited capacity to cope with environmental stress (Rees, 1990). An ecosystem is thought of as being able to absorb up to a certain amount of pollution and a renewable resource as capable of providing a maximum yield above which additional harvest begins to deplete it ('sustained yield'). Above a certain amount of stress from human activity there are catastrophic consequences and the ecosystem cannot continue to function and provide its services. For example, there are maximum admissible pollutant levels for the global atmosphere or a river, and maximum yields that a stock of fisheries or a water resource can sustain. From this perspective, sustainability of a given geographic area is equated with sustainability of the ecosystem that supports it. Ortolano (1984) for example, defines carrying capacity as 'the growth limits an area can accommodate without violating environmental capacity goals'.

The strategies for attaining it relate to policies for constraining the scale (intensity) of human activities within such limits. Proponents of this 'limits-based' strategy stress the importance of regulations on human activities to stop unlimited or excess use of environmental goods and services and to reduce negative environmental impacts (Rees, 1990). Related policies include, among others, limits to population and controls on its spatial distribution, standards for the protection of species, ambient standards, maximum acceptable levels of pollutant emissions, limits on the use of renewable resources and enforcement of resource-saving technologies. Policies for controlling the flow or number of visitors or limiting the number of beds allowed in tourist destinations pertain to this logic.

The Limits of Limits

It is difficult or impossible to prove that environmental limits exist and, if they do, what they are. It is perhaps even more difficult to convince people to respect those limits and to provide strategies for doing so...This strategy overestimates our knowledge of human carrying capacity and underestimates the importance of socioeconomic factors (Graaf et al., 1996).

Norgaard (1995) is concerned that 'even though "limits" is the most widely understood metaphor, it seems to have reached the limits of its scientific and political implementation'. The idea of the objective scientist who can quietly sit in a lab and identify the actual level of 'limits' and inform the regulator has become increasingly under fire. The politically heated debate on climate change serves as a vivid example. It is not only a case of lack of data, gaps in science or bias of the scientists themselves. As argued below, the very notion of 'limits' as conventionally perceived has insuperable conceptual problems.

Limits are Difficult to Determine

Ecosystem processes are too complex and uncertain to be easily reduced to thresholds in certain parameters which, if surpassed, lead to catastrophes. In most cases it is a combination of or synergies between different parameters – conditions that lead to certain impacts. For example, in the past the maintenance of a minimum river flow above a threshold at all times was thought of as critical for the sustainability of the aquatic ecosystem. Now it is accepted that flushes of water at certain times might be equally important. Several qualitative elements might also combine with quantitative elements in determining the ecological condition of a river. Different parameters are important for different systems and settings and at different times.

Limits are conceptual constructs which meet with additional difficulties when seen in spatial terms, as quite often for management purposes geographic areas of interest (as is the case with tourist areas and tourist destinations) do not necessarily coincide with functional boundaries of natural processes and ecosystem functions. It is even ambiguous if it is possible to identify the geographical boundaries or area limits of natural ecosystems, much more to assess 'ecosystem's limits'.

Furthermore, for operational policy-making it does not suffice to decide on the ecosystem's limits, but there is a need to translate them into limitations and controls on human activities, that is, it is necessary to distinguish between the relative contribution of different human activities and natural environmental processes on an ecosystem (more so, taking into account temporal and spatial distributions). There are direct and indirect effects involved as well as linkages, conflicts, complementarities and synergies which render the isolation of impacts and their attribution to a single activity often an impossible task. Much more so this is difficult in the case of tourism which is a complex of activities.

Improved monitoring, data collection and scientific knowledge may allow more accurate estimations. These however entail a significant economic cost. Setting monitoring networks and laboratories for bathing water quality and monitoring micro-pollutants is very expensive. And even with the best, state-of-the-art knowledge there is a degree of irreducible complexity and uncertainty in environmental processes, and even more so in the human processes that cause them.

Note that such complications are vastly more intense when moving from limits to certain parameters or resources and to carrying capacity limits for a whole area, as in the case of tourism carrying capacity. Water, for example, for which only some of the complications in defining qualitative and quantitative limitations were raised above, is only one of several ecological resources of importance. Similarly, tourism related stress may be only one of the number of activities (for example agriculture, industry, other land-use) and natural processes relating to ecological impacts in a certain areas. The task of defining such standards tests the limits of scientific capacity and certainly the financial, intellectual and scientific resources of the locales where they would have to be defined and implemented. Hence the main limitations to the application of tourism carrying capacity that Mexa and Coccossis identify in their overview (following chapter of this book): the lack of scientific objectivity; its collapse 'to a few measurable dimensions which however substantially restrict its potentially in planning', the futility of trying to arrive at a desirable unique number (for example maximum number of visitors) as an increased number of dimensions need to be considered, and the failure to take into account relationships between use and impact.

Limits are not Universal or Static

Limits are not important in themselves, but with respect to some function or use the system serves, for example public health, tourism, and so on. Standards for these functions need not be 'objectively' definable or universal. Different standards are relevant for the quality of bathing water depending on whether the sea is used by regular bathers (for example clarity, moderate waves) or by surfers. In a similar manner different tourist destinations raise different expectations (and thus 'activity patterns and uses'), so in an 'urban' or 'cosmopolitan' beach overcrowding might be more tolerated than in a remote island destination.

It follows that 'limits' are not static but they change in the long term, as levels of knowledge, perceptions, expectations and uses change. Fifty years ago recreational and tourism activities and preferences were not what they are today and given continuously changing socioeconomic, cultural and international economic conditions they may be very different in a few decades' time. Complicating things further, the value of nature itself is not a constant but may increase the more it is exploited and the more 'scarce' it becomes.

The importance of perceptions and changing values has been recognized in the debate over tourism carrying capacity. Assessment has extended from ecological thresholds to include notions of visitors' recreational experience, indicators and criteria of psychological satisfaction, and so forth. Note however that in making this shift much of the determinism characterizing initial ecological limits-based perceptions of carrying capacity is being lost and it can no longer be treated as a scientifically objective concept. Universal standards or even methodologies cannot be applied and findings about carrying capacity are not constant but subject to change and certain dilemmas arise on the normative value of assessment. An example of this can be found in a destination attracting low-income and low-education level tourists who do not appreciate quality of services or quality of the environment, but only low cost. In this situation, should carrying capacity be adjusted to their preferences and their sense of 'recreational experience'?

Limits at What Spatial Scale?

Since ancient times, societies have 'traded their way out' of the limits of their immediate locales. The very existence of trade discards the notion of an absolute carrying capacity for a certain socio-spatial system. Cities, regions, countries are all open systems which can both import resources and export wastes. Even a relatively closed system, such as an island, can import natural resources from farther away (for example water by tankers and underground pipes). It is total costs that matter in this case, not absolute limits. The carrying capacity of the island defined in physical terms is not a constant but can be 'expanded'.

Deciding the appropriate scale for setting limits is arbitrary. Administrative or other geographical borders are often arbitrary but so are ecosystem borders, often invoked as the appropriate unit of reference. As Norgaard (1994, p. 85) notes, the very notion of an ecosystem is to a large extent a mental construct of the discipline of ecology. 'Ecosystem boundaries vary depending on whether one is studying microbes, ants or elephants ... and time may affect the definition of the boundaries as well...The boundary problem is not trivial, and there are no perfect ways of contending with it'.

Imposing on an island community, for example, the requirement to live within the limits of its local ecosystem and resources is as arbitrary as asking a metropolitan area to stop offering jobs to non-city-dwellers or transferring natural resources from beyond its administrative borders or bioregion. Defining and enforcing limits to growth in a given area (a tourist destination in this case) becomes problematic, in so far as these limits are not 'fixed' in a deterministic way but can be 'expanded' and their spatial scale of reference is more or less arbitrary. Carrying capacity assessment has tried to incorporate this dimension by extending assessment to infrastructural, economic and other dimensions. Each frame of reference though implies possibly a different 'appropriate' geographical area of reference. In addition, in this way the essence of carrying capacity as an ecological limitation is conceptually reduced, for example, to a question of economics and technical planning (for example installing the necessary infrastructure in due time to accommodate an increase in the number of visitors).

On the other hand, in modern society much of the environmental impact of certain localities (tourist areas) does not relate only to their stress on local resources and ecosystems but to their relative importance or contribution to broader regional and global environmental problems (through import of resources and export of wastes). Focusing on local carrying capacity limits may result in a loss of the broader picture. Islands for example may overcome local water resource limitations by importing water with tankers from the mainland or desalination but in fact they are displacing their problem to the areas from where they draw water and to the global environment or to other sectors, in terms of the emissions related to intensified sea transport or the energy resources used.

'Dead is Dead' and the Cost of Staying Within Limits

Most ecosystems do not have a single unique limit, but one or more thresholds where severe changes in their characteristics occur. In certain instances, it might be considered as preferable to concentrate activity on a developed, 'dead' or 'severely affected' system whose carrying capacity has been exceeded rather than allocate the same activity to a new, 'virgin' system. Imagine a scenario of two neighbouring islands, the one intensely developed for tourism and the other untouched. Even in strict environmental terms, it might be a much wiser strategy to concentrate tourism in the first island where certain carrying capacity limits of its ecosystems and its natural resources may have been exceeded, increasing the transfer of resources from overseas instead of, say, developing infrastructure in the 'virgin' island and affect an untouched natural ecosystem there. In certain instances policies based on 'carrying capacity may encourage widespread degradation of the environment, rather than protect it' as they allow increase of stress 'on the limit' in all systems (in comparison to a 'dead is dead' policy which could apply stricter standards in some areas and looser in others, Mar, 1981).

More importantly, there are certain economies of scale related to the concentration of population and activities in one geographical area instead of distributing them among many. In a group of islands and for a given number of tourists, it would be much more expensive to distribute them evenly on all islands (and stay within the limits of each) than to concentrate them on one. This is not only a case of monetary cost. A 'dead is dead' policy of concentration instead of a carrying capacity one, might be much more resourceful in terms of less material and energy demands per 'product output' (for example tourist product) due to scale effects. The above observation brings back the importance of scale. Focusing at the local level may lead to worst overall outcomes at higher scales (regional, national or global) particularly if cumulative effects are ignored. Inversely, what might be better at higher scales of spatial reference may imply uneven distributions at lower levels.

Limits are Not Socially Neutral

The imposition of limits on human activities has certain distributional implications (Martinez-Alier and O'Connor, 1999). Hence there is fierce opposition or defiance and reluctance of politicians to implement limits, especially if scientific facts are intensely disputed. Imposing limits on one locale, while other areas have developed (or are still developing) without respecting similar limits, raises an important issue of equity (the 'north versus south' debate in the control of greenhouse gases emissions is a characteristic example. Is it justifiable for northern countries that have developed without respecting global ecosystem limits to impose now those standards on the less-developed regions?). The same questions of social or geographical equity are applicable to tourist destinations as well. Why should there be limits in a developing destination when the one next to it of similar size has far exceeded any sense of limits?

All the above suggests that it makes little sense to talk about limits as constant parameters that 'exist out there' and can be identified, given the necessary knowledge and time, and enforced given the necessary political 'will'. What is at stake in reality are questions of complex and dynamic *trade-offs* between impacts, different uses, economic cost and risk in a context of inherently limited knowledge and irreducible uncertainty. Crucially, these trade-offs are not socially neutral. The crucial policy question therefore is not one of limits, but one of *choice*.

'No Limits': Economic Efficiency and Anti-Carrying Capacity Views

Many economists consider theirs as the science of choices and trade-offs in the 'allocation of scarce means to multiple ends'. They were quick to dismiss as irrelevant the propositions of Meadows and others for 'limits to growth' and rejected the idea that carrying capacity limits put constraints on economic development (Kahn et al., 1976). From an economist's point of view, scarcity is the mother of invention and reaching limits prompts experimentation with and development of new technologies that will eventually overcome these limits. For Fedorov and Novik (1977) 'as science progresses and production processes change, possibilities change, owing to a more efficient use of each resource and exploitation of new resources of natural wealth and to the quest for fundamentally different solutions. If this were not so, mankind would long since have found itself at an impasse...Not only the present population of earth, but even a smaller number, could not have been fed by hunting as our remote ancestors practiced it'.

From an economic point of view, the criterion of sustainability is equated to either non-declining utility through time (put into operation as non-declining consumption and measured by income) or maintenance of production opportunities for the future (Perman et al., 1999). Production opportunities are related to capital; the objective is that the total capital stock, 'natural', man-made and 'intellectual' does not decrease in time (Ayres et al., 2001). This reduces sustainability to 'sustainable economic growth' (Solow, 1992), or what is commonly referred to as 'economic sustainability'. Put simply, development is sustainable no matter how much environment we 'consume' as long as we offset these losses by passing on more roads, infrastructure and other productive machinery or knowledge to future generations, giving them the opportunity to achieve an equal standard of living (Pearce and Turner, 1990).

Although in theory there are several provisos, in practice most economists (especially at the level of policy advisor) reduce sustainability into the criterion of intra and inter-temporal efficiency (Bergh, 2000). A change is efficient when those who gain could compensate those who lose (although actual compensation is not required) and still be better off, or in real-life practice, when net benefits surpass costs.

Environmental problems are reduced to cases of 'internalizing' unpriced environmental goods and services within markets (real or hypothetical) by making them a commodity so that 'decision-makers' (individuals, groups or policy-makers) experience the real costs and benefits of their decisions. Hence the two guiding economic policy principles: private 'property rights' and 'full cost pricing'. The first focuses on turning the environment into a property that its holders can trade (setting property rights and allowing their market exchange) and the second in valuing it monetarily (through proxy-valuation techniques) and taxing or pricing accordingly the consumptive or polluting uses (Tietenberg, 2003). Common-held policy proposals include cost-benefit analysis in all sorts of decisions (projects, policies), full and marginal-cost pricing, establishment of tradable pollution or resource-use rights (Bergh, 2000). Such 'economic' instruments are often contrasted to the coercive 'command and control' instruments favored by a limits-based perspective.

Even though 'economic' and 'ecological' sustainability are often mentioned in one and the same breath and tend to be combined in policy documents, they differ markedly in their formulation. They represent two partially contrasting and irreducible perspectives. While in the limits vision, the economy is confined within the boundaries of nature, in the economic vision nature is only one among several inputs to the economy (Daly, 1999).

From a mainstream economic perspective, there should be no interference in the works of the 'market' via planning processes or 'artificial' limits. People are 'voting' with their money in the market and it is markets that should decide the optimal level of resource use or pollution. For example, locals and tourists should be free to decide on the mix of environmental quality versus income mix they prefer. Locals might wish to sacrifice some of the ecology of their islands in order to increase their income from tourism activities and tourists may prefer to do with lower environmental quality in their destination than with a higher travel budget. Water can be over-abstracted and then imported from far way as long as users are willing to pay for it. Then again, preservation of 'environmental quality' or provision of 'green tourist products' may be taken on, if and when they become profitable market activities.

Government interference is allowed from a mainstream economic perspective only in order to correct market imperfections, such as for example, 'internalizing' environmental externalities. This means that at least in principle policies should be in place so that visitors and locals in a tourist destination face the real (including environmental) cost of their decisions and this cost is reflected in the provision of services and the cost of goods. In practice of course, this is far from happening. Economists have an answer for this. Correcting market imperfection itself should be undertaken only to the extent that the benefits from the change exceed the costs (administrative costs for changing pricing systems or imposing taxes, and so on). As Bromley (1991) observes, this comes perilously close to supporting that whatever exists is efficient, otherwise it would change.

Therefore from the mainstream economic perspective carrying capacity limits and the need for limitations simply do not exist; it is costs and benefits that matter. Although the economic perspective appears irrelevant to the science of carrying capacity assessment, in the dominant present-day neo-liberal political environment, public policies in all sorts of areas are based on market principles and decisions are taken on strict cost-benefit criteria. Imposing limits or investing to understand these limits runs counter to this dominant political environment and the theoretical economic model presented above provides the justification. The public too, be it the inhabitants of a country of the poor south or of a less developed Mediterranean island, feel outraged at the suggestions of the 'environmentalists' from developed, urban areas that they should constrain their activities within the limits of some hypothetical carrying capacity and sacrifice their immediate income. Yet, there is a growing sense, among many, that it is exactly these dominant economic trends and public perceptions that are unsustainable.

Economists have got it right in so far as they see the policy question as one of choices and trade-offs rather than external limits. The problem is that many are advocating a wrong type of choice.

Efficient in What and for Whom?

Economists have implicitly assumed that maximum growth of GNP is the primary goal regardless of the inadequacy of the measure, of how it is generated, and of who receives it ... Any other goal is seen to be a constraint on the primary goal and hence a limitation on efficiency. While this conflation has become customary in economic discourse, it is theoretically incorrect. In political discourse it relegates all societal goals besides raw GNP growth to a secondary status, as things which conflict with the ideal of efficiency (Norgaard, 1992).

The dominant, efficiency focused ('neo-classical' and the like) economic model has been challenged at its very theoretical and methodological foundations (see Potts, 2002 for the definitive review). Several contemporary economists have criticized its treatment of environment and development issues (Bromley, 1991; Harvey, 1996; Gowdy, 1994, Norgaard, 1994; Martinez-Alier et al., 1998).

Values are Not and Should Not be a Given

Efficiency as commonly understood is a measure of how well a target ('ends') is being met. Nobody could argue against being efficient (Bromley, 1991). The problem, however, arises in defining and measuring the 'ends' that the multiple means come to serve.

The economic model considers maximization of utility vis-à-vis maximization of material wealth (put into operation through monetary value), as the universal and given end of all human action. There are several problems with this assumption. As Norgaard (1994, p. 18) asks, if values and preferences are considered as a given, what if development has not been sustainable because society's value system in the past has put too little weight on the environment and the future. Even if 'humans "prefer" to use fossil fuels rather than solar energy, "prefer" to trade the earth's biological diversity for consumer goods, still acting on these preferences will change the physical world we live in, probably for the worse. Such an outcome would presumably not be preferred' (Ayres et al., 2001). Locals in a tourist destination for example, may not continue increasing their income to the detriment of the local environment if only they know the long-term implications. Reducing the value of the environment to its monetary value is a risky undertaking; a level of environmental quality may need to be sustained irrespective of its net present economic benefit.

Economic reasoning rests on individualistic, utilitarian and materialistic theory of value. This is in no way ethically or philosophically superior to alternative stances such as, for example, consequentalist non-utilitarian, ethical or deontological (Jacobs, 1994). Maximization of individual material wealth is in no way the only type of goal held by humans nor can all other goals be reduced into monetary value (Jacobs, 1994). Humans hold multiple values, and different values may be applicable to different circumstances. In some aspects they might act as consumers-maximizers, in others as citizens-altruists. Indeed, much of the debate around sustainability concerns resolving the relative importance of the different 'ends', important for different peoples. Even distinguishing what counts as 'means' and what as an 'ends' may not be that straightforward. As Latour (1997) agues, the distinction of the ecological movement is that it sees nature not only as a 'means' to production and material wealth, but also as an 'end' in itself. Ecologists want the environment sustained, irrespective of its exact cost or its contribution to utility. Locals may wish to have the environment and the heritage of their area sustained no matter what the sacrifice for short-term income from tourism. A future with the ecological base of an island destroyed, for some may be a future not worth living.

All the above suggest against the economic paradigm which tends to reduce all human values into monetary values, attach a price to the 'environment' and reduce the complexity of human decisions (and sustainability in this respect) into the maximization of net present monetary benefit (Jacobs, 1994, Vatn and Bromley, 1994).

Efficiency Depends on Distribution

What is efficient depends on how rights and income are distributed (Bromley, 1991; Norgaard, 1992). For example, the 'efficient' level of pollution depends on the relative rights and incomes of the polluter and the polluted (Bromley, 1991). The institutional structure determines which costs will be reckoned by which decision-makers, and hence arrangements over natural resources determine which outcomes appear to be efficient. As long as transaction costs (costs of negotiation, legal procedures, acquiring information) are positive and they typically fall on the polluted, predicating change only upon the criterion of short-term efficiency is biased towards maintenance of the dominant status quo. Bargaining power in a market depends on existing income. The 'market vote' thus, unless counterbalanced, will tend to favour the already advantaged to the detriment of the disadvantaged. The proclaimed indifference of the efficiency criterion to distribution is in fact a strong stance: one that favours the existing status quo (Livingston, 1993).

Therefore letting the markets decide may not only lead to detrimental environmental effects but also to intensifying social inequality. One can well imagine a plausible future scenario under unrestricted global, neo-liberal market processes where tourism saturates island destinations, islands look increasingly like cities, crime increases, bathing and drinking waters become contaminated and local fisheries are destroyed. All this might be the efficient outcome of acting on short-term, individualistic values and preferences and positive net discounted benefits. New values might then dominate, rendering profitable 'enclave hotels' for the rich with protected views to the sea, swimming pools, unlimited supplies of bottled water and imported food. The poor would still be 'willing' to swim in polluted waters, buy drinking water of questionable quality from vendors and might well survive without fish in their diet. Indeed, this is not far from what is already the case in many third world tourist destinations. From an economic perspective there is nothing inherently 'bad' in such an outcome, if this is what the outcome of preferences expressed in a market leads to. But as Bromley (1991) stresses, public policy is first and foremost about reallocating costs, benefits and opportunities. It is about safeguarding a broader social and public good and expressing a shared notion of what is proper and fair to do in order to achieve a desired future.

Substitution, Irreversibility and Technological Progress

Most of the debates of 'limits versus no limits' have been centred on the question of the ability of technological progress to overcome temporary limits and scarcity in specific environmental resources. This relates to the question over the potential of physical capital to substitute for natural resources (Ayres et al., 2001). Limits' advocates have resorted to the laws of thermodynamics (entropy and conservation of matter) to suggest that there are finite limits on planet earth to the level of human activity it can sustain. These relate to limits of energy availability (eventually, the rate of solar influx) and waste absorption, as by definition waste recycling will be always less than 100 per cent. Therefore both the limits of resources and of natural sinks will be eventually reached (Daly, 1999). Although some see evidence of these limits being reached (Costanza et al., 1997), the consensus is that such limits and the eventual increase of entropy are probably irrelevant for the present timescale of decisions.

On the other hand, this does not mean that past experience and the technological progress in the previous two centuries can be lightheartedly extrapolated indefinitely into the future. There is an inherent risk in assuming that the next technology in the sequence will always be there, as the economic model suggests, substituting whatever resource is depleted. Especially for pollutant emissions and the sink functions of ecosystems there is little experience up to now to reassure that technology can cope with changes. There is also a growing sense that many new technologies are simply pushing and extending boundaries, externalizing costs and risks or shifting them to the future, rather than really overcoming the limitations. Nuclear energy and, possibly, genetically modified organisms are characteristic examples.

It is important here to clarify the differences in perspectives. In the economic model no ecological change or loss is 'irreversible' in so far as the utility it provides can be substituted by other forms of capital (Norton and Toman, 1997). A species (for example of fresh fish) may be lost, but the services it provides can be substituted (for example aquaculture or food substitutes). For ecologists on the other hand, substitution and reversibility refer to specific ecosystem characteristics. Once a species of fish has become extinct, this is irreversible, although the economic welfare it contributed to can be substituted by other factors of production.

Economists refer to total outcomes: a certain species, natural area, group of people or activity may lose if total utility is to increase. In real life though, the emphasis is often on specific outcomes and rightly so. McDaniel and Gowdy (1999) document the story of the island nation of Nauru, where the richest phosphate deposits of the world were discovered in 1900 and after ninety years of phosphate mining, about 80 per cent of the island was totally devastated. The people of Nauru benefited from a high per capita income and accumulated a trust fund as large as US$ 1 billion. But this vanished in the Asian financial crisis and islanders now face a bleak future. The authors make the case that while nature can be substituted for money, this substitution is one-way and not reversible. The fate of Naurians is highly relevant to what might be happening to many tourist destinations that may be sacrificing their ecological base for short-term profits from tourism and when and if the markets shift, might be left devastated. Economists would see Nauru as a specific case, unimportant from a global economic perspective. But for the Naurians it was certainly important.

Beyond Limits and Efficiency

Ayres et al., (2001) make a fundamental distinction that helps us push the debate on sustainability forward from the dichotomy on limits versus no limits. 'Much of the confusion in the discussion arises from the failure to distinguish between two assumptions ... The first is the assumption of substitutability between natural and manufactured capital. The second is that economic well-being "covers" all other concerns. If the second assumption is accepted, then the argument boils down to a purely economic debate...If on the other hand, substituting financial capital for natural resources is incompatible with maintaining a suitable physical environment for human species, then sustainability implies that we must step outside the conventional market framework in order to establish the conditions for maintaining human happiness'.

In the case of tourism, this means that if the discussion is reduced to one of maintaining a growing income from tourism (or more generally, income from economic activities), then economists might be right: there is no need for carrying capacity assessments, limits and the like (assuming unlimited prospects of substitution vis-à-vis technological progress). Let the markets decide, they would argue, and if and when 'limitations' become profitable, let them be undertaken. If however as Ayres et al. suggest the discussion is about a broader sense of public good and sustainable living, then precaution, maintenance of some level of environmental quality and some conscious limitations on the scale and intensity of economic activity and the rate of destruction of the ecological base become important. That is we might collectively decide to set limits on tourism flows and constrain some of its impacts on the local (natural, built, cultural) environment, no matter how economically beneficial in the short-term tourism activities may be.

A Third Way to Sustainability: An Alternative, Ecological-Economic Perspective

Ecological economics is a multi-disciplinary field of research which addresses the relationship between ecosystems and the economy with an emphasis on non-linear irreversible interactions and processes and with a use of multiple ecological and economic theory tools (Costanza et al., 1997; Bergh, 2000). There are significant differences between researchers who consider themselves as ecological economists (Spash, 1999). Many do not reject the mainstream theoretical economic model presented above. They do make, though, some steps towards a more sensitive treatment of environmental issues, by linking economic models with ecological models or by combining economic efficiency goals with some sort of ecosystem scale constraints. Pearce and Turner (1990) for example, although they convey standard economic policy prescriptions (cost-benefit analysis, pricing and taxation instruments), advocate a more careful treatment of critical ecosystems given uncertainty and irreversibility (they name their view as a 'strong' approach to sustainability, distinguishing it from the 'weak' approach of mainstream economists and the 'very strong' of ecologists).

The framework put forward below deviates from these. Instead, it draws from the work of scholars at a political ecological-economic line of theorizing within ecological economics, who combine elements from political, institutional, evolutionary and other heterodox economic approaches that reject the concept of economic efficiency as perceived in mainstream economics and see in nature an importance beyond simply a means to economic production. Borrowing from their ideas, an alternative framework is sketched below for approaching sustainability issues.

A Co-Evolutionary Perspective of Society and Nature

Environmental and social changes co-determine each other (Norgaard, 1994). Nature is to an extent social just as society is to an extent natural. Societies mould their environments and in turn, the new environment that is being created affects the path society follows in the future. This is a reciprocal, positive-feedback, cumulative, 'co-evolutionary' relation. This conception breaks the dichotomy of 'limits vs. no limits to growth'. There are no absolute, mechanistic limits but relative distributions of the (non-linear) impacts of environmental change among different groups of people, in space and time. There are multiple potential co-evolutionary socio-ecological paths towards the future, more or less certain, with different implications for different peoples and less, or more, compatible with their values (Swyngedouw, 2002). For example, in a worst-case scenario of climate change, the world will not vanish in a day. Different forms of human communities may evolve in a context of harsh climatic conditions and find a new balance (most probably much worse with respect to expected standards of living of western civilization, but not necessarily worse by those standards experienced in some under-developed regions even today).

Values are endogenous to this process of co-evolutionary change, humans refashion their environments both physically and cognitively. In turn the resulting environments, real and perceived, select for the dominant human demands, values and technological or institutional responses. There might be more or less desirable co-evolutionary paths towards the future from our perspective, but it should be remembered that future generations will be born within a very different 'selection milieu'.

This argument in relation to tourism was repeatedly made above. Perceptions of the recreational experience differ and change. Tourism (together with other activities) changes local environments; in turn, these changes 'select' for new types of tourism (unspoilt beaches became popular only after many beaches had been 'spoilt'). New technologies make new forms of recreation possible or bring new data about problems and dangers in the spotlight (for example threats from polluted bathing waters). The process of evolution is by definition uncertain and unpredictable. Historical 'accidents' may change the co-evolutionary path dramatically. In a worst-case scenario of a 'clashes of civilizations' in the 21st century, international tourism may disappear altogether. The best we can strive for in this context of continuous and unpredictable change is to maintain diversity and some sort of system resilience in order to be able to adapt to changing conditions.

Diversity (ecological, cultural and political) is supported *a priori* from a co-evolutionary perspective, as otherwise co-evolution would stagnate (Norgaard, 1994). Mono-cultural development of tourism in a tourist destination is inherently risky. Maintaining by proper limitations a certain ecological base and differentiated productive base is a much wiser approach. Ability to adapt is also an important policy criterion. Managing co-evolutionary change is a process of shaping shared and collective visions about the possible, the desirable and the feasible and how to achieve them.

Post-Normal Science

Environment and development issues present new challenges for science. They are characterized by uncertain facts, disputed values, high stakes and urgent decisions (Funtowisz and Ravetz, 1991). Contrary to economic and ecological thinking which recognize only one set of values, an alternative ecological economic perspective is based on the premise of 'weak comparability' of values (Martinez-Alier et al., 1998). Weak comparability implies 'incommensurability', in other words there is not one common unit of measurement across plural values. This rejects not only monetary reductionism but also physical reductionism (such as ecological footprints, eco-energetic valuations). However, 'it does not imply incomparability. It allows that different options are weakly comparable, that is comparable without recourse to a single type of value' (Martinez-Alier et al., 1998). Decisions about sustainability issues are therefore multi-dimensional, multi-criteria problems where the different dimensions (criteria) are only weakly comparable. Deciding on the relative weight of the different dimensions held by the different legitimate 'stakeholders', choosing the appropriate numerical scale upon which they will be compared and handling the different degrees of scientific certainty and risk in the assessment of each, can only be a matter of democratic discourse and agreement.

Furthermore, scientific complexity and uncertainty are so high that the notion of the 'objective' scientist who can get all facts and suggest the best course of action is becoming obsolete. Judging on acceptable levels of uncertainty and reliability of information vis-à-vis risk, is a case of 'judgement' and hence 'justice', in the broadest sense. Funtowisz and Ravetz (1991) refer to a new scientific paradigm they call 'post-normal science', in which lay persons become effective participants in dialogue and decisions.

This marks a shift from a 'substantive' to a 'procedural' approach to decisions and to what can be called (as per Herbert Simon) 'satisficing' choices; not best in some superior sense, but selected as satisfactory through an appropriate process. Ecological and economic thinking implicitly assume that there is some sort of a sustainability calculus, a golden rule (criterion) by which actions can be judged as sustainable or not ('optimality' or carrying capacity limits, respectively). A procedural perspective in contrast does not focus on outcomes or constraints. It emphasizes that the rationality of evaluation relates to the decision-making process. Inclusiveness becomes a goal in itself, and a criterion for the 'quality' of the process and the decision. It is not a means by which to get people to agree to the 'right' decisions, as is often perceived in planning and sustainability literature. It is about defining what is right per se, as common value is formed through dialogue and consensus. The lack of 'objectivity' thus is not seen as a failure but as an inherent characteristic of the process towards defining sustainability.

'Subjectivity' and plurality of perspectives are accepted and systematically treated in order to arrive at compromises and sustainable agreements.

The process of Integrated Assessment (Abaza and Baranzini, 2002) refers to just such a multi-dimensional and participatory type of evaluation. Environmental criteria are important though by no means the only criteria of a comprehensive evaluation. Information on costs and benefits or thresholds and carrying capacity limits can all feed in a participatory discourse based on multiple types and sources of scientific information and multiple stakeholders' and participants' values and perspectives (Martinez-Allier et al., 1998). Assessment is not seen as an absolute and deterministic evaluation but more as a tool to foster strategic conversation and shaping of shared visions. Tools such as scenarios, stakeholder-based modelling, technological assessment, and so on, can all complement traditional scientific methodologies.

The above resonate well with recent developments in the practice of tourism carrying capacity assessment and the shift from the search for absolute values to more multi-dimensional and policy oriented assessments where carrying capacity is no longer considered as simply a technical act but as an exercise facilitating political choice of objectives and management actions (see discussion in the overview by Mexa and Coccossis in this volume). The shift from thresholds to 'desired conditions' reflects the shift from limits to shared visions and from the search for 'objective' scientific standards to debated alternative scenarios. This is not to say the information and debate about limits and limitations is deemed irrelevant, but that it assumes a new role (see more below).

Reapproaching Sustainability

Sustainability can then be related to an institutionalized process of finding 'satisficing' (and not 'optimal') solutions to conflicting and dynamic (evolutionary) problems. It is about deciding on the 'kind of world we want to live in and then try to manage the process of change as best as we can approximate it' (Lewontin, 1997; Swyngedouw, 2002). It refers to 'the ability of a given society to move, in a finite time, between satisficing, adaptable and viable states' (Giampietro, 1999). Development then is the improvement of the well-being of the people to the extent that their ways of knowing, social organization and technologies select for an evolutionary course of the environment that complements their values (Norgaard, 1994).

Sustainable tourism is that one which contributes to the above process towards sustainability for both the destination area and its broader region. It is one in which the different co-evolutionary paths that tourism development (perceptions, technologies, products, environmental conditions) can – and should – take are analysed and choice is the outcome of a collective, open and democratic debate with the best use of science and with due recognition to irreducible uncertainty and complexity.

The above is not a call for relativism. Participatory and negotiated compromises might well be fallacious, in the sense of misreading the conditions and leading to outcomes that were not intended. The fallacy of consensus means that even if a group of people agrees that 1+1=3, this does not mean that this can ever become realized. Quality criteria for the best possible use of science are necessary (Funtowisz and Ravetz, 1991). Note that 'markets' or 'cold-blooded technocrats' can equally well lead to fallacious decisions, as the management of environmental and public health crises such as mad-cow disease demonstrates. Criteria should be set for what constitutes an informed public scientific discourse of acceptable scientific quality.

Prudence and Conscious Limitations

Consensus might still select for catastrophic co-evolutionary paths. A community might easily agree to live to the maximum in the present no matter what the consequences will be for the far future. Indeed such an outcome is very probable given the present, dominant materialistic values. Furthermore, we know little about the future and might agree to follow paths that surpass certain ecological thresholds leading to unintended and undesired consequences; indeed, this is the core of the environmental debate. This of course can also be the outcome of a 'market' or centralized decision-making. But is this 'sustainable'?

We suggest that a notion of 'prudence' about the future and about the ecological consequences of our actions is necessary to complement the emphasis on democratization and inclusiveness. This suggests a democratic agreement on acceptable, precautionary social and ecological 'minima' (Kapp, 1983) and the transfer of 'social bequests' to future generations (Norgaard, 1992; Bromley, 1998). If the sustainability problem is seen as 'how much, this always implies that some amount of resource should be used and some left. We use 25 per cent of a rainforest and leave the rest, for example. But then the next time we make a decision we start all over again and use 25 per cent of what's left, and so on, until it's all gone' (Ayres et al., 2001). 'Regard for the future through social bequests shifts the analytical problem to a discussion about what, rather than how much, to leave to those who will follow' (Bromley, 1998). Transfer mechanisms might include setting aside natural resources and protecting environments, educating the young, and developing technologies for the sustainable management of renewable resources (Norgaard, 1992). A community might collectively decide to pass on to future generations more (or less) as a social bequest what is suggested by ecological limits (for example a protected natural area, control on pollution or ban of certain activities and pollutants). Biophysical or ecological thresholds, carrying capacity assessments or ecological footprint appraisals have all a role to play in the scientific debate about social and ecological minima and inter-generational transfers without however claims of supremacy in an integrated decision-making process.

In our perspective, prudence means also that material growth and the related preferences cannot continue to be treated as a given. For Norgaard (1994, 1995), the roots of contemporary environmental crisis rest on materialism and the unrestrained appetite of our civilization for more and more material goods and wealth. 'More' should not always mean better and a prudent policy would impose limits not only on the impacts of our behavior but directly on our consumption patterns. Conscious limitation on the scale, intensity and type of tourism activity may have to be imposed, irrespective (or simply informed) by the carrying capacity limits.

Mainstream economists might argue for the 'inefficiency' of inclusive and democratic decisions and the arbitrariness of transfers or controls on consumption. But as agued above, efficiency is a criterion of how well a goal is being met. What is at stake is defining the goal itself. Bromley (1991) distinguishes between 'universal efficiency' and 'effectiveness', the latter referring to reaching a socially defined goal, for example as defined by socio-ecological minima or within the limits of social bequests, in a cost-wise manner. Economic instruments and economic valuations are not discarded all together; they are meant though, to serve social goals and not dictate them. Note that to an extent the above reduction of the economic perspective in a 'free market' dogma may make a caricature of a great diversity of theoretical works by economists. While in the policy implementation phase, a great many adopt an 'efficiency' perspective many environmental economists are advocating an 'effectiveness' approach with a more careful treatment of 'natural capital' and recognize that certain natural values or ecological limits may need to be respected irrespective of their strict efficiency rationale (Pearce and Turner, 1990). In their view, economic instruments (pricing, and so on) can be used as tools to achieve desired goals and these might include for example, not only maximization of wealth but also respect of certain limitations (for example the use of economic instruments as a tool to control tourist flows within carrying capacity limits).

Note also that, even in monetary terms, there is growing evidence that participatory, consensual decisions in conflicting, sustainability-related issues come at a lower overall cost. Enforcement by the government or application of unrestrained market mechanisms often entail considerable implementation and transaction costs (legal disputes, delays due to social opposition).

From Carrying Capacity to Integrated Assessment and Policy

The discussion in this chapter argued that:

1. Carrying capacity cannot be about absolute, constant and universal limits, reducible to single numbers. Such a task is beyond the reach of our intellectual capacity and far beyond the resources available for the task.
2. Carrying capacity can not be a scientifically objective concept. This should not be seen as a limitation or a drawback as it is an inherent characteristic of the notion of sustainability. Sustainability is not a universal, value-free objective criterion that can be defined with recourse only to science. It depends also on dynamic perceptions and values and on a plurality of perspectives. It is

through an institutionalized process of dialogue, compromises and value resolution that shared visions should be developed about what citizens want to achieve. This suggests a move from the identification of thresholds to the envisioning of 'desired conditions'.

3. The above mark a shift from an assessment of carrying capacity to a broader, multi-dimensional and participatory assessment based on various sources of information and with the use of multiple indicators, the aggregation of which should be part of a politicized, scientific discourse. Development of shared visions (through the use of techniques such as strategic scenarios, stakeholder mediated dynamic modelling, and so on) can complement strict scientific assessments.   Information on the 'carrying capacity limits' and the various 'thresholds' of certain systems, with due consideration to the complexity and uncertainty involved, can still be vital parts of this discourse providing guidance for certain impacts (economic, ecological, distributional) to be faced if certain courses of action are followed. The objective should be to inform on trade-offs and to facilitate, not to dictate choice.

Regarding the policy role of carrying capacity based limitations:

1. Limits on human activities on the basis of ecological thresholds are unjustifiable. On the other hand, this does not mean that 'business-as-usual' or 'free market' policies are better as they entail considerable risk and may run counter to certain acceptable human values. Conscious limits to consumption and human activities can still be set, but only as part of democratic and politicized debate.

2. Plurality and diversity are inherently good. Controls (for example on tourist flows or maximum number of tourists in certain periods or in certain areas) can still be part of broader integrated strategies, together with other regulatory and economic, voluntary and coercive, instruments. Again, such controls should not be only the subject of ecological, biophysical or other considerations, but subject to a broader debate where equity issues would feature prominently.

Mexa's and Coccossis' review of the discussion over the application of tourism carrying capacity assessment in the next chapter shows that many practitioners are reaching similar conclusions to those suggested by the theoretical exploration pursued in this chapter.

References

Abaza, H. and Baranzini, A. (eds) (2002), 'Implementing Sustainable Development: Integrated Assessment and Participatory Decision-Making', Edward Elgar, Cheltenham, UK, Northampton, MA.

Arrow, K., Bolin, B., Costanza, R., Dasgupta, P., Folke, C., Holling, C.S., Jansson, B.O., Levin, S., Maler, K.G., Perrings, C., Pimentel, D. (1995), 'Economic Growth, Carrying Capacity and the Environment', *Science*, 268, pp. 520-521.

Ayres, R.U., Bergh, J.C.J.M. van den, Gowdy, J. (2001), 'Strong Versus Weak Sustainability: Economics, Natural Sciences and Consilience', *Environmental Ethics*, 23(1), pp. 155-168.

Bergh J.C.J.M. van den, (2000), 'Ecological Economics: Themes, Approaches and Differences with Environmental Economics', *Regional Environmental Change*, 3(1), pp. 13-23.

Boulding, K. (1966), 'The Economics of Coming Spaceship Earth', in Jarett, H. (ed), *Environmental Quality in a Growing Economy*, Johns Hopkins Press, Baltimore, pp. 3-14.

Bromley, D. (1991), *Environment and Economy. Property Rights and Public Policy*, Blackwell, Oxford, UK, Cambridge, USA.

Bromley, D. (1998), 'Searching for Sustainability: the Poverty of Spontaneous Order', *Ecological Economics*, 24, pp. 231-240.

Costanza, R., Cumberland, J., Daly, H., Goodland, R., Norgaard, R. (1997), 'An Introduction to Ecological Economics', *International Society for Ecological Economics*, St Lucie Press, Florida.

Daly, H.E. (1999), *Ecological Economics and the Ecology of Economics. Essays in Criticism*, Edward Elgar, Northampton, MA, USA.

Fedorov, E. and Novik, I. (1977), 'Man, Science and Technology', in Deutsch, K.W. (ed), *Ecosocial Systems and Ecopolitics*, Paris, UNESCO, pp. 45-48.

Funtowisz, S.O. and Ravetz, J.R. (1991), 'A New Scientific Methodology for Global Environmental Issues', in Constanza, R. (ed), *Ecological Economics*, Columbia, New York, pp. 137-152.

Giampietro, M. (1999), 'Implications of Complexity for an Integrated Assessment of Sustainability Trade-offs', in *Advanced Study Course on Decision Tools and Processes for Integrated Environmental Assessment*, University of Barcelona, Barcelona.

Gowdy, J.M. (1994), *Coevolutionary Economics: The Economy, Society and the Environment*, Kluwer Academic Publishers, Dordrecht.

Graaf, H. J. de, Musters, C. J. M., Ter Keurs, W. J. (1996), 'Sustainable Development: Looking For New Strategies', *Ecological Economics*, 16, pp. 205-216.

Harvey, D. (1996), *Justice, Nature and the Geography of Difference*, Blackwell. Oxford.

Jacobs, M. (1994), 'The Limits to Neoclassicism: Towards an Institutional Environmental Economics', in Benton, T. and Redclift, M. (eds), *Social Theory and the Global Environment*, Routledge, London, New York, pp. 67-91.

Kahn, H., Brown, H., Martel, L. (1976), *The Next 200 Years: a Scenario for America and the World*, William Morrow, New York.

Kapp, K. (1983), *Social Costs, Economic Development and Environmental Disruptions*, University Press of America, London.

Latour, B. (1996), 'To Modernize or to Ecologize? That's the Question', in Braun, B. and Castree N. (eds), *Remaking Reality – Nature at the Millennium*, Routledge, London, pp. 221-242.

Lewontin, R. (1997), 'Genes, Environment and Organisms', in Silvers, R.B. (ed), *Hidden Histories of Science*, Granta Books, London, pp. 115-139.

Livingston, M.L. (1993), 'Normative and Positive Aspects of Institutional Economics: The Implications for Water Policy', *Water Resources Research*, 29, 4, pp. 815-821.

Mar, B.W. (1981), 'Dead is Dead – An Alternative Strategy for Urban Water Management', *Urban Ecology*, 5, 103-112.

Martinez-Allier, J. and O'Connor, M. (1999), 'Distributional Issues: an Overview', in Bergh J.C.J.M van den (ed), *Handbook of Environmental and Resource Economics*, Edward Elgar, Northampton, MA, pp. 380-391.

Martinez-Allier, J., Munda G., O'Neill, J. (1998), 'Weak Comparability of Values as a Foundation for Ecological Economics', *Ecological Economics*, 26, pp. 277-286.

McDaniel, C. and Gowdy, J.M. (1999), *Paradise Lost: Markets, Myths and Ecosystem Destruction*, University of California Press, Berkeley.

Meadows, D.H. and others, (1972), *The Limits to Growth; a Report for the Club of Rome's Project on the Predicament of Mankind*, Universe Books, New York.

Norgaard, R. (1992), 'Sustainability as Intergenerational Equity: Economic Theory and Environmental Planning', *Environmental Impact Assessment Review*, 12, pp. 85-124.

Norgaard, R. (1994), *Development Betrayed: The End of Progress and a Coevolutionary Revisioning of the Future*, Routledge, London.

Norgaard, R. (1995), 'Metaphors we Might Survive By', *Ecological Economics,* vol. 15, pp. 129-131.

Norton, B.G. and Toman, M.A. (1997), 'Sustainability: Ecological and Economic Perspectives', *Land Economics,* 73(4), pp. 553-568.

Ortolano, L. (1984), *Environmental Planning and Decision Making*, John Wiley and Sons, New York.

Pearce, D.W. and Turner, R.K. (1990), *Economics of Natural Resources and the Environment*, Harvester Wheatsheaf, Hemel Hempstead.

Perman, R., Ma, Y., McGilvray, J., Common, M. (1999), *Natural Resource & Environmental Economics*, Longman, London.

Potts, J. (2002), *The New Evolutionary Microeconomics : Complexity, Competence, and Adaptive Behaviour*, Edward Elgar, Cheltenham, UK, Northampton, MA, USA.

Rees, W.E. (1990), 'The Ecology of Sustainable Development', *Ecologist*, vol. 20 (1), pp. 18-23.

Solow, R.M. (1992), *An Almost Practical Step Toward Sustainability*, Washington D.C., Resources for the Future.

Spash, C.L. (1999), 'The Development of Environmental Thinking in Economics', *Environmental Values*, 8, 413-435.

Swyngedouw, E., Kaïka, M., Castro, E. (2002), 'Urban Water: a Political Ecologic Perspective', *Built Environment*, 28 (2), pp. 124-137.

Tietenberg, T. H. (2003), *Environmental and Natural Resource Economics*, 6th ed, Addison Wesley, Boston.

Vatn, A. and Bromley, D.W. (1994), 'Choices Without Prices Without Apologies', *Journal of Environmental Economics and Management*, 26, pp. 129-148.

Chapter 3

Tourism Carrying Capacity:
A Theoretical Overview

Alexandra Mexa and Harry Coccossis

Defining Tourism Carrying Capacity

In any locality there is a strong relationship between society, economy and environment. Environmental and other geographic features create locational advantages attracting people and economic activities. Human activities and patterns of living are often based on local environmental conditions and resources while at the same time they may affect them. Quite often the degradation of the environment may have impacts on people and their activities, as in the case of tourism. To the extent that such effects do not significantly disturb the structure and dynamics of local human and natural ecosystems there is a perceived state of balance or 'harmony' perceived in a dynamic sense of continuing gradual change and adaptation. A critical issue in this perspective is the capacity of a system to assimilate change, which also brings forward also the notion of its thresholds or limits. This is the conceptual basis of carrying capacity in tourism planning and management (Coccossis, 2002; Coccossis and Parpairis, 2000).

Early definitions of carrying capacity have concentrated on a unidisciplinary/one-dimensional perspective (for example from biology). Some other issues related for example to the impacts of tourism on local economy or society (economic and social capacity) were also gradually introduced (O' Reilly, 1986). Recent interpretations underline the need for a multi-dimensional approach (PAP/RAC, 1997). Definitions have attempted to relate the capacity issue to qualitative aspects such as visitor satisfaction. The existence of three different types of carrying capacity – environmental, physical and perceptual or psychological – of an area has been suggested by Pearce (1989), referring mainly to negative impacts from tourism such as degradation of the environment, saturation of facilities and decline in enjoyment by visitors. It thus became evident that carrying capacity needs to be determined not only in terms of ecology and generally the deterioration of the area but furthermore it needs to incorporate the visitors' experiences thus human values (Manning, 2002). There are various definitions of tourism carrying capacity (TCC), none of which is universally accepted, and there is no unique, standard procedure for assessing tourism carrying capacity (Saveriades, 2000); developing a quantitative methodology for measuring carrying capacity in various sites, satisfying different management needs is considered a 'mission impossible' (Kun, 2002). Most definitions of tourism carrying capacity combine two aspects: the 'capacity issue' of a destination (how many tourists are wanted, or how much tourism can be accommodated before negative impacts are evidenced) and the 'perception of capacity issue' (how much tourism is acceptable before a decline in the level of satisfaction and ensuing decline in tourism) (O' Reilly, 1986; Saveriades, 2000; Glasson et al., 1995).

In the following paragraph some of the commonly used definitions of tourism carrying capacity are presented in an effort not only to highlight their differences but also their contribution to an understanding of a complex and multi-dimensional issue: carrying capacity. References include both tourism and recreational carrying capacity.

From a general point of view tourism carrying capacity is 'the maximum number of people that may visit a tourist destination at the same time without causing destruction of the physical, economic and sociocultural environment and an unacceptable decrease in the quality of visitor satisfaction' (WTO, 1981). In ecological terms carrying capacity can be defined 'as the maximum number of visitors that can be accommodated by a given destination under conditions of maximum stress' and in economic terms 'as the maximum number of visitors that can be accommodated at a constant quality of their experience' (Canestrelli and Costa, 1991, p.296). Tourism carrying capacity can be also defined as 'the maximum use of any site without causing negative effects on the resources, reducing visitor satisfaction, or exerting adverse impact upon the society, economy and culture of the area' (McIntyre, 1993, p.23). For tourist destination resorts tourism carrying capacity can be defined as the number of user unit use periods that a tourist area can provide each year without permanent natural/physical deterioration of the area's ability to support recreation and tourism and without appreciable impairment of the visitors' recreational experience (Coccossis and Parpairis, 1995, p.119). In referring to carrying capacity of parks and wilderness areas carrying capacity can be defined as 'the amount of types of visitor use that can be accommodated without unacceptable resource and social impacts' (Manning and Lawson, 2002, p.157). Carrying capacity can also be understood as a function of various factors such as 'quantity of available resources, tolerance of available resources to use, number of visitors, type of use, design and management at place, attitude and behaviour of tourists' (Lindsay in Glasson et al., 1995, p. 45).

Different definitions, as those above may suggest different interpretations of tourism carrying capacity. Manning and Lawson as well as WTO relate tourism carrying capacity to *unacceptable* impacts introducing explicitly the – no doubt existent in the other definitions – subjective nature of the carrying capacity concept. Canestrelli and Costa suggest that there are different types of capacity, or different components of carrying capacity, such as the ecological and the economic and the limits implied by each type do not necessarily have to coincide. As a result, managers face the prospect of making decisions on the basis of arbitrary trade-offs, probably in favour of the most limiting factors. From an extreme position, implying that tourism always has negative impacts, McIntyre correlates intensity of use with impacts and visitor satisfaction, suggesting that an increase of use may increase or provoke impacts and reduce satisfaction. However, it has been argued by several researchers that the use is not always related to impacts and satisfaction through a linear relationship; season and type of use can be more significant factors than the intensity for the appearance of certain impacts (Shelby and Heberlein, 1986; Sofield, 2002). Coccossis and Parpairis associate exceeding of carrying capacity limits with the natural/physical deterioration of the area's *ability* to support recreation, which could be different from the actual natural/physical deterioration of the area. Recreation and tourism might be more sensitive to declining characteristics of the natural environment, not affecting other sectors (for example agriculture). Conversely, recreation may continue to be supported (even in the case where some qualitative changes have occurred due for example to the change in the type of tourists visiting the area) although natural deterioration has been observed. Lindsay's definition highlights the multi-dimensional character of tourism carrying capacity; the existence of several interrelated and interdependent factors indicates the complexity of the system itself.

The above simply highlight the richness of interpretations of carrying capacity, and the various aspects (or dimensions) of tourism carrying capacity. These differences among definitions also imply differences in ways of *measuring* tourism carrying capacity, therefore differences in approaches to be adopted for that purpose. This is also suggested by the following definition according to which carrying capacity is:

> ...the amount of tourism damage a site can assimilate without long term damage, which can be *measured* against the total number of tourists visiting the site to determine whether the social optimum has been exceeded and the site is being over-utilized (Steele, 1995).

However for many researchers carrying capacity still remains ill-defined, encouraging debate in respect to its use for tourism management (Butler, 1997; Glasson et al., 1995).

Some definitions of carrying capacity are more targeted, as is the case of protected areas (national parks, wilderness areas) focusing on the *acceptability* of natural resource and human impacts of visitation and considering biophysical characteristics, social factors and management policies (visitor use restrictions) to be more important determinants of carrying capacity than the number of visitors (Prato, 2001). Within this context limits on the number of visitors are not to be directly interpreted as carrying capacity (Sofield, 2002).

Criticism of the Tourism Carrying Capacity Concept

In tourism planning, carrying capacity is often interpreted as the maximum acceptable level of tourism development in an area. Although at a conceptual level carrying capacity is easily understood and accepted, in operational terms it meets with considerable difficulties (Williams, 1998). There are several interrelated factors, which need to be considered, rendering the determination of a desirable 'unique' number difficult, or in general of explicitly carrying capacities and consequently the application of tourism carrying capacity in tourism planning and management (Gold, 1980; Farrell and Runyan, 1991; Ferreira and Harmse, 1999). This difficulty has led some researchers to characterize carrying capacity as a 'flawed concept' (Sofield, 2002). To overcome such limitations some site or destination managers prefer to focus on the acceptable changes in the environment or recreation experience (characterized as outputs) instead of trying to estimate the 'magic number' of users (inputs) (Sofield, 2002).

Empirical evidence in Europe (EC, 2002) indicates that the analysis of tourism carrying capacity is often exhaustive, although at the implementation stage the focus is on a few critical factors (consumption of scarce resources like water, the relationship or ratio between inhabitants and tourists, and so on). To the extent that this reduction is based on a broad consideration of both the structure and the dynamics of the system under study, it can probably overcome the dissonance between the concept and its operationalization identified earlier. Monitoring, evaluation and appropriate adaptation could provide the core of a process in applying tourism carrying capacity assessment.

Criticism of carrying capacity is also related to the fact that it '...is often addressed theoretically in a modeling approach, divorced from reality – that is the political solution to inadequate development control' (Clark et al., 2002).

Lindberg, McCool and Stankey (1997) summarize criticisms of tourism carrying capacity in three points, identified also as limitations: the first is that carrying capacity definitions often provide little guidance for practical implementation, the second relates to the perception of carrying capacity as a scientific objective concept, while the third relates to the fact that 'carrying capacity typically focuses attention on use levels or numbers of visitors, yet management objectives typically relate to conditions'.

In respect to the first point of criticism it is noted that definitions of complex concepts such as tourism carrying capacity, or sustainability, need to be regarded more as *guiding frameworks* and less as scientific and operational definitions, which are rigorous and precise, providing detailed guidance, enabling researchers to compare results, allowing transfer of experience, and so on. Lime (in Shelby and Heberlein, 1986) notes that carrying capacity should be considered as a 'framework', a way of thinking, for planning and managing tourism and as such it cannot provide the basis for some 'magic formula' for estimating 'how much is too much'. The inability to arrive at such a definition needs not to be regarded as a weakness but more as the result of the inherent characteristics of the concept itself.

Carrying capacity by definition opens new horizons and this is both demanding and challenging. If carrying capacity definitions are perceived as guiding frameworks then it becomes apparent that the quest for a unified, universal set of criteria or an approach to specify/measure carrying capacity will not be necessary, since it is understood that this needs to be dealt within each case separately. Such a framework needs to provide *guiding principles* so as to pursue further action and research taking into account local characteristics and particularities.

The second point of criticism of Lindberg, McCool and Stankey has become the center of an interesting debate. For some, the fact that carrying capacity is based to a great extent on subjective perceptions is believed to render it problematic (Priestley and Mundet, 1998). However several other researchers refer to carrying capacity as a management notion and not as a scientific concept or formula to obtain a number, beyond which development should cease (Stankey in Lindberg et al., 1997; Saveriades, 2000, p. 151). The eventual limits must be considered as guides. They should be carefully assessed and monitored, complemented with other tools such as standards, and so on. In this sense, carrying capacity is not a unique unchangeable number, on the contrary it changes with time and is related to the patterns of growth of tourism (for example it may be diminished by uncontrolled growth and unregulated overuse) and it can be altered by management action (Hendee, et al., 1990; Saveriades, 2000). Technology and organization, for example, can play an instrumental role towards this direction. Researchers have highlighted the implications that technological achievements may have on tourism. Electronic reservation, use of intelligent cards, opportunities to control visitor flows, new ways of interpretation will undoubtedly provide new perspectives in tourism demand and tourist supply (Lindsay 1992; Martin and Mason, 1993).

Carrying capacity does not involve only technical issues, but political ones as well (the choice of a managerial objective is a political and not just a technical act) (McCool, 2002). Carrying capacity reflects to an extent the expectations and goals of the various actors involved and their identification may arise as a central issue/question instead of the question, 'how many visitors can the resources bear?' (Ashworth, 1995, p. 57-58). The subjective component of carrying capacity is not necessarily something negative. As Cole (in Sofield, 2002) notes, 'recreation carrying capacity is not an inherent value; it must reflect value judgments'.

However tourism carrying capacity does not only revolve around management subjective issues but also around scientifically objective issues as well. It incorporates matters of both science and values, which need to be integrated into 'informed judgments' (Manning and Lawson, 2002).

The third critical limitation relates to the fact that 'carrying capacity typically focuses attention on use levels or numbers of visitors, yet management objectives typically relate to conditions' (Lindberg et al., 1997). The emphasis put on imposing limits on the number of visitors as a key action to limit impacts, which as a result leads to the use of limits as an end in itself, is wrong (McCool, 2002). Tourism carrying capacity fails 'to take into account relationships between use and impact or to consider prescriptive measures regarding what kinds of conditions should be sought in a place' (Ahn et al., 2002, p.4).

It is widely understood that the identification of desired conditions is at the core of tourism destination management. These reflect two types of concern: the desired level of key conditions (characteristics) of the destination and the level of user satisfaction. It is also understood that there are significant difficulties in linking numbers of users/visitors to levels of impacts, therefore with 'conditions after use' and their impacts on user satisfaction. However the definition of a desirable number of tourists or of use levels is also a practical and operational tool in management. Adopting a *two-tier approach* (identify desired conditions as well as limits on the number of tourists) provides the opportunity to evade the issue and shift the focus of management on monitoring both 'ambience' conditions: (desirable state of the 'environment' and user satisfaction) and the number of users as an indicator of pressures. It is the latter which provides the opportunity for action.

In spite of all limitations (e.g. relating uses and impacts) a return to the concept of identifying maximum appropriate numbers of users and limits on the amount of development needs to be encouraged (Butler, 1997). '...In the absence of such control (on levels, type and time of use), overuse, misuse and abuse of the resource are likely to occur over time' (Boyd and Butler, 1996, p.559). In certain cases, particularly in the cases of small areas such as monuments, sites or natural areas, for practical reasons a threshold needs to be identified (whenever this is possible, even though it may change over time, across seasons or a week, and so on) which could easily be implemented/monitored without excessive demands on the ground.

Limitations of Tourism Carrying Capacity Assessment

As noted earlier carrying capacity is not a matter of identifying a fixed value. It can change over time due to several internal or external factors. Carrying capacity can also take various values at a given time as well. For example different perspectives (or emphases on a certain dimension or component) may lead to different measurements of tourism carrying capacity. These are limitations, on the basis of which a lot of the criticism presented in the previous section is rooted. These usually focus on two issues: 'capacity' and the 'perception of capacity'. They reflect difficulties in understanding and measuring tourism dynamics, in identifying which impacts are caused – or to what extent – by tourism, to difficulties arising from the fact that there are different types of impacts on the host community that need to be studied (McElroy and de Albuquerque, 1998) but also to difficulties in determining how much impact is too much, or what is the maximum amount of crowding (or of some other condition or impact) which might be acceptable (Manning, 2002). Furthermore the environment is dynamic and varied as both natural and human ecosystems are characterized by change and adaptation, while any human presence will influence and eventually modify the environment. Ecological capacities are difficult to define. In reality there is a complex pattern of interaction among levels deriving from the composite character of tourism and the dynamic nature of systems involved (Pearce, 1989). Furthermore ecosystems are characterized by complex feedback loops making the assessment of cause and effect relationships related to tourism particularly difficult. It has been suggested that tourism carrying capacity is rooted in a false assumption that of a stable ecosystem, characterized by harmony (McCool and Lime, 2001).

Similar difficulties are confronted in defining perceptual capacities, which are subject to variations between and within individuals and groups, as well as to management objectives (Williams, 1998).

For example different perspectives often exist among managers or regulators and visitors or tourists. The first may focus, on the biological and ecological factors whereas visitors are concerned with the 'perceptions of must-see attractions' (Sofield, 2002). Their views may be completely different (Stewart and Cole, 2003). For example in a survey for mountain activities it was found that in general bikers enjoy the challenge of obstacles on the trail many of which are present due to erosion. It is a case where what is acceptable and desirable for managers and visitors respectively may be in total conflict, although there are ways to achieve a point of equilibrium. It is however the concept of carrying capacity that revealed these issues/conflicts in the first place, 'forcing' managers to search for appropriate solutions that could accommodate ecological but also social concerns (Symmonds et al., 2000).

Different perspectives can be observed among visitors as well, resulting in differentiated satisfaction levels (Lindberg et al., 1997). These differences effect prioritization of desired conditions, therefore affecting the measurement of tourism carrying capacity. The visitors might also be unaware of the underlying causes of the threat that may be imposed in a particular area, or perceive impacts improperly or underestimate their significance; they might also underestimate the impacts which they themselves can cause when compared with the impacts caused by another group; they may also not understand the complexity of the issues faced by managers (Sofield, 2002; Symmonds et al., 2000; Stewart and Cole, 2003).

Research on visitor satisfaction indicates that often the level of use has limited, if any, influence on overall visitor satisfaction, although it may affect the type of tourists attracted; certain types of tourists will not visit the area and this group will be replaced by another one (Lindberg et al., 1997). For many to determine social carrying capacity a more precise tool than that of satisfaction is requested (e.g. perceived crowding may be more appropriate), since there were cases where people complained about crowding, feeling that carrying capacity had been exceeded, even though the satisfaction levels recorded were quite high (Shelby and Heberlein, 1986). In cases of crowding perception psychological factors seem to be far more influential (Lee and Graefe, 2003).

It is therefore a complex mix of objectivity and subjectivity that governs differential perspectives on what is and what is not acceptable capacity (Haas, in

Sofield, 2002). That suggests that tourism managers need to participate in a dialogue, which will pursue a convergence of the various, often diverging perspectives of visitor capacity (ibid).

The Emergence of Other Approaches to Capacity for Tourism Assessment

Carrying capacity can be a powerful concept for policy making although from a scientific perspective it has met with considerable controversy due to the analytical difficulties in arriving at a 'calculated' capacity (threshold or limit). This difficulty as noted stems from the multiple dimensions of the concept and the inherent constraints in estimating limits in natural and human ecosystems. It is for this that several researches prefer to use other vocabulary like 'limits of acceptable change' because it better encompasses their understanding of the critical interaction between human and natural systems at every level (Howard and Potter, 2002).

In recent literature the interest in carrying capacity has shifted from an 'objectively' assessed threshold to (policy useful) *desired conditions* providing more advantages to planning and decision making. Instead of searching for precise limits concerning the number of users who would be sustained by an area it was recognized that a number of alternative capacity levels exist, some based on human preferences. Following this, emphasis was placed on management policies that meet visitor expectations and preferences rather than on determining limits to use (Boyd and Butler, 1996).

Alternative concepts have been suggested reflecting *Management-By-Objectives (MBO) approaches* such as Visitor Impact Management (VIM), Limits of Acceptable Change (LAC), Visitor Experience and Resource Protection (VERP), Tourism Organization Management Model (TOMM), and so on.

These tools are based on a more or less similar process (Manning, 2002), as demonstrated in Table 3.1. Indicators and standards of quality can be used to determine carrying capacity, furthermore managed with the help of a monitoring program. This approach to carrying capacity is central to LAC, VIM and VERP (Manning, 2002).

Table 3.1 Some alternative approaches to tourism carrying capacity

The *'Limits of Acceptable Change (LAC)' approach* (McCool, 1994; Stankey et al., 1985; Glasson et al., 1995; Ahn et al., 2002)

The LAC approach aims at defining those conditions which are recognized as desirable in an area and sets up management strategies to maintain or restore these conditions and achieve specified goals.
This approach does not search for use limits; it utilizes land use zoning where a set of desired conditions in terms of social, ecological, physical and economic impacts are maintained. Standards are defined and indicators

utilized, to identify when unacceptable impacts emerge, along with appropriate actions so as to achieve management objectives. Indicators may relate to the various types of tourism impacts.

The 'Visitor Impact Management (VIM)' approach (Graefe et al., 1990; Glasson et al., 1995, p.150)

The VIM approach identifies what are considered to be unacceptable visitor impacts, their likely cause and the appropriate actions to anticipate the problems. Like LAC approach it does not seek a numeric value, instead it identifies a set of standards which can be used to compare with existing conditions. VIM is a process of adaptation, which describes desirable conditions and evaluates current activity as a basis for setting tourism management objectives. It does not consider tourism in isolation but integrates the sector within other socioeconomic development activities, thus forming an element of comprehensive local (and regional, as appropriate) development plans.

The 'Visitor Experience and Resource Protection (VERP)' approach (Manning, 2002)

The VERP framework had been initially applied for park management. VERP constitutes of four main phases. The first comprises, in a way, all preparatory activities such as the establishment of an interdisciplinary project team, the development of a strategy to ensure public participation during the entire process and last but not least the development of statements with reference to the purpose, significance and primary interpretive themes. The second phase is the analysis of resources and of existing visitor use. The third phase includes the description of a potential range of visitor experiences and resource conditions (on the basis of which potential prescriptive zones will be identified). Specific indicators and standards will then be selected with the aim to develop a monitoring plan. The final phase of the VERP process is the monitoring and management phase.

The rise of these approaches such as LAC, ROS (Recreation Opportunity Spectrum), and so on is partially explained by the increased interest in social aspects, overuse and crowding and their management implications (Butler, 2002).

Some of these approaches (e.g. Tangible Resource Limits, Tolerance by the Host Population, Satisfaction of Visitors, Excessive Rate of Growth of Change) are considered as different *approaches of interpretations or methods of determining* carrying capacity (Getz, 1983) or (e.g. LAC, VIM and VERP) as *contemporary carrying capacity frameworks* (Manning and Lawson, 2002), or *a reformulated view of carrying capacity* (Stankey et al., in Sofield, 2002), suggesting that they are closely linked to the basic concept of tourism carrying capacity.

Limitations of Alternative Approaches

The approaches described above do not 'escape' from the criticism that refers to tourism carrying capacity (e.g. criticism related to the subjectivity of the method (Lindberg, McCool and Stankey, 1997). For example the LAC framework in its search for relationships between existing and desired or 'acceptable' conditions relies on management judgment (Ahn et al., 2002). Furthermore visitor satisfaction is a multidimensional concept that is influenced by a potentially broad assay of elements of the resource, social and managerial environments (Manning, 2003), suggesting that one cannot escape from the numerous factors that need to be considered as in the case of carrying capacity. The difficulty of tourism carrying capacity assessment to arrive at the calculation of a unique number that would successfully incorporate environmental and socioeconomic constraints is present in the LAC framework as well. Furthermore it is recognized that conditions and thus their acceptability vary considerably, whether planning for a specific wilderness or an urban area (Ahn et al., 2002). This is the result of the fact that at the heart of the LAC process is acceptability of an amount of change (ibid) which, however, can be influenced by several factors such as education, level of awareness regarding for example impacts from tourism, age, and so on. Williams (1998) identifies two limitations regarding LAC approach, the first relates to difficulties in agreeing and assessing qualitative aspects and the second has to do with the fact that the process is dependent upon the existence (or we could say upon the hypothesis of the existence) of a structured planning system, of sufficient resources (human and monetary) that could assist the monitoring and review stages. Others (Glasson et al., 1995) refer to difficulties arising from the need for detailed information (compromises to this may lead to more or less arbitrary conclusions) and the fact that the LAC approach is part of an on-going process of planning, management and monitoring and as such it could not be used as an 'on-off' tool.

Concerning the VIM approach several limitations are recognized, mainly related to the relationship between use and impact, including among others the recognition that there is no predictable response between use and experiences, that impacts do not relate through a linear relationship with user density, that different groups have different levels of tolerance, that some types of activities have different impacts and that site-specific and seasonal variables influence impacts (Glasson et al., 1995, pp.59-61).

Butler (1997, p.12) argues that 'the adoption of approaches like LAC and ROS results in a form of creeping incrementalism of development and with it cumulative change, shifts in tastes and types of tourists, and essentially a shifting of capacity limits in favour of even higher levels of use'. Furthermore what is of critical importance and most worrying is that these approaches have encouraged a shift in emphasis from determining maximum acceptable levels of use and corresponding visitor numbers to determining acceptable and desirable levels of environment and experience; although these approaches can be of great help they should not be regarded as substitutes for carrying capacity (Butler, 2002). It is also interesting to note that although in the early stage of the research for carrying capacity the emphasis was placed on the ecological component, now the reverse is evident, since the emphasis is placed on the social elements of tourism carrying capacity (ibid). This shift however could become a threat for the environmental conservation of several destinations.

Prerequisites for Applying Tourism Carrying Capacity

Lindberg, McCool and Stankey (1997, p.463) refer to seven requirements that need to be satisfied so as to render carrying capacity a useful framework: agreement on the type of desired social and resource conditions, agreement on the desired level of these conditions and thus the standard for each indicator, known relationship between use levels and impacts for each indicator, use level must be more important than other factors such as visitor behavior or management actions in determining the amount of impact, the management agency must have the legal, human resource and financial ability to limit access to the area, there must be agreement on the rationing system, (such as price or first-come, first-served) used to limit access the gain to admitted visitors must implicitly outweigh the loss to excluded visitors.

As the authors suggest these requirements are rarely, if ever, met. This is the reason of a shift from 'how many?' to 'what are the desired conditions?' that encouraged the development of various approaches such as LAC, VIM and VERP.

The requirements introduced reflect a more or less *rational* approach, based on several assumptions, according to which cause-effect relationships can be traced, agreement can be achieved on the basis of scientific evidence, trade-offs can be estimated (i.e. cost-benefit analysis is possible), decision-making is rational, implementation is given and is not the result of a continuous struggle involving a lot of uncertainty, the power of the agency responsible for implementation is given, and so on. However reality does not resemble such an ideal situation, suggested preconditions are rarely met. In implementing tourism carrying capacity some of the aforementioned preconditions need to be regarded more as expected or desirable outcomes, goals to be pursued. For example agreement may not be the starting point for TCCA but it may emerge through a process of dialogue and negotiation among the actors involved.

Carrying capacity needs to be regarded as an ongoing process. Incremental decisions may be taken often based on incomplete knowledge concerning for example, the relationship between use levels and impacts. Visitors' expectations and satisfaction levels need to be incorporated and balanced over long-term conservation goals, while gains and losses from applying TCC may not always be possible to identify.

Major Shifts in Applying Tourism Carrying Capacity: From Controlling to Planning for Tourism Development

During the past decades in spite of criticism the concept of carrying capacity has re-emerged at the centre of scientific debate. This possibly underlines the fact that tourism carrying capacity is a powerful concept which has succeeded in evolving and embracing new concerns in planning and in managing impacts from tourism development. These past decades are characterized by major shifts in assessing tourism carrying capacity, highlighted below (some of which have been discussed already).

A gradual *broadening of the scope* of tourism carrying capacity assessment has been noticed, from ecological, physical to social and economic carrying capacity, also resulting in the increase of the factors to be considered.

In addition *the focus has shifted* from the idea of determining maximum numbers of users towards the achievement of desirable conditions, identification of limits of acceptable change, and so on. This kind of shift also underlines a shift in emphasis: from impacts to the perception of impacts. This was partially necessary since at the early stages social aspects, and general subjective concerns were neglected. However scientific issues need not be played down and capacity issues as well as perception of capacity considerations need to be addressed with equal importance.

The prevailing concern for a scientific approach to tourism carrying capacity has been gradually broadened *towards a management approach*. This implies moving from explicit and numerical values towards more indicative systems. This has been the result of various changes (more factors to be considered, changes in the spatial scale to be studied, and so on). Numerical capacities may be still appropriate in a few cases (McCool and Lime, 2001), but in general a unique numerical number for carrying capacity may not always be attainable. Carrying capacity needs not to be regarded as an end in itself. It is not realistic to expect or pursue a finite carrying capacity for a specific area. On the contrary it is more realistic to expect many different, possible carrying capacities depending on management goals, resiliency of the systems and types of activity (Saveriades, 2000). In addition it is not only the maximum number of visitors that need to be defined, but also the optimal number that is the number that maximizes positive impacts in the host community (Kun, 2002).

The above had several implications on the process of defining and assessing tourism carrying capacity which gradually 'escaped' from the field of a scientific and experts discourse moving *towards a process of dialogue,* which involves not only key stakeholders but also tourists themselves, allowing for the incorporation of their perceptions and expectations.

Sustainability has brought new impetus to the concept of carrying capacity in tourism planning literature. Sustainability has re-oriented assessments of policy towards social and environmental issues. A lot of concern revolves around the issue of sustainable tourism. Sustainability also brought into perspective the need to deal with relative weights and values. So Pforr (2001, p.70) argues that:

> ...the debate about definitions and how concepts of sustainable development, sustainable tourism and ecotourism can be translated into the real world, however often remains a highly technical, scientific one and neglects the consideration of values and interests of the various actors involved.

This is understandable, as in a process of dialogue and compromises, one cannot ignore the 'power arrangements' taking place since the whole process is a 'highly political phenomenon, a process that governs how these concepts are defined and translated into action or non-action'. *The same argument applies for tourism carrying capacity assessment.* After all it is often stressed that carrying capacity conflicts do not revolve around resource questions but also involve issues concerning values (Ferreira and Harmse, 1999). In reality managers increasingly deal more with values than with facts, while to a great extent the uncertainty in many carrying capacity decisions is largely value-based (Stewart and Cole, 2003).

What is also of great interest is that tourism carrying capacity assessment is not considered only for limited, confined sites (hosting mainly recreational activities) but for various types of large tourist destinations such as cities, coastal areas and islands. The transition from a smaller to a significant larger spatial scale, combined with the tendency to include more parameters renders the whole attempt of capacity assessment far more difficult. Concerns relate also to 'how much and what type of development?', and not only to 'how many and what type of tourists and tourist activities?'. These concerns are rooted to a great extent in an increased awareness regarding sustainable tourism development.

There is also a general shift from 'isolated' tourism carrying capacity initiatives to the integration of capacity assessment into broader planning and management schemes. Although the application of TCCA is not always explicitly stated, the basic concept is present, the need to impose some kind of limits (e.g. Local Agenda 21). TCC for example has been regarded as part of an ongoing management process for coastal areas that of Integrated Coastal Zone Management (PAP/RAC, 1997; PAP/RAC, 2003).

Tourism Carrying Capacity: (Still) a Powerful Concept?

Beyond criticism, tourism carrying capacity, remains a powerful concept and as such can serve planning and management towards sustainable tourism.

Long-term considerations are inherent in the carrying capacity concept. Sustainable tourism development is defined as the development that is (Janssen et al., 1995, p.65):

both in volume and in direction of development evolving in such a way that the pressure on the natural environment remains below the level of the *carrying capacity* for both the *present* and the *future generation.*

Carrying capacity can contribute to managing tourism on the basis of sustainability principles. It is considered as a well-established approach inherent in the notion of sustainability (Williams, 1998; Glasson et al., 1995). As such carrying capacity needs to be regarded as a *guiding framework* that could help in revealing policy, contributing to achieving consensus over the need to pursue sustainable tourism development. The difficulties arising from the interpretation of the concept so as to guide concrete action need to be regarded not as a failure of the initial idea and corresponding definition but more as a challenge for further research as well as political debate.

Furthermore to a certain extent problems and issues for management relate to levels of use and levels of development. Therefore although carrying capacity does not always coincide with use/development limits it can help in identifying these limits. The imposition of limits does not have to be seen as negative since it can provide a positive perspective as well, as it may encourage the 'discovery' of new areas in an effort to control carrying capacity in a given area (Haas, in Sofield, 2002).

In addition carrying capacity can be used in combination with several other approaches providing an appropriate tool kit for tourism managers. The application of use limits needs to be regarded as one of many other management options that could assist anticipation of impacts from tourism development (McCool, 2002). Buckley (1998, p.209) stresses the need to recognize the different approaches to managing tourism (carrying capacity, LAC, ROS, VIM) as different aspects of a single all-encompassing monitoring and management strategy.

Furthermore carrying capacity is a concept, which seems to be familiar and comprehensible to non-experts such as decision-makers, other key stakeholders, and so on. This can serve as an advantage in management.

Regarding criticism of tourism carrying capacity, mainly rooted in the limitations previously discussed it should be stressed that limitations on carrying capacity are closely linked with *expectations*, often unrealistic, related among others to scientific progress (increased knowledge could lead to an increased capability in providing answers to (all) problems), to institutional and planning settings, to the rational character of decision-making, and so on. Given that these expectations are to a great extent either unrealistic or conditioned to several other factors it becomes evident that as far as the (success of the) decision for implementing tourism carrying capacity is linked to all these limitations/factors no progress is expected to be recorded. Limited implementation of tourism carrying capacity will no doubt inhibit the understanding of several methodological issues related to measurement of tourism carrying capacity.

References

Ahn, B., Lee, B., Shafer, S.C. (2002), 'Operationalizing Sustainability in Regional Tourism Planning: An Application of the Limits of Acceptable Change Framework', *Tourism Management*, Vol. 23, No. 1, pp.1-15.

Ashworth, G. (1995), 'Environmental Quality and Tourism and the Environment' in Coccossis, H. and Nijkamp, P. (eds), *Sustainable Tourism Development*, Avebury, Aldershot, pp. 49-63.

Boyd, S. and Butler, R. (1996), 'Managing Ecotourism: An Opportunity Spectrum Approach', *Tourism Management*, Vol. 17, No. 8, pp. 557-566.

Buckley, R. (1998), 'Tools and Indicators for Managing Tourism in Parks', *Annals of Tourism Research*, Vol. 25, No. 4, pp. 208-211.

Butler, R. (1997), 'The Concept of Carrying Capacity for Tourist Destinations: Dead or Merely Dead?', in Cooper, C. and Wanhill, S. (eds), *Tourism Development. Environmental and Community Issues*, Wiley, Chichester, pp. 11-21.

Butler, R. (2002), 'Issues in Applying Carrying Capacity Concepts: Examples from the United Kingdom', *WWF Hellas Conference on Methods for Tourism Carrying Capacity Measurement and Visitor Management in Protected Areas: Presentations and Conclusions*, Athens, 31/5-1/6/2002.

Canestrelli, E. and Costa, P. (1991), 'Tourist Carrying Capacity. A Fuzzy Approach', *Annals of Tourism Research*, Vol. 18, No. 2, pp. 295-311.

Clark, J.R., Clifford, G., Khanna, S., Padamsee, Y., Potter, B., Towle, E. (2002), 'Small Island Carrying Capacity, Vulnerability and Indicators'.
http://www.csiwisepractices.org/?review=441

Coccossis, H. (2002), 'Tourism Development and Carrying Capacity', in Apostolopoulos, G. and Gayle, D. (eds), *Island Tourism and Sustainable Development: Caribbean, Pacific and Mediterranean Experiences*, Praeger, Westport, Connecticut, pp. 131-144.

Coccossis, H. and Paprairis, A. (1995), 'Assessing the Interaction between Heritage, Environment and Tourism: Myconos' in Coccossis, H. and Nijkamp, P. (eds), *Sustainable Tourism Development*, Avebury, Aldershot, pp.107-125.

Coccossis, H. and Parpairis, A. (2000), 'Tourism and the Environment – Some Observations on the Concept of Carrying Capacity', in Briassoulis, H. and van der Straaten, J. (eds), *Tourism and the Environment. Regional, Economic, Cultural and Policy Issues*, Kluwer Academic Publishers, Dordrecht, pp. 91-106.

European Commission (EC) (2002), *Defining, Measuring and Evaluating Carrying Capacity in European Tourism Destinations. Material for a Document.* Prepared by Coccossis, H., Mexa, A. and Collovini, A., University of the Aegean, Department of Environmental Studies, Laboratory of Environmental Planning, Greece. http://europa.eu.int/comm./environment/iczm/tcca_material.pdf

Farrell, B. and Runyan, D. (1991), 'Ecology and Tourism', *Annals of Tourism Research*, Vol. 18, No. 1, pp. 26-40.

Ferreira, S. and Harmse, A. (1999), 'The Social Carrying Capacity of Kruger National Park, South Africa: Policy and Practice', *Tourism Geographies*, Vol. 1, No. 3, pp. 325-342.

Getz, D. (1983),'Capacity to Absorb Tourism – Concepts and Implications for Strategic Planning', *Annals of Tourism Research*, Vol.10, No.2, pp. 239-263.

Glasson, J., Godfrey, K., Goodey, B., Absalom, H., Borg, J. van der (1995), *Towards Visitor Impact Management: Visitor Impacts*, Avebury, Aldershot.

Gold, S.M. (1980), *Recreation Planning and Design*, Macgraw-Hill Books, New York.

Graefe, A.R., Kuss, F.R., and Vaske, J.J. (1990), *Visitor Impact Management: The Planning Framework*, National Parks and Conservation Association, Washington, D.C.

Hendee, J., Stankey, G., Lucas, R. (1990), *Wilderness Management*, 2nd ed, Golden, North America Press.

Howard, M. and Potter, B. (2002), 'Small Islands: Limits of Acceptable Change'. http://www.csiwisepractices.org/?review=420

Janssen, H., Kiers, M., Nijkamp, P. (1995), 'Private and Public Development Strategies for Sustainable Tourism Development of Island Economies', in Coccossis, H. and Nijkamp, P. (eds), *Sustainable Tourism Development*, Avebury, Aldershot, pp. 65-83.

Kun, Z. (2002), 'Assessment of Sustainable Tourism Development Potential: a Manual for Pan Parks', *WWF Hellas Conference on Methods for Tourism Carrying Capacity Measurement and Visitor Management in Protected Areas: Presentations and Conclusions*, Athens, 31/5-1/6/2002.

Lee, H. and Graefe, A. (2003), 'Crowding at an Arts Festival: Extending Crowding Models to the Frontcountry', *Tourism Management*, Vol. 24, No. 1, pp. 1-11.

Lindberg, K., McCool, S., Stankey, G. (1997), 'Rethinking Carrying Capacity', *Annals of Tourism Research*, Vol. 24, No. 2, pp. 461-464.

Lindsay, P. (1992), 'CRS Supply and Demand', *Tourism Management*, Vol. 13, No. 1, pp. 141-144.

Manning, R. (2002), 'How Much is too Much? Carrying Capacity of National Parks and Protected Areas', *WWF Hellas Conference on Methods for Tourism Carrying Capacity Measurement and Visitor Management in Protected Areas: Presentations and Conclusions*, Athens, 31/5-1/6/2002.

Manning, R. (2003), 'What to do about Crowding and Solitude in Parks and Wilderness? A Reply to Stewart and Cole', *Journal of Leisure Research*, Vol. 35, No. 1, pp. 107-118.

Manning, R. and Lawson, S. (2002), 'Carrying Capacity as "Informed Judgment"': The Values of Science and the Science of Values', *Environmental Management*, Vol. 30, No. 2, pp.157-168.

Martin, B. and Mason, S. (1993), 'The Future for Attractions: Meeting the Needs of the New Consumers', *Tourism Management*, Vol. 14, No. 1, pp. 34-40.

McCool, S. (2002), 'Principles and Concepts for Managing Visitor Impacts in Protected Areas', *WWF Hellas Conference on Methods for Tourism Carrying Capacity Measurement and Visitor Management in Protected Areas: Presentations and Conclusions*, Athens, 31/5-1/6/2002.

McCool, S. and Lime D. (2001), 'Tourism Carrying Capacity: Tempting Fantasy or Useful Reality?' *Journal of Sustainable Tourism*, Vol. 9, No. 5, pp. 372-388.

McCool, S.F. (1994), 'Planning for Sustainable Nature-Dependent Tourism Development: The Limits of Acceptable Change System', *Tourism Recreation Research*, Vol. 19, No. 2, pp. 51-55.

McElroy, J. and de Albuquerque, K. (1998), 'Tourism Penetration Index in Small Caribbean Islands', *Annals of Tourism Research*, Vol. 25, No. 1, pp. 145-168.

McIntyre, G. (1993), *Sustainable Tourist Development: Guide for Local Planners*, World Tourism Organization, Madrid.

O'Reilly, A.M. (1986), 'Tourism Carrying Capacity. Concepts and issues', *Tourism Management*, Vol. 7, No. 4, pp. 254-258.

PAP/RAC (1997), *Guidelines for Carrying Capacity Assessment for Tourism in Mediterranean Coastal Areas*, Priority Actions Programme Regional Activity Centre, Split, pp. viii+51.

PAP/RAC (2003), *Guide to Good Practice in Tourism Carrying Capacity Assessment*, Priority Actions Programme, Regional Activity Centre, Split.

Pearce, D. (1989), *Tourist Development*, Longman Scientific and Technical, Essex.

Pforr, C. (2001), 'Concepts of Sustainable Development, Sustainable Tourism and Ecotourism: Definitions, Principles and Linkages', *Scandinavian Journal of Hospitality and Tourism*, Vol. 1, No. 1, pp. 68-71.

Prato, T. (2001), 'Modelling Carrying Capacity for National Parks', *Ecological Economics*, Vol. 39, No. 3, pp. 321-331.

Priestley, G. and Mundet, L. (1998), 'The Post-Stagnation Phase of the Resort Cycle', *Annals of Tourism Research*, Vol. 25, No. 1, pp. 85-111.

Saveriades, A. (2000), 'Establishing the Social Tourism Carrying Capacity for the Tourist Resorts of the East Coast of the Republic of Cyprus', *Tourism Management*, Vol. 21, No. 2, pp. 147-156.

Shelby, B. and Heberlein, T. (1986), *Carrying Capacity in Recreational Settings*, Oregon State University Press, Corvallis, OR.

Sofield, T. (2002), 'Is the Glass Half-Empty? No, it is Half-Full', *WWF Hellas Conference on Methods for Tourism Carrying Capacity Measurement and Visitor Management in Protected Areas: Presentations and Conclusions*, Athens, 31/5-1/6/2002.

Stankey, G., Cole, D., Lucas, R., Petersen, M., Frissell, S., Washburne, R. (1985), *The Limits of Acceptable Change (LAC) System for Wilderness Planning*, USDA Forest Service General Technical Report INT-176.

Steele, P. (1995), 'Ecotourism: An Economic Analysis', *Journal of Sustainable Tourism*. Vol. 3, pp. 29-44.

Stewart, W. and Cole, D. (2003), 'On the Prescriptive Utility of Visitor Survey Research: A Rejoinder to Manning', *Journal of Leisure Research*, Vol. 35, No. 1, pp. 119-127.

Symmonds, M., Hammitt, W., Quisenberry V. (2000), 'Managing Recreational Trail Environments for Mountain Bike User Preferences', *Environmental Management*, Vol. 25, No. 5, pp. 549-564.

Williams, S. (1998), *Tourism Geography*, Routledge Contemporary Human Georgaphy Series, Routledge, London.

World Tourism Organization (WTO) (1981), *Saturation of Tourist Destinations: Report of the Secretary General*, Madrid.

Chapter 4

Tourism Carrying Capacity: Methodological Considerations

Harry Coccossis and Alexandra Mexa

Introduction

Conceptualizing tourism carrying capacity from a policy analysis perspective requires a multi-dimensional approach, inclusive of environmental, social, political and economic aspects of the tourist destination under consideration.

The scope of this chapter is to discuss some methodological aspects and present a framework for measuring and implementing tourism carrying capacity (TCC). It is a process which is closely related to the planning process for tourism development. It reflects a rational approach in examining and delimiting options for future tourism development with a view to taking early action. Measuring and implementing tourism carrying capacity requires an appropriate framework considering the particularities of each case regarding the characteristics of the destination in relation to the characteristics of tourists who visit the area. It also has to take account of the stage of tourism development, as carrying capacity may be applied in developing destinations as well as in mature ones, which may even be considered as saturated. The application of tourism carrying capacity can thus focus on the appropriate type of future tourism development in respect to certain key limits of local significance, or it may prescribe actions to be taken to change the type of tourism development. In any case an intrinsic component is monitoring the interface of tourism and locality and reference is made to the use of indicators for measuring and implementing TCC. At the end of the chapter an annex has been included where three types of indicators are presented following the logic of the area-basic-core model: indicators for sustainable development, indicators for sustainable tourism development and indicators for tourism carrying capacity. The presentation is by no means exhaustive but it suggests that tourism carrying capacity assessment needs to be regarded in close relation to the planning process for sustainable tourism development.

Measuring and Implementing Tourism Carrying Capacity

A Process Driven by Local Particularities

Obviously in considering carrying capacity the various issues (for example ecological, sociocultural) should be considered with different weight (or importance) in different destinations. These differences stem from the type (characteristics/particularities) of the place, the type(s) of tourism present and the tourism/environment interface. The three are interrelated to some extent (Coccossis, 2002):

- The characteristics of locality provide the basic structure for the development of tourism. These can be evidenced in terms of local resources, the vulnerability of local natural ecosystems, population size, economic structure, culture and local heritage, and so forth. Size, the structure and dynamism of the local society, culture and economy, organizational and management capacity can be also significant factors which influence the local ability to cope with pressures and impacts from tourism.

- The type of tourism determines the basic characteristics of tourist behaviour in terms of using space and tourism resources and conditions the tourist/local community, tourism/local economy and tourist development/environmental quality relationships. The type of tourism can be expressed in terms of the motive(s) for visiting a place, the mode of mobility and transport, the frequency and length of stay and activity range of tourists, daily expenditure, and so forth. In this context it is important to consider differences among types of tourists in terms of expectations, attitudes, behaviour and spatial activity patterns as these condition the pressures and impacts of tourism on a place. Furthermore other issues related to the structure of the tourism system (the role of tour-operators, the existence of major hotel chains and of other international firms and their role in local tourism development, and so on) need to be carefully considered in defining the type of tourism.

- The tourism/environment interface is a composite of the previous two factors mainly in the form and type of tourist development (spatial patterns), the phase in a life-cycle context of the destination, the level of organizational and technological systems employed, the management regime, and so on. The tourism/environment interface is expressed in terms of constraints evolving either from the impacts of tourism on the environment or from the degradation of the environment on tourism and the tourism product.

Carrying Capacity for Various Types of Tourist Destination: Focusing on Particularities

In applying tourism carrying capacity it is possible to put different emphasis or significance on the various components (or dimensions) to be considered (for example ecological, sociocultural) for different types of tourist destination (ibid.):

Coastal areas: Coastal areas are often associated with mass tourism, large scale construction and infrastructure, intensive land development and extensive urbanization, a prevalent model in most Mediterranean destinations. Carrying capacity issues revolve around considerations about tourist density, the use of beaches and tourist infrastructure, congestion of facilities, sea pollution, etc.

Islands: Island tourism, if not falling within the previous category, is more of the selective type with small and medium scale accommodation, often in (or around) existing settlements, rural local societies, small communities, etc. Carrying capacity considerations focus on the relationship of tourism with the local society and culture, the effects on local production systems and the economy of the island, quality of life but also the demands and impacts on resources such as water and energy, the management of waste, etc.

Protected areas: Tourism in protected areas is associated with appreciating and observing nature, scientific endeavor and education. This type of tourism is associated with minimal development of infrastructure and small scale interventions in areas normally under strong control and restrictive management. Carrying capacity issues concern the number of tourists, visitor flows and spatial patterns of concentration and dispersion vis-à-vis the protection of nature and the functioning of ecosystems but also the quality of visitors' experience.

Rural areas: Tourism in rural areas covers a wide range of purposes (motivations) and is usually associated with visiting areas of special beauty, being in nature, low intensity activities but widely dispersed around low density rural communities often in remote locations. In some areas agro-tourism falls within this category. Carrying capacity issues involve questions about visitor flows, impacts on local society and culture, effects on rural economies, the spatial patterns of visitor flows, etc.

Mountain resorts: These are likely to fall within the intensive development, mass tourism category, often centered on winter sports. Carrying capacity issues include environmental impacts from large scale infrastructure or access roads on natural ecosystems, microclimate change from artificial snow, vegetation cover losses and soil erosion, landscape deterioration, but also congestion of facilities and waste management.

Historical settlements and towns: Tourism is attracted to historic towns as a result of the built cultural heritage, urban amenities, lifestyle and cultural traditions, cultural events, etc. There can be several types of tourism in this category. The dominant mass tourism associated with large numbers of visitors centring on monuments, museums, and so on, often of a short stay (even daily visits) in which case carrying capacity issues centre around congestion of facilities, traffic, urban land-use change, waste management, etc. In some other cases at the other end of the spectrum, tourism in historic settlements could be more of the selective type associated with small groups of visitors, low pressures for development and so on, in which case carrying capacity considerations could be limited to urban fabric change, and such like.

The Components of Tourism Carrying Capacity

Carrying capacity considerations revolve around three basic components: physical-ecological, sociocultural and political-economic. These components reflect also the range of issues considered in practice (Shelby and Heberlein, 1986; PAP/RAC, 1997; Symmonds and Hammitt, 2000; O'Reilly, 1986; Williams, 1998; Curtis, 1998).

A. Physical-Ecological Component

The physical-ecological component comprises elements of the natural and built-cultural environment as well as infrastructure and social amenities needed for tourism development.

Ecological capacity is concerned with impacts on the ecosystems and resources. It refers to the capacity of natural systems, that is to their assimilative capacity which allows them to absorb certain loads of pollutants, emissions, and so on, without this causing the loss of their essential characteristics, or of ecological functions. It cannot be easily manipulated by human action and to the extent that some limits can be estimated they should be carefully observed and respected as such.

Physical capacity refers to elements of the built-cultural environment including infrastructure. In some cases the term 'physical capacity' has been used to make reference to the availability of space needed for the various activities, while another term, that of 'facility capacity', has been suggested to describe characteristics of spaces intended to support the tourists'/visitors' activities and needs (Shelby and Heberlein, 1986; Symmonds and Hammitt, 2000).

For this analysis, the term 'physical capacity' will be used with its first meaning. In particular the physical capacity refers primarily to infrastructure systems (and their characteristics) like water supply, sewerage, electricity, transportation and to social amenities like postal and telecommunication services, health services, banks, etc. The capacity limits of the infrastructure component can rise through investments in infrastructure, imposition of taxes, adoption of organizational-regulatory measures, etc. For this reason they cannot be used as the only basis for determining carrying capacity but rather as a framework to guide decision making regarding management options. It should be noted however that the capacity limits of the infrastructure component might not always be so 'flexible', suggesting that it may not be possible to change them, for example, due to excessive costs for both construction and operation of infrastructure. In this case, limits of the infrastructure component may prove to be the real constraint on future tourism development. In several small island communities the operation costs involved in environmental protection infrastructure (for example waste treatment or desalination plants) can be prohibitive. Also focusing on managing environmental problems (for example sea pollution) resulting from seasonal tourist flows may require investments for required infrastructure which means foregoing other local priorities.

Limits related to built-cultural environment aspects also need to be taken into account. Cultural sites (ancient theatres, temples, museums, etc.) may have their own capacity limits, different from those of the entire destination, thus limiting tourism.

Levels of capacity for the component can be set, for example, in terms of:

- Acceptable level of congestion or density in key areas or spatial units such as parks, museums, city streets, etc.
- Maximum acceptable loss of natural resources (for example water or land) without significant degradation of ecosystem functions or biodiversity or loss of species.
- Acceptable level of air, water and noise pollution on the basis of tolerance or the assimilative capacity of local ecosystems. The existence of standards (for example concentration of various elements in drinkable water, or standards for bathing water) can help in determining acceptable levels.
- Intensity of use of transport infrastructure, facilities and services.
- Use and congestion of utility facilities and services of water supply, electric power, waste management of sewage and solid waste collection, treatment and disposal and telecommunications.
- Adequate availability of other community facilities and services such as those related to public health and safety, housing and community services, etc.

B. Sociocultural Component

Social carrying capacity is used as a generic term to include both the levels of tolerance of the host population as well as the quality of the experience of visitors to the area.

The sociocultural component refers primarily to those social aspects which are important to local communities, as they relate to the presence and growth of tourism. Social and demographic issues such as opportunities for local manpower or availability of trained personnel, and so on, changes in family patterns and social relations extending also to sociocultural issues such as the sense of identity of the local community are included. Although some of these issues (for example available manpower) may relate more to the political-economic component, they are included in the study of this component due to their relevance to social structure and potential social implications. For example the lack of manpower availability may lead to an increased dependence on foreign labor, which under certain conditions may result in social conflicts and tensions, particularly in small islands with small, traditional local communities.

Some of these can be expressed in quantitative terms but most require suitable socio-psychological and anthropological research. Social capacity thresholds are perhaps the most difficult to evaluate as opposed to physical-ecological and economic ones since they depend to a great extent on perceptions and values (Saveriades, 2000; Symmonds and Hammitt, 2000).

The notion of social carrying capacity is often used to focus on the concept of crowding and its effects on local community and tourist/visitor (dis)satisfaction. Models based on various theories such as expectancy theory, stimulus-overload theory and social interference theory have been used to define perceived crowding (Lee and Graefe, 2003). Social psychological factors seem to have a rather significant influence on the tourists' perception of crowding than the actual level of density or the number of visitors encountered. The characteristics and values, the activities and behavior of the local community and visitors, as well as destination management may all influence the perception of crowding.

Political and economic decisions such as, for example, migration policies, may affect some of the socio-demographic parameters. The same applies for decisions related to the physical-ecological aspects of the area. All three components are interrelated and are mutually influenced.

Levels of capacity for the sociocultural component may be expressed, for example, in terms of:

- Number of tourists and types of tourist recreation activity which can be absorbed without affecting the sense of identity, life-style and social patterns and activities of host communities.
- Level and type of tourism which does not significantly alter local culture in direct or indirect ways in terms of arts, crafts, belief systems, ceremonies, customs and traditions.
- Level of tourism that will not be resented by local population or pre-empt their use of services and amenities.
- Level of tourism (number of visitors and compatibility of types of activities) in an area without unacceptable decline of experience of visitors.

C. Political-Economic Component

The political-economic component refers to the impacts of tourism on the local economic structure, activities, and so on, including competition with other sectors. Economic carrying capacity is the ability to absorb the various tourist functions without squeezing out desirable local activities (O' Reilly, 1986). Exclusivity is not always assumed. Recreational economic carrying capacity applies to situations where a resource is simultaneously utilized for outdoor recreation and another economic activity. In this case the concern is to establish an acceptable recreation use level that does not interfere with the non-recreational activity so as to reduce the economic viability of the resource (Sowman, 1987). Obviously conflicts and complementarities are of major interest in this context as well as competition and dominance. A related concept might be crowding-out, which refers to the total number of visitors that can be allowed in a locality (for example in a city) without hindering or displacing the other functions that the locality needs (Borg, et al., 1996).

Of special concern is social equity or the degree to which profits from tourism are distributed in a way to create opportunities for the improvement of social and economic conditions of the local society, not only those directly involved in tourism. Within this context it is significant whether tourism is a reliable source of income and employment. Economic carrying capacity is often overlooked. In a study for the Nepalese Himalaya it was noted that although there has been some effort to improve social and environmental carrying capacity, little or no attention has been paid to economic carrying capacity which is so vital for improving the economic conditions of the local people and promote sustainable mountain tourism (Nepal, 2000).

Institutional, policy and decision-making issues are also included in the political-economic component to the extent they involve local capacities to manage the presence of tourism. Considerations of political-economic parameters may also be necessary to express divergence in values and attitudes within the local community vis-à-vis tourism.

Levels of capacity for the political-economic component may be expressed, for example, in terms of:

- Level of specialization in tourism.
- Loss of human labor in other sectors due the attraction of tourism.
- Income distribution issues at local level from tourism.
- Level of tourism employment in relation to local human resources.

Methodology for Measuring and Implementing Tourism Carrying Capacity Organized by Component

As already discussed, TCC involves setting levels of acceptable tourism (expressed often in numbers of tourists per unit of time or density) which are derived from an analysis of key features (like natural resources, species under protection, cultural and social patterns and traditions, etc.) which may intervene in the tourist development of a place, felt or perceived as limits on the basis of which tourism management decisions have to be taken. These can be set on the basis of any one of the various components (as presented in the previous paragraphs) or a combination of them.

The process of defining TCC comprises descriptive as well as evaluative elements (it follows in principle the framework for TCC as described by Shelby and Heberlein, 1986). These elements are not separate, but included in the various steps in a process as described below.

Descriptive elements These describe the system (tourist destination) under study functions, including physical, ecological, social, political and economic aspects of tourist development.

Within this context, of particular importance is the identification of:

- *Constraints:* Limiting factors which cannot easily be managed. They are not flexible, in the sense that the application of organizational, planning, and management approaches, or the development of appropriate infrastructure does not easily alter the thresholds associated with such constraints, or the cost, in its broader sense, is significant.
- *Bottlenecks:* Limiting factors of the system which managers can manipulate through organizational or technological means, for example (e.g. number of visitors at a particular place).
- *Impacts:* They concern elements of the system affected by the intensity and type of use. The type of impact determines the type of capacity (ecological-physical, social, and so on). Emphasis should be placed on significant impacts.

Evaluative elements These describe how an area should be managed and the level of acceptable impacts. This part of the process starts with the identification (if it does not exist already) of the desirable condition/preferable type of tourism development. Within this context goals and management objectives need to be defined, alternative fields of actions evaluated and a strategy for tourist development formulated. On the basis of this, tourism carrying capacity can be defined.

Within this context of particular importance is the identification of:

- *Goals/objectives:* (i.e. define the type of experience or other outcomes that a recreation setting should provide). Objective setting is a critical step of the whole process as objectives identify the appropriateness of management actions or indicate acceptable resource and social conditions (McCool, 2002). Objectives therefore serve as a means of defining how much change is acceptable, and as such they need to be examined from time to time; as the types of recreation experience might change so therefore may the levels of acceptable change. Establishing objectives is a highly political process. Within this context it is important to ensure participation of all key stakeholders and the local community so as not only to ensure legitimacy of the planning process but furthermore to increase possibility of success through achievement of consensus (ibid).
- *Evaluative criteria:* These specify acceptable levels of change (impacts).

As mentioned both descriptive and evaluative elements are present in the various steps of the process for defining and implementing tourism carrying capacity. The process is described in the following paragraphs and it includes eight steps:

1. Analysis of the system.
2. Analysis of tourism development.
3. Analysis of the implications of tourism development for each component.
4. Impact assessment.
5. Definition of tourism carrying capacity for each component.
6. Elaboration of alternative tourism development options and alternative courses of action.
7. Definition of total carrying capacity for the system.
8. Implementation of total carrying capacity.

1. ANALYSIS OF THE SYSTEM

1.1 Analysis of the physical-ecological characteristics of the system

(a) Analysis of general ecological and physical characteristics of the area. Data collection – analysis.

Within this context it is necessary to define the boundaries of the system. It is useful if the area under study can be matched to the boundaries of data units such as census areas or municipalities for which data is likely to exist. Analysis is a cyclical process. Although the identification of problems usually follows the analysis of the system and therefore of data collection, in reality, data collection is often driven by key issues/problems. This cannot exclude the possibility of enriching the analysis, at a later stage, by adjusting the relevant boundaries of the area concerned. Special consideration is normally given to key features and processes depending on the geographical characteristics of the area as locality and as tourist destination, such as hydrology, coastal dynamics (in cases of coastal areas and islands), vegetation patterns and cover, wildlife species distribution, natural and cultural landscape, urban (and tourist) development patterns, urban sprawl, land-use patterns and dynamics, transport network, water supply and sewage disposal, wastewater treatment facilities, energy production, presence of a variety of services necessary to support tourism (for example health facilities), etc.

(b) Study of the relationships with the adjacent/neighbouring areas on the basis of strong linkages with the system under study (for example linkages may relate to existing infrastructure or key ecological processes). The presence of technical and tourist infrastructure and of tourist attractions in neighbouring areas may contribute to the pressures exerted on the area under study, or alternatively it may provide opportunities for future growth. The existence of pollutant activities for example in the adjacent areas may prevent the development of tourism or of certain types of activities in the area under study.

1.2 Analysis of the sociocultural characteristics of the system

(a) Analysis of general demographic and social characteristics of the area. Data collection – analysis.
Analysis of population growth and density, age structure, education levels, etc., within this context.

(b) Analysis of cultural patterns and social relations. Particular emphasis is often placed on those aspects which might affect the use of resources and the relationship between the local community and the tourists/visitors, expressed often in terms of conflicts, perceived threats, or such like.

(c) Study of the relationship with the broader system (cultural and social conditions in the wider region) which may influence the system under study. The relationships between local neighborhood communities are often conflicting, characterized by increased competitiveness. This inhibits cooperation.

1.3 Analysis of the political-economic characteristics of the system

(a) Analysis of general political and economic characteristics of the area. Data collection – analysis.
Some of the issues that may be considered are:

- The state and structure of the economy: employment and unemployment, presence of traditional activities like agriculture and fishing, seasonality of activities, average income, public, private investments for the area.
- Political issues, decision-making process, major actors and community participation.
- Administrative, organizational aspects, mechanisms in place, scientific, technical and management capabilities to manage problems, distribution of responsibilities.
- Regulatory and institutional context, goals and policies for tourism, development and environment, land-use plans, regulations and standards in force at the tourist destination, pattern of tourist development related to overall sensitivity of the area (highly restricted, controlled, intensive). Existence of voluntary agreements, and so on.

(b) Study of the relationship with the broader system (political-economic conditions that influence the system under study). The adjacent area may be a higher administrative unit (prefecture or region) where the area under study belongs.

2. ANALYSIS OF TOURISM DEVELOPMENT

(a) Analysis of *tourist supply and demand.*

(b) Exploration of *future trends, prospects for tourism development, potential tourist demand (international, domestic), emerging types of activities.*

(c) Definition of the *type of tourism development*, for example mass versus selective types of tourism development like agro-tourism, cultural, religious, and so on. The development of an inventory of activities may be also useful to highlight the temporal dimensions.

(d) Definition of the *level of tourist activity.* In this case data like tourist arrivals, overnight stays will be necessary.

(e) Identification of *patterns of behavior.* The level of use of various facilities, visitor densities, length of stay, activities at the destination and levels of tourist satisfaction are also important factors.

(f) Identification of the *characteristics of visitors.* Characteristics of the visitors such as age, sex, income, motivations, expectations, race, ethnic origins could provide valuable information. Identification of main groups: tourists, excursionists, and so on.

(g) Identification of *spatial patterns* of tourism development, for example tourism development in coastal areas is often highly concentrated in a narrow zone in close proximity to the coastline. This often results in serious impacts on the vulnerable coastal resources and ecosystems or 'betonization' of coastline. Quite often tourism development follows a dispersed spatial model causing several environmental problems as well.

(h) Identification of *tourist attractions.* Identify resources and particular areas, which constitute now or in the future significant poles of attraction for many tourists (for example beaches, natural areas, wild life, etc.). Classification of these tourist attractions including those of the associated region and neighboring area. Are these attractions of a seasonal function (for example sea, beaches), or not (a casino, monuments, historic areas, and so on)? Gastronomy, traditions, festivals, performances, life-style, and so forth need to be included as well. An inventory of key events may be of some use.

(i) Analysis of *tourist spatial and temporal (seasonality) flows.* Duration of stay (within this context it would be interesting to identify the duration of stay for certain key tourist attractions, the 'favorite' tourist routes, and so on).

(j) Definition of the *profile of the area* in terms of its key characteristics.

(k) Analysis of *tourist revenues.*

(l) Analysis of *current policy in relation to tourism development.*

(m) Analysis of *national and local strategies for tourism development.*

(n) Analysis of *strategies of key actors in the tourism sector. (*As Russo and van der Borg (2002) note, the destination needs to be attractive not so much to the individual tourist, but to the tourist industry and in particular to the transnational players that dominate it. Within this context their strategies are of critical importance).

3. ANALYSIS OF THE IMPLICATIONS OF TOURISM DEVELOPMENT FOR EACH COMPONENT

3.1 Implications for the physical-ecological component – identification of impacts, driving forces, causes

Seasonality may be, for example, the driving force for several environmental problems. In many coastal areas and islands the tourist season has a rather limited duration, usually no more that a couple of months. The large number of arrivals and of overnight stays may result in significant pressure on limited natural resources like water, while the physical capacity of the systems in respect to waste management and in certain cases energy production is usually surpassed.

Quite often the cause for many impacts is not related to the number of tourists but to the type of their activities. Impacts on the environment often result from activities that are quite often classified as environmental friendly. Trekking and paragliding can cause severe threats to fragile ecosystems.

3.2 Implications for the sociocultural component, identification of impacts, driving forces, causes

For example tourism development may have major repercussions on employment opportunities, family structures and social relations (divorces, etc.). The study of these impacts will highlight the vulnerability of the sociocultural component in respect to tourism development.

3.3 Implication for the political-economic component, identification of impacts, driving forces, causes

Tourism may encourage abandonment of traditional activity patterns. However in several cases the influence of other factors besides tourism (for example media) may be stronger.

4. IMPACT ASSESSMENT

4.1 Assessment of the physical-ecological component of the system
    This may include among others:

- Natural environment (the deterioration occurred from existing development, assessment of resources and vulnerability of ecosystems).
- Built-cultural environment.
- Technical infrastructure and services.
- Tourist superstructure (requirements for technology used in respect to conserving key resources like water and managing key problems like waste, and so on).
- Tourist attractions.

(a) Assessment of *impacts* on local environment and infrastructure.
(b) Identification of *problems, conflicts, threats* and *risks*.
Certain impacts may result in the deterioration of the physical-ecological characteristics of the area and eventually lead to the disaffection of tourists and to the increase in the cost for providing various services, imposing threats on the identity of the area. Evidence from practice has indicated that local people, planners, decision-makers and entrepreneurs have a relatively good knowledge of what the major problems are. Most of these problems are those exerting significant pressure (for example lack of water resources), imposing major costs (for example waste management) and threatening the base of tourism development.
The identification of key problems, threats and risks should be done for both the:

- Environment (for example problems caused due to tourism development)
- Tourism development (for example problems caused due to environmental deterioration). Potential threats as well as risks to tourism development due to future environmental problems need to be carefully considered.

Conflicts among activities over the use of resources need to be carefully considered, as they are often the cause for overexploitation.
(c) Identification of *issues and opportunities for management* (for example visitor flows).

4.2 Assessment of the sociocultural component of the system

(a) Assessment of impacts on the local community. Identification of local population preferences. Residents are an important part of the tourism system, an important ingredient of 'hospitality' in a destination. The reaction of the inhabitants towards tourism development determines the social impact of tourism on the local society and thus the social-carrying capacity of the destination.
(b) Assessment of the tourist's satisfaction level.
(c) Identification of problems, threats and sociocultural conflicts.
(d) Identification of *issues and opportunities for management*.

4.3 Assessment of the political-economic component of the system

(a) Assessment of impacts on local economy and community (for example impacts of tourism on traditional activities may include loss of agricultural land, which may be encouraged by the inefficient regulatory provisions, the inadequate mechanisms for implementation and control, etc.).
(b) Identification of problems, threats, conflicts and risks.
Conflicts may arise between different policy goals.
(c) Identification of *issues* and *opportunities* for management.

5. DEFINITION OF TCC FOR EACH COMPONENT

(a) Identification of *bottlenecks* for the physical-ecological, sociocultural and political-economic component (the assessment may lead to numerous problems and threats. Some of them will be selected on the basis of certain criteria as the most critical).

(b) Identification of *constraints* for all three components. Criteria constraints need to be identified.

(c) Definition of *thresholds* for bottlenecks and constraints. Maximum but also minimum values need to be identified. (In Malta an increase in foreign exchange earnings from tourism by a minimum average annual increase of 6 per cent had been suggested.)

- Selection of *indicators*.
- Definition of desired level of each indicator/threshold (for example a ratio of visitors to the local population). *Standards* related to the capacity of the physical environment, to the construction of tourist accommodation establishments and facilities, to protection against various forms of pollution, infrastructure and transportation standards can be very useful. Where standards exist, the monitoring of indicators is carried out in relation to established standards.

6. ELABORATION OF ALTERNATIVE TOURISM DEVELOPMENT OPTIONS AND ALTERNATIVE COURSES OF ACTION

Alternative options (development options and courses of action) contain:

- Constraints (remain unchangeable in the various options)
- Bottlenecks (changeable given the various courses of action). For example, the capacity of a beach may not necessarily pose restrictions on the number of beds, given that new activities in the hinterland are provided for tourists.

(a) Formulation of goals and objectives taking into account future trends and prospects for tourism development. Goals are important in planning for tourism development by providing broad directions and clarifying that some aims are more important than others. Furthermore the establishment of priorities is important to the concept of capacity and will determine whether some obstacles can be overcome in pursuit of objectives. In the light of goals and objectives, management parameters can be introduced to reduce impacts.

(b) Elaboration of alternative courses of action.

(c) Analysis and assessment of the impacts of the various options for each of the three components (costs related to envisaged projects, measures).

(d) Definition of the carrying capacity of each one of the components for each option.

(e) Selection of preferable option.
(f) Elaboration of a strategy for tourism development.

7. DEFINITION OF TOTAL CARRYING CAPACITY FOR THE SYSTEM

(a) Definition of bottlenecks for the preferable option.
Total TCC does not necessarily have to take the form of a unique numerical value, resulting from a 'calculation' of the various TCC for each component. At this stage having selected the desired option it would be possible to identify the final key factors and therefore the thresholds and indicators to be considered. It may be possible that only one proves to be the real key factor and therefore total TCC of the whole system coincides with, for example, the TCC of the physical-ecological component.

8. IMPLEMENTATION OF TOTAL CARRYING CAPACITY

(a) Elaboration of TCC policy measures.
(b) Selection of a final list of indicators for the constraints and bottlenecks identified.
(c) Definition of thresholds and standards.

9. MONITORING
Monitoring of the system as well as of visitors is required. Visitor monitoring compromises three components: visitor counting (including total usage, usage variations, distribution of visitors), visitor profiling (including demographic, socio-economic data, recreational pursuit participation information about users in order to describe visitors to a resource) and finally surveying of visitor opinions (drawing information regarding attitudes, perceptions and motivations of visitors to a resource) (Cope et al., 2000, p.60).

Information collected through monitoring may help site planning and development, policy-making and the review process of management performance (ibid). Regular monitoring of visitor flows and impacts and the ability to produce comparative time-series data can assist decision making (Ferreira et al., 1999).

Of critical importance are the approaches used for monitoring the mechanisms applied so as to use the outcomes of monitoring to assist management and planning as well as the managers' perceptions of the value of such data in order to take some decisions (ibid). Monitoring can assist the development of long-term trends indices, the generation of performance indicators, the formulation of policy and informing management strategies, among others (ibid).

The Role of Indicators in Measuring and Applying Tourism Carrying Capacity

Indicators provide significant opportunities for defining and implementing TCC, a process which does not necessarily have to follow the steps as described in the previous paragraphs. Evidence from practice indicates that in several cases a core set of indicators, reflecting pressures and state of key factors (for example endemic and threatened species) has been used as a way to monitor the state of the system and identify the violation of tourism carrying capacity limits. Changes could guide the identification of carrying capacity limits, which are not necessarily defined in advance. The implications of an indicator's measurement need to be examined in terms of the goals that have been defined and the sensitivity of the sites under study. The use of indicators as a way to identify and define TCC limits is a simpler and more flexible approach compared to the process described. It could also be also effective in the short term, enabling managers to confront increasing pressures from tourism development. This kind of approach has been widely used in the cases of natural parks and generally areas of high ecological value.

Of particular importance are the efforts towards the elaboration of complex and integrated indicators. McElroy and Albuquerque (1998) describe the construction of a Tourism Penetration Index compromised of three indicators: visitor spending per capita, average density per 1000 population and number of hotels per km^2.

Indicators are essential, but not the only building block for managing tourism development. Reflecting on the components of TCC three types of indicators are suggested: physical-ecological indicators, sociocultural indicators and political-economic indicators.

In the following tables the main topics/thematic areas (for example employment and demography) addressed by the indicators are presented for the various types of tourist destinations. An attempt has been made to assign priority to those thematic areas that are considered more important. They should however be considered as indicative only.

Table 4.1 Thematic areas of the physical-ecological indicators

PHYSICAL-ECOLOGICAL INDICATORS

THEMATIC AREAS	Coastal areas	Islands	Protected areas	Rural areas	Mountain resorts	Urban areas, Historic sites
Natural Environment and Biodiversity	H*	H	H	H	H	
Air Quality			H			H
Noise			H		H	H
Energy		H				
Water	H	H	H		H	H
Waste	H	H		H	H	H
Cultural Heritage	H	H	H	H	H	H
Tourist Infrastructure	H	H	H	H	H	H
Land	H	H	H		H	H
Landscape	H	H		H	H	
Transport and Mobility					H	H

H* = Major importance

Table 4.2 Thematic areas of the sociocultural indicators

SOCIOCULTURAL INDICATORS

THEMATIC AREAS	Coastal areas	Islands	Protected areas	Rural areas	Mountain resorts	Urban areas, Historic sites
Tourism Earnings and Investments	H*	H		H	H	H
Employment	H	H		H	H	
Public Expenditure and Revenue	H	H		H	H	H
Policy for Tourism Development	H	H	H	H	H	H

H* = Major importance

Table 4.3 Thematic areas of the political-economic indicators

POLITICAL-ECONOMIC INDICATORS

THEMATIC AREAS	Coastal areas	Islands	Protected areas	Rural areas	Mountain resorts	Urban areas, Historic sites
Demography		H*	H	H	H	
Tourist Flows	H	H	H		H	H
Employment	H	H		H	H	
Social Behavior		H		H	H	
Health and Safety	H	H		H		H
Psychological Issues	H	H	H	H	H	H

H* = Major importance

Each one of the thematic areas can be represented by more than one indicator following the logic of the DPSIR framework (OECD, 1998) (Figure 4.1). Within this context indicators for carrying capacity may focus on:

- pressures and stresses
- the state of the natural environment and of the resources
- impacts and consequences
- the effectiveness of management efforts and implemented actions.

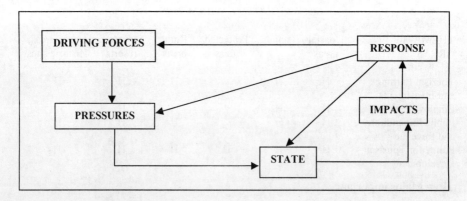

Figure 4.1 1: DPSIR framework

In Tables 4.4 to 4.6 (annex of this chapter) indicators for each one of the thematic areas are suggested. Indicators are further divided into three major categories:

1. Sustainability Indicators
2. Sustainable Tourism Indicators

3.   Tourism Carrying Capacity Indicators

If with sustainable tourism development a type of development is implied where the pressure on the natural environment remains below the level of the carrying capacity, then sustainable tourism indicators can help in determining whether tourism is damaging the environment and to what extent (Janssen et al., 1995). Sustainable tourism indicators are directly linked with the definition and implementation of TCC. They aim to describe the general relationship between tourism and the environment, the effects of environmental factors on tourism, the impacts of the tourism industry on the environment and the responses required for promoting and safeguarding a more sustainable development of tourism and recreational activities. Sustainability indicators are also useful since they provide an overall indication of the state of the system in respect to sustainability. Tourism carrying capacity indicators aim at describing the pressures that are exerted, the state of the system and the impacts from tourism development. However in this case only the *key* factors, problems, and so on are considered.

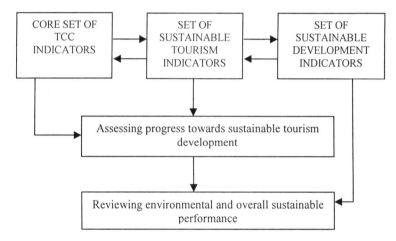

Figure 4.2 TCC, sustainable tourism and sustainable development indicators

The list of indicators (as presented in Tables 4.4 to 4.6) is indicative and should be considered as neither exhaustive nor mandatory. Planners and decision-makers could select some of the suggested indicators on the basis of local particularities and priorities and formulate a new set of indicators for TCC.

Issues to Consider in Applying Tourism Carrying Capacity

In the process of defining and implementing tourism carrying capacity some issues may need to be addressed:

Long-term considerations vis-à-vis environmental conservation, protection of cultural heritage, etc., need to remain at the core of measuring tourism carrying capacity, balanced however with *short-term priorities and demands*. Tourism products and services, as several other products, are susceptible to pressures from a globally competitive market, often imposing severe pressures on local communities (entrepreneurs, decision-makers and so on) who, although they realize the need for a long-term strategy, often find it difficult to balance these considerations under immense short-term pressures.

Following the above a *balance between ecological/environmental aspects and satisfaction of visitor's aspirations* needs to be pursed. This more or less reflects the need to balance between long-term considerations and immediate pressure imposed by tourism demand (either for cheaper products rendering environmental protection rather costly, or for increased consumption of space, new resources, etc.). This will probably require enlightened management.

The decision on the approach for defining and measuring tourism carrying capacity needs to be based on the analysis of the characteristics and problems of the area under study (ecological, sociocultural, institutional, and so on). There is no such thing as a 'prêt-a-porter' approach for defining tourism carrying capacity which is appropriate and effective for all tourist destinations. The application of carrying capacity seems to be easier in limited well-defined areas, often under a single management regime, such as for example cultural sites, in comparison to other types of tourist destination such as coastal areas or mountain resorts. It should also be taken into account that tourism carrying capacity could vary among the different parts of an area (for example the centre of the town as opposed to the surrounding areas, or in various sub-areas within ecologically sensitive areas, etc.). In certain cases like islands it may be more appropriate to consider the entire region when defining and implementing carrying capacity limits.

Overall measuring tourism carrying capacity does not have to lead to a *single number* (threshold), like the number of visitors. Hall and Lew (1998) state that carrying capacity is increasingly being identified as:

...a management system directed towards maintenance or restoration of ecological and social conditions defined as acceptable and appropriate in area management objectives, not a system directed toward manipulation of use levels *per se*.

Carrying capacity analysis helps establish a development benchmark which is certainly more important than 100 per cent accuracy. Even when this is achieved, this limit does not necessarily obey to objectively, unchangeable, everlasting criteria. An upper and a lower limit of TCC can be of more use than a fixed value. TCC assessment should provide not only the maximum but also the minimum level of development, that is the lowest level necessary for sustaining local communities. In addition, TCC may contain various carrying capacity limits in respect to the three components (physical-ecological, socialcultural and political-economic).

In applying tourism carrying capacity it is possible to set priorities and avoid a tourism carrying capacity process of a broader spectrum, as the one described. Curtis (1998) notes that there are cases where a single type of carrying capacity may be considered. He mentions the cases of historic cities where the most appropriate type is the physical carrying capacity.

The approach for defining tourism carrying capacity and the emphasis in its measurement may change or shift over time in order to reflect changes to a system's structure and dynamic as well as changes in management goals and priorities, in visitors' values and expectations, and so on. Carrying capacity is not a fixed value, instead it acts as a guidance for tourism sustainability. As the system changes, guidance needs to reflect new problems and threats as well as new challenges and aspirations. Visitors and local communities, for example, tend to alter their behavior over time and often adapt to worsening or different conditions, resulting in a different social response.

The implementation of TCC can be facilitated, guided and monitored, with a coherent set of *indicators*. During the process of defining TCC an initial set of indicators may be developed, finalized following the final decision on TCC of the entire system. The whole process is dynamic and, as already noted, since TCC is not a fixed concept, it should be regarded as a tool for guiding policy formulation and implementation towards sustainable tourism.

The opinion of visitors as well as of decision-makers is of critical importance in measuring and implementing tourism carrying capacity. However as Stewart and Cole (2003) note:

> By focusing on the opinions of visitors the questions that are most fundamental to prescriptive decisions are largely ignored. ...institutional initiatives, collaborative learning and stakeholder dialogue processes are more suitable pathways to develop answers....Prescriptive decisions should be based on agency mission, legal mandates and careful consideration of the needs of many legitimate stakeholders. The opinions of current users, who are just one of several stakeholder groups, comprise only a small portion of the input needed to make prescriptive decisions.

Within this context consensus of key stakeholders on the definition of TCC is critical. An agreement on the goals of tourism and a vision for development is necessary. The results of the TCC study should be communicated to stakeholders, local people and users who will have to support the implementation of envisaged measures. The participation of tourist agents (for example tour operators) is essential too in those cases where they may have a prominent role (for example mass tourism destinations such as coastal zones).

Tourism Carrying Capacity as Part of a Planning Process

The measurement, assessment and implementation of tourism carrying capacity may be considered as a process within a planning process for tourism development. Figure 4.3 outlines the main steps of a process, which could be used to measure and implement tourism carrying capacity. In this respect, the following should be noted:

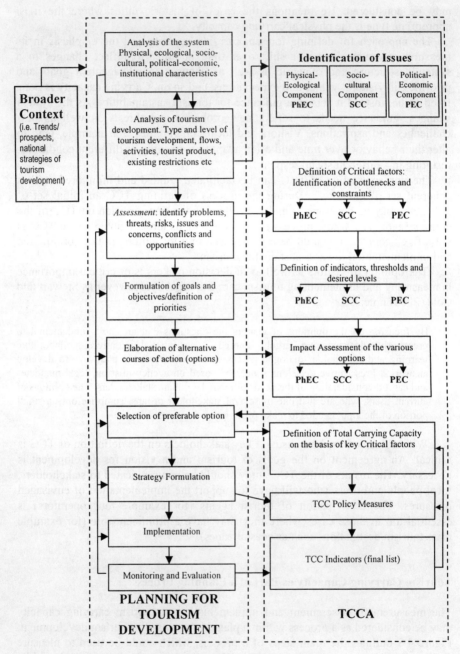

Figure 4.3 Planning for tourism development and TCCA

The process of defining and implementing tourism carrying capacity and a broader process of planning for sustainable tourism, which are parallel and complementary processes, can provide a general framework guiding local community, planners and decision-makers. This framework consists of principles, goals, objectives and policy measures in regard to tourist development in an area on the basis of the area's distinctive characteristics/features respecting local capacities to sustain tourism.

Setting capacity limits for sustaining tourism activity in a place involves a *vision* about local development and decisions about managing tourism. These should be considered in the context of democratic community strategic planning, which requires participation of all major actors and the community at large.

The process described for measuring and implementing tourism carrying capacity needs to be regarded as an indicative framework (despite its detail) in seeking for some limits on tourism development. The process is cyclical and repetitive, comprising of steps, which are not always so distinct in practice.

Monitoring is an essential component of it, providing essential feedback. The process is adaptive and could help us tune the various measures adopted to mitigate impacts from tourism development.

As noted the process includes descriptive as well as evaluative elements. No doubt that consultation with all stakeholders will be essential in order to ensure an effective implementation of capacity limits. This, coupled with political willingness, will play an instrumental role, probably more than any methodological deficiencies and weakness related to the various tools that will be applied so as to implement tourism carrying capacity limits.

References

Borg, J. van der, Costa, P., Gotti, G. (1996), 'Tourism in European Heritage Cities', *Annals of Tourism Research*, Vol. 23, No. 2, pp. 306-321.

Coccossis, H. (2002), 'Island Tourism Development and Carrying Capacity', in *Island Tourism and Sustainable Development: Caribbean, Pacific and Mediterranean Experiences*, Y. Apostolopoulos and D. Gayle (eds), Praeger, Westport, Ct. pp. 131-144.

Cope, A., Doxford, D., Probert, C. (2000), 'Monitoring Visitors to UK Countryside Resources. The Approaches of Land and Recreation Resource Management Organizations to Visitor Management', *Land Use Policy*, Vol. 17, pp. 59-66.

Curtis, S. (1998) 'Visitor Management in Small Historic Cities', *Travel and Tourism Analyst*, No. 3, pp. 75-89.

Ferreira, S. and Harmse, A. (1999), 'The Social Carrying Capacity of Kruger National Park, South Africa: Policy and Practice', *Tourism Geographies*, Vol. 1, No. 3, pp. 325-342.

Hall, M.C. and Lew, A.A. (eds) (1998), *Sustainable Tourism: A Geographical Perspective*, Longman, Harlow.

Janssen, H., Kiers, M., Nijkamp, P. (1995), 'Private and Public Development Strategies for Sustainable Tourism Development of Island Economies', in Coccossis H. and Nijkamp P. (eds), *Sustainable Tourism Development*, Avebury, Aldershot, pp. 65-83.

Lee, H. and Graefe A. (2003), 'Crowding at an Arts Festival: Extending Crowding Models to the Frontcountry', *Tourism Management*, Vol. 24, No.1, pp. 1-11.

McCool, S. (2002), 'Principles and Concepts for Managing Visitor Impacts in Protected Areas', *WWF Hellas Congress on Methods for Measuring Carrying Capacity and Visitor Management in Protected Areas: Presentations and Conclusions*, 31/5-1/6/2002, Athens.

McElroy, J. and de Albuquerque K. (1998), 'Tourism Penetration Index in Small Caribbean Islands', *Annals of Tourism Research*, Vol. 25, No. 1, pp. 145-168.

Nepal, S. (2000), 'Tourism in Protected Areas. The Nepalese Himalaya', *Annals of Tourism Research*, Vol. 27, No. 3, pp.661-681.

O'Reilly, A.M. (1986), 'Tourism Carrying Capacity. Concepts and Issues', *Tourism Management*, Vol. 7, No. 4, pp. 254-258.

OECD (1998), 'Towards Sustainable Development. Environmental Indicators', Paris.

PAP/RAC (1997), 'Guidelines for Carrying Capacity Assessment for Tourism in Mediterranean Coastal Areas', PAP-9/1997/G.1. Split, Priority Actions Programme Regional Activity Centre.

Russo, A. and Borg, J. van der (2002), 'Planning Considerations for Cultural Tourism: a Case Study of Four European Cities', *Tourism Management*, Vol. 23, pp. 631-637.

Saveriades, A. (2000), 'Establishing the Social Tourism Carrying Capacity for the Tourist Resorts of the East Coast of the Republic of Cyprus', *Tourism Management*, Vol. 21, No. 2, pp. 147-156.

Shelby, B. and Heberlein, T. (1986), *Carrying Capacity in Recreational Settings*, Oregon State University Press, Corvallis, OR.

Sowman, M.R. (1987), 'A Procedure for Assessing Recreational Carrying Capacity of Coastal Resorts', *Landscape and Urban Planning*, 14, pp. 331-344.

Stewart, W. and Cole, D. (2003), 'On the Prescriptive Utility of Visitor Survey Research: A Rejoinder to Manning', *Journal of Leisure Research*, Vol. 35, No. 1, pp. 119-127.

Symmonds, M. and Hammitt W. (2000), 'Managing Recreational Trail Environments for Mountain Bike User Preferences', *Environmental Management*, Vol. 25, No. 5, pp. 549-564.

Williams, S. (1998), *Tourism Geography*, Routledge Contemporary Human Georgaphy Series, Routledge, London.

ANNEX
INDICATIVE LISTS

Table 4.4 Physical-ecological indicators

PHYSICAL-ECOLOGICAL INDICATORS

ISSUES	SUSTAINABILITY INDICATORS	SUSTAINABLE TOURISM INDICATORS	TOURISM CARRYING CAPACITY INDICATORS
1. Natural environment and biodiversity			
1.1. Ecosystems			

1.1.1.Ecological destruction, beach degradation, etc.	-Total area of natural and semi-natural areas
	-Surface of natural and semi-natural areas/Total area
	-Percentage of natural areas:
	   • in good condition
	   • heavily degraded
		-Change in vegetation cover due to tourism activities
		-Change in biodiversity due to tourism/recreation activities
		-Change of critical areas due to tourism development
		-Length of unspoiled coastline/total length of coastline
		-Length of artificially developed coastline/Total length of coastline
		-Beach length/Total length of coastline
			-Area of key ecosystems (wetland, forest, etc)/Total area

1.1.2.Disruption – loss of fauna and flora	-Number of endemic and threatened species -Number of endemic species/Number of endemic species at national level -Area occupied by endemic or threatened species/Total land (%)		

PHYSICAL-ECOLOGICAL INDICATORS

ISSUES	SUSTAINABILITY INDICATORS	SUSTAINABLE TOURISM INDICATORS	TOURISM CARRYING CAPACITY INDICATORS
1.1.3. Overcrowding			-Number of tourists per ▪ km of (accessible) coastline ▪ sq. m of (accessible) coast ▪ sq. km of natural site -Number of tourists/Protected key ecosystems surface
1.2. **Protection**	-Percentage of areas under protection status (protected land/ total land) -Protected land of various key ecosystems (wetland, forest, etc)/ total key ecosystem land (i.e. Protected forest land/total forest land) -Protected Areas as % of threatened		
2. **Cultural heritage**		-Loss or degradation of built structures and other archaeological or historical sites due to tourism development -Degradation of aesthetic values	
3. **Tourist infrastructure**		-Number of bed places per tourist accommodation type /Total number of bed places -Percent of occupancy of key facilities	-Tourist beds/Permanent population

PHYSICAL-ECOLOGICAL INDICATORS

ISSUES	SUSTAINABILITY INDICATORS	SUSTAINABLE TOURISM INDICATORS	TOURISM CARRYING CAPACITY INDICATORS
		-Tourist accommodation units that have been awarded with an eco-label (recognized at international, EU, national, regional or local level), that follow eco-audit, etc/Total tourist accommodation units	
4. Air quality	-Average number of days in which pollution standards are exceeded per year -Level of pollution due to exhaust fumes per year		-Average number of days during tourist season in which pollution standards are exceeded per year
5. Noise pollution	-Average number of days per year when noise pollution standards are exceeded (number of reports)		-Average number of days during tourist season when noise pollution standards are exceeded
6. Energy *6.1. Energy consumption*	-Per capita consumption of energy (from electric power and petrochemical fuels)	-Average annual consumption of energy/Average consumption during tourist season	

PHYSICAL-ECOLOGICAL INDICATORS

ISSUES	SUSTAINABILITY INDICATORS	SUSTAINABLE TOURISM INDICATORS	TOURISM CARRYING CAPACITY INDICATORS
	-Energy consumption per source (from renewable and non- renewable sources)/Total energy consumption)	-Energy consumption of tourism related activities/Total energy consumption • Annual • Monthly -Consumption of energy from renewable sources/Total consumption of energy (in tourist units) -Preventive actions for minimising energy consumption for clients	-Energy consumption of tourism related activities/Local capacity for energy supply
6.2. *CO$_2$ emissions*	-Total CO$_2$ emissions per year -CO$_2$ emissions per capita -CO$_2$ emissions for each type of fuel sources (GPL, natural gas, electric energy, etc)/Total CO$_2$ emissions	-CO$_2$ emissions from tourism related activities/Total CO$_2$ emissions (per year)	
7. Water *7.1. Water consumption*	-Water consumption/resident/per day	-Water consumption per bed or per tourist/per day	-Water consumption of tourism related activities/Total consumption

PHYSICAL-ECOLOGICAL INDICATORS

ISSUES	SUSTAINABILITY INDICATORS	SUSTAINABLE TOURISM INDICATORS	TOURISM CARRYING CAPACITY INDICATORS
	-Seasonal withdrawals/Seasonal available resources (Seasonal exploitation index of water resources) -Water consumption per sector (industry, tourism related activities, primary, etc)/Total consumption -Abstraction/Renewable water resources -Water consumption/Water supply (Water unaccounted for)	- Average water consumption during peak season/Average annual water consumption - Tourist beds in tourist units where practices for water consumption minimization are followed/Total tourist beds	- Water consumption of tourism with respect to total available resources
7.2. Water quality *7.2.1. Water quality*	-Percentage of water samples under the quality standard at the water treatment outflow site per year	-Cleanness index of the water available in tourist complexes (is the water drinkable or not?) -Index of the number of pollutants (coliform bacteria and concentration of heavy metals)	-Percentage of coastal water quality samples, which conform to bathing quality standards per year
7.2.2. Water management	-Wastewater undergoing first, second and third stage treatment/Total wastewater	-Annual cost of water supply/Number of tourists -Annual cost of drinking water supply/Number of tourists	

PHYSICAL-ECOLOGICAL INDICATORS

ISSUES	SUSTAINABILITY INDICATORS	SUSTAINABLE TOURISM INDICATORS	TOURISM CARRYING CAPACITY INDICATORS
8. Waste			
8.1. Waste production			
8.1.1. Solid waste production	-Daily solid waste production per capita -% composition of waste (organic, plastic, metal, etc.)	-Daily solid waste production per tourist -% composition of waste during peak season	-Daily average solid waste production in peak period/Daily annual average solid waste production
8.1.2 Liquid waste production	-Daily liquid waste production/person		-Daily average liquid waste production in peak period/Daily annual average liquid waste production
8.2. Waste management			
8.2.1. Solid waste management	-Solid waste disposal for each treatment type (incinerator, landfill, recycling, reuse)/Total solid waste -Solid waste collection or landfilling capacity/day -Percentage of persons served by organized and hygienic solid waste management systems	-Tourist units (tourist beds) that follow recycling or waste minimization approaches/Total tourist units (total tourist beds) -Recyclable waste produced in tourist units/Total waste produced in tourist units -Existence of preventive actions for clients with the scope of minimizing solid waste productions -Cost of waste management/Number of tourists	-Daily solid waste production during peak season/Daily solid waste collection capacity or capacity of the disposal systems
8.2.2. Liquid waste management	-Liquid waste treatment capacity/day	-Share of tourist beds in tourist units that have their own waste water treatment plant	-Daily liquid waste production during peak season/Daily liquid waste treatment capacity

PHYSICAL-ECOLOGICAL INDICATORS

ISSUES	SUSTAINABILITY INDICATORS	SUSTAINABLE TOURISM INDICATORS	TOURISM CARRYING CAPACITY INDICATORS
	-Share of local population served by waste water treatment plants -Share of collected and treated wastewater by the public/private sewerage system	-Cost of liquid waste management per tourist	- Share of tourist beds in TU served by waste water treatment plants
9. Land *9.1. Land use* *9.1.1. Intensity*	-Urbanized land/Total land -Green area ratio per person (sq. m./per capita)	-Number of secondary houses/Total houses -Percentage of land use per sector	-Urbanized land for tourism (second houses, hotels, recreation centres, etc.)/Total urbanized land -Density of tourism development (No. of beds/tourism urbanized land)
9.1.2. Changes	-% of land abandonment in the last decade	-Loss of agricultural, forest, wetland land, etc., in the last decade due to tourism development -% of natural area spoiled by skiing activities/facilities	
9.2. Soil erosion	-Eroded land/Total land		-Rate of coastal erosion
10. Landscape *10.1.Loss of aesthetic values*		-Average and maximum height of construction	

PHYSICAL-ECOLOGICAL INDICATORS

ISSUES	SUSTAINABILITY INDICATORS	SUSTAINABLE TOURISM INDICATORS	TOURISM CARRYING CAPACITY INDICATORS
11 Transport and mobility			
11.1. Accessibility (loss of access to key sites)		-Configuration of the land and the architectural aspects	-Average travel distance and time per tourist to reach the destination -Waiting time to use facilities (i.e. time at ski lifts, museum entrances, queuing, etc.)
11.2. Infrastructures	-Road density (road length/total area) -Telecommunication networks	-Seasonal day average traffic (no. of domestic and international flights, no. of boats arriving, no. of cars, etc)/ Annual day average traffic	-Number of parking places/ Average number of cars per day, coaches etc. in critical areas (i.e. along a beach, historic center, etc.)
11.3. Mode of transportation		-People using public transport/ Resident population + tourists	
11.4. Safety		-Accident levels: number of car/water etc. related, etc. accidents during the year	-Frequency of accidents

Table 4.5 Sociocultural indicators

SOCIOCULTURAL INDICATORS

ISSUES	SUSTAINABILITY INDICATORS	SUSTAINABLE TOURISM INDICATORS	TOURISM CARRYING CAPACITY INDICATORS
1. Demography	-Population growth rate, age structure -Population density (persons/km^2)		
2. Tourist flow			-Tourists/inhabitants: • Max value (peak period) • Min-Average value -Number of beds places per 100 inhabitants -Number of overnights per 100 inhabitants -Number of arrivals per 100 inhabitants -Number of tourists per area unit of site/key area (i.e. beach, square, museum, natural/cultural site, etc): ▪ Max value (peak period) ▪ Min-Average value -Tourists/density area: • Max value (peak period) • Min-Average value

SOCIOCULTURAL INDICATORS

ISSUES	SUSTAINABILITY INDICATORS	SUSTAINABLE TOURISM INDICATORS	TOURISM CARRYING CAPACITY INDICATORS
			-Tourists/month (distribution during the year/seasonality)
3. Employment	-Employment record in traditional activities (agriculture, fishing, etc.) -Decrease in employment in traditional activities (i.e. agriculture, fishing)	-Part-time or seasonal employment/ Employment throughout the year	-Tourist bed places/Local people employed -Migrant labor/Local population Comparison with national average
4. Social behavior	-Number of marriages compared to national average -Number of divorces compared to national average	-Percentage of tourists understanding/using language of the destination -Number of mixed couples compared to national average -Rate of premature school leavers	
5. Health and safety *5.1. Health*		-Average first aid emergencies during tourist season/annual average	
5.2. Criminality	-Crime levels: Distribution of the number of crimes reported (theft, assault) during the year	-No. of crimes in which tourists were involved/Total no. of crimes -No. and type of crimes against tourists	

SOCIOCULTURAL INDICATORS

ISSUES	SUSTAINABILITY INDICATORS	SUSTAINABLE TOURISM INDICATORS	TOURISM CARRYING CAPACITY INDICATORS
6. Psychological issues			
6.1. Tourists' satisfaction level		-Rate of tourists satisfied with their vacation	-Number of tourist complaints
6.2. Residents' satisfaction level		-Rate of residents satisfied with current level of tourism development -Number of retail establishments/Number of establishments serving local needs (as opposed to tourists) -Number of local establishments open year round/Total number of local establishments	-Number of resident complaints (i.e. from noise) -Rate of residents benefiting from tourism (local employers + local employees /total population) -Displacement of members of local population due to tourism development

Table 4.6 Political-economic indicators

POLITICAL-ECONOMIC INDICATORS

ISSUES	SUSTAINABILITY INDICATORS	SUSTAINABLE TOURISM INDICATORS	TOURISM CARRYING CAPACITY INDICATORS
1. Tourism earnings and investments	-Average per capita income of resident population	-Ratio of net foreign exchange earnings relating to the tourist investments or to the functioning of tourist activity -Inflow earnings from expenditure prior departure -Per capita tourist expenditure during stay -Tourism receipts (in absolute terms)	-Average per capita income in catering and tourism
2. Employment	-Employment by economic sector -Unemployment ratio -Number of unemployed residents	-Average annual employment (directly or indirectly) in tourist sector/Total employment -Number of seasonal workers	-Percentage of seasonal labour force in the total number of workers employed in tourism

3. Public expenditure and revenue	-Public expenditure on
	  ▪ conservation and value enhancement of natural, cultural and historic patrimony
	  ▪ protected area management/Total public expenditure
		-Tourist tax revenue/Total tax revenue
		-Tourist tax revenue/Public expenditure on tourism development	

Chapter 5

The Use of Various Tools for Implementing Tourism Carrying Capacity

Alexandra Mexa

Introduction

The implementation of tourism carrying capacity (TCC) requires the use of various tools. The term tool as employed in this chapter encompasses simple or more complicated techniques applied at a site (for example signing, reservation and booking, market control), more sophisticated methods (for example computer simulation modeling), policy measures adopted to manage visitor flows (for example dispersion vs. concentration), along with several other more 'conventional' means such as institutional and regulatory and more recently economic instruments.

Some of these tools have a broader scope, that of natural conservation, tourism and environmental management for example, and were not necessarily developed for limiting the number of tourists or their activities in a certain area. Their analytical presentation is beyond the scope of this contribution.

This variety and the respective lack of homogeneity make it hard to classify all these tools into specific categories, although some effort has been made to organize them into seven main groups, not necessarily always distinct in character, those of institutional, regulatory, economic, organizational-management and information technology tools. A short description of their characteristics, in some cases of the advantages and disadvantages of their use, is presented in the following paragraphs.

Tools differ in several ways and their selection may reflect in some cases a differentiated view of planning and management for sustainable tourism development and differentiated views in applying in practice the tourism carrying capacity concept (for example for implementing tourism carrying capacity limits emphasis may be placed more on the use of 'soft' approaches like education and planning and less on 'hard' approaches like physical and financial restrictions, see Glasson et al., 1995 for this distinction).

Most of the tools described are focusing on controlling *demand* through for example the diversification of accessibility for various types of visitors, 'rationing' the use through price or reservation policies and less on the *supply* side (see also van der Borg et al., 1993).

The selection of the various tools would probably influence, if not determine, the effectiveness of the application of tourism carrying capacity limits in a particular area and by extension on tourism development in the area.

Institutional Tools

At the European level there are several institutional instruments that may encourage and facilitate the application of tourism carrying capacity. Furthermore there are opportunities to include TCC (as guidelines) in existing well-established institutional mechanisms. Some of them are presented below.

Global and Community provisions such as the *Fauna-Flora-Habitat Directive,* the *Natura 2000* (a European network of special protected areas foreseen by the FFH Directive), and the *Red Lists* are valuable instruments for nature protection and for defining carrying capacity levels for ecologically sensitive sites so as to limit tourism development. The *Alps Convention* along with the *Barcelona Convention for the Mediterranean Sea* can also be useful tools for providing a framework for nature protection. Of significant value can be for example the *Bern Convention, UNESCO World Heritage Convention, Ramsar Convention, Convention on Biological Diversity,* and so forth which set the protection of these areas as a priority; tourism is among the activities that usually have to be regulated (German Federal Agency for Nature Conservation, 1997).

In addition to this, most countries have their own legislation that provides for the conservation of the areas, which are ecologically sensitive and valuable. The implementation of the various provisions can be realized through land acquisition, the establishment of a specific authority, the appointment of a management organization, the elaboration of management plans, and other special provisions (for example the delimitation of buffer zones around nature reserves where activities are allowed given certain conditions) (Leitmann, 1998). This legislation coupled with EU and international institutions form a complex grid, which is however not always so effective due to difficulties in implementation. In Greece for example the implementation is often prohibited or delayed due to the lack of appropriate mechanisms and funds, increasing pressures for land development and land speculation, deficiencies of the existing administrative system, and so on (Coccossis and Mexa, 2002).

Respective mechanisms and other institutional decisions often exist for other areas besides those of natural and cultural significance, guiding their development while providing some opportunities for implementing TCC. Lately in Greece a decision of the State Council closely associated the demand for the development of infrastructure for energy production in four small *islands* (through an underwater connection with the corresponding power network of the mainland) with the carrying capacity of these islands (Andros, Tinos, Syros and Myconos) suggesting that interventions in islands should consider needs arising from the growth and needs of local population and not from uncontrolled tourism development. It was noted that the suggested option would encourage excessive tourism and urban development. With this decision the need to apply limits to tourism development was implied.

In another case the European Commission in its document 'Towards an Integrated European Strategy for the Management of Coastal Zones', and in its Communication to the Council and the European Parliament on Integrated Coastal Zone Management, defines integrated coastal zone management as a dynamic, continuous and interactive process, which aims at balancing profits from economic development and human uses, with those from conservation and rehabilitation of coastal zones, from the prevention of human losses and increased social accessibility to the coast, within the *limits* defined by the natural dynamics and the *carrying capacity;* as such the European Commission encourages member states to promote ICZM of their coastal areas (EC, 1999; EC, 2000). However decisions do not always have a binding character. The lack of specific reference to the capacity limits of these areas (for example small islands) and the need to consider them when planning for future development or providing approval for various projects, will no doubt inhibit the promotion of tourism carrying capacity assessment.

Another commonly used tool that could assist the implementation of tourism carrying capacity is *Environmental Impact Assessment.* It should be applied to proposed development projects in order to evaluate the potential impacts (environmental, social and economic) in light of forecasted tourism growth and peak demand and determine whether they are acceptable. Alternative sites for development should be considered, taking into account local constraints and carrying capacity limits. The project is granted permission, usually with some conditions so as to ensure mitigation of impacts.

TCC could be a central concern required in *SEA* (Strategic Environmental Assessment) since this reflects anticipating development on the basis of the capacity of local systems to support it. Policies and programs are subject to an integrated evaluation.

Regulatory Tools

Institutional as well as 'command and control' instruments are commonly applied. Some of these tools will be presented below:

Zoning is a rather useful tool, easy to apply, considered as the most widely applied regulatory technique (Buckley, 1998). It may succeed in limiting use, encouraging dispersal, managing and eliminating conflicts mainly through the separation of non-compatible activities, keeping sensitive, ecologically or recovering areas free from use (Kuo, 2002; Day, 2002). It is applied mainly in protected areas since their special status allows the definition and delimitation of zones where protection, conservation and limitations in the various uses are imposed. A typical division in zones is the following:

- Zone A – Most valuable and vulnerable. Entry only to authorised scientific teams
- Zone B – Highly sensitive. Escorted visits in small groups
- Zone C – Considerable natural interest. Some traditional and tourism activities, limited car access
- Zone D – Mild development, serves as a buffer zone. Tourism and visitor facilities, car access and parking, compatible activities.

Zoning is also a commonly applied mechanism in planning for the future development in coastal areas, islands, and so on. In Greece such zones are used for building and land use control. This relates to provisions for anticipating future development through land development regulation, mostly relating to physical planning issues (Coccossis and Mexa, 1997).

Limits to free access: It can contribute significantly to environmental protection and seems to be applicable in some cases of tourism development, notably areas with significant ecological and cultural value, often vulnerable sites.

However, many European laws protect free access, suggesting that it is not possible to discriminate on the basis of various factors. Imposing limits to accessibility is allowed only in certain cases.

In the context of a recent EU Demonstration Project on Integrated Coastal Zone Management in the Greek island region of Cyclades the authorities of the unique traditional settlement of Oia (located in the northern part of the island of Santorini, situated in the central Aegean) complained of the 'massive' visitor flows throughout summer evenings coming to enjoy the spectacular view of the volcano during the sunset. The visitors who did not use local accommodation (as it is more expensive compared to the other parts of the island) caused significant disturbance (noise, littering, traffic problems, overcrowding, increased danger for car accidents, and so on) to both locals and tourists (overnight tourists in the settlement of Oia) in the area. The desire however of the local authorities to exclude these tourist flows, which were failing to have any positive impacts on the village, could never be realized as this would have been against the Constitution (University of the Aegean, 2000).

Physical interventions: It comprises all actions to minimize interaction between visitors and environment – applied usually in ecologically sensitive areas – such as building animal viewing platforms, pathways, erection of fences to prevent tourists from entrance, resource hardening such as repairing heritage monuments and buildings, limiting car parks and other tourism facilities to reduce numbers (Kuo, 2002). These constructions may however have negative impacts on the natural environment of the area, not to mention the impacts on the expectations and experiences of tourists themselves (ibid). They are considered along with the financial restrictions as 'hard methods' (Glasson et al., 1995).

Limitations on specific activities: Some activities may be forbidden given particular conditions while others may be just limited to certain periods of the year or to a limited number of users. For example, paragliding is forbidden in some French National Parks because it disturbs birds and lately free camping in most of the coastal areas of Greece.

Within this context all kinds of tourist activities need to be evaluated in order to prevent environmental impacts or conflicts among different users. In the future special permits or the application of EIA in the case of new forms of activities as in the case of infrastructure development can be foreseen.

Other limits: Seasonal closures (for example in case of significant breeding or nursery sites), site duplication, limits on visitor numbers are quite often used in heavily used national parks. Bans and restrictions on motorized vehicles and watercraft, prescriptions of maximum party size are some examples (Buckley, 1998; Kuo, 2002; Day, 2002).

Imposition of fines: Penalties may be applied, particularly in ecologically sensitive areas as well as cultural sites, so as to secure conformance with the various rules.

Concentration or dispersion of development pressures and tourist flows: The former maintains areas characterized as not yet 'contaminated', by concentrating tourism into 'honeypots of visitor attraction', while the latter opens up new areas for tourism development (Collins, 1999; Ferreira and Harmse, 1999). From an environmental point of view concentration may not always be the best approach to manage tourist flows; infrastructure burdens, impacts on social cohesion, negative impacts on local business besides tourism, ribbon development may be some of the impacts (Collins, 1999). Dispersal might be a preferable option as externalities appear only when the system reaches certain threshold levels.

Dispersion has both advantages and disadvantages (Glasson et al., 1995): advantages include the relief of the area from the pressures exerted by the increased number of visitors, the maintenance of numbers within limits, the disappearance of social costs related to excess demand, the diffusion of benefits among more inhabitants and entrepreneurs. However there are certain disadvantages, the most important probably being that there is no permanent relief of the congested part. Furthermore it is not always easy to persuade tourists to follow alternative routes, while even if this happens there is always the possibility of transferring the problem of crowding and congestion and therefore of increased pressure on resources elsewhere. Last but not least locals may be opposed to such an option at the fear of losing some of the economic benefits they possess or anticipate.

The dilemma of concentration or dispersion does not necessarily arise only for the purpose of managing visitor flows, more apparent in the case of areas with ecological significance. It may be a central point in planning for the future development for example of a coastal resort. Within the context of a Coastal Area

Management Program for the island of Rhodes (a well known tourist destination located in the southern part of Greece), conducted in the early nineties, an exploration of the future options with the help of Development and Environment scenarios was pursued. For each one of these scenarios different spatial strategies (for example concentrated, bipolar, linear along the coast) were considered. Impact assessment indicated that dispersion, although preferable for most scenarios since it contributed increased economic benefits for several local communities (mainly through land development), imposed severe stress on coastal resources, mainly through the loss of agricultural land and in general through the permanent alteration of land uses (Coccossis and Mexa, 1995).

The selection of the optimum in each case policy option is above all a matter of policy choice: is it better to concentrate tourists or to disperse them? Alternatively, could it be better to promote the creation of several poles of tourist development? The concept of carrying capacity can be applied in all cases. However, even in cases where a plan for tourism dispersion exists, it would be difficult to manage and guide tourist flows. This may be easier in cases where there is a single authority responsible for management.

Economic Tools

The changing role of both the state and the market encourages the adoption of other tools, besides the institutional and the regulatory. Some of them are presented below.

Pricing systems: Economic management strategies involve discriminating pricing systems (both incentive and disincentive strategies) to maximize economic gain and to spread visitor pressure throughout the year (Kuo, 2002). Price strategies include among others (ibid):

- Reduced fees for entrance (it may encourage visitation during off-peak periods within the week or throughout the year), for the use of public transportation, and so on (the application of entrance fees is presented more extensively in the following paragraphs)
- Park-and-ride schemes as well as on-site transportation to manage traffic problems
- Regulations and fines for inappropriate behavior (see previous paragraphs)
- Charges (so as to discourage for example the use of private cars).

Some kind of pricing to maximize economic profits is promoted, often indirectly and in a fragmented manner, in other types of destinations (besides areas with ecological or cultural value), such as coastal areas or islands where tourism is highly seasonal. In an effort to safeguard both employment and income opportunities and not so much to cope with seasonal pressure on resources, it is common to apply lower prices for accommodation for periods which are not peak months such as July and August. A more coordinated approach inclusive of other services may have additional positive impacts arising from an extended tourist season.

Pricing is a mechanism where by changing the fee at least during the times where demand exceeds capacity managers could control flows, under the assumption that the fee would be high enough to cause those less willing or less able to pay to drop out of the market therefore decreasing demand until it equalled supply (Shelby and Heberlein, 1986). It can help in prioritizing desires (at least to some of the visitors), it could secure experience to those who value it the most, while those who would make use of the resource would be the ones to pay, thus avoiding subsidizing recreation. However this may discriminate against those who cannot afford to pay, not to mention that it would no doubt raise several ethical questions and at the end of the day the irritation of the visitors, even of the broader public. (ibid; Butler, 1997). It is probably for this reason that managers are reluctant to consider pricing as a mechanism for limiting use. One may perhaps decide to consider such mechanisms during peak periods.

In cases of heritage tourism there may be numerous factors that need to be considered in elaborating a pricing strategy, encompassing financial constraints, competition, visitor profile and managing access (Garrod and Fyall, 2000).

Entrance fees: It is a particularly commonly applied mechanism. Visitors to cultural sites, publicly owned national parks and other natural areas often pay entrance fees and other charges for access and use. It is not always the most appropriate tool to use in order to limit and control tourism development and growth.

Fees and charges for entrance, camping, and so on are now applied by many protected areas, with the primary aim to raise funds and less to influence visitors behavior. (Buckley, 1998). However:

> ...entrance fees and other charges for access to such areas are frequently below amounts visitors are willing and able to pay, and below amounts required to finance park operating budgets...the generation of only small revenue flows from parks and reserves provides governments with little political or fiscal rationale to augment funding for them in strategies of national development. The vicious circle is one of low fees, inadequate revenue and deficient public investment – followed by continued low fees, revenue and investments (Laarman and Gregersen, 1996, p.247).

As noted the application of fees is not always welcomed. In the heritage sector although financial prospects are not promising, managers do not consider increased admission prices as an appropriate response to this development, suggesting as an alternative physical restraints and increase of visitors' secondary spending; However this last strategy seems to be viable in cases of constant or increasing number of visitors, which may prove inappropriate in cases where carrying capacity limits have been reached (Garrod and Fyall, 2000).

Taxes may be used as a way to incorporate in market prices various externalities like environmental degradation. However increased prices can discourage tourists and entrepreneurs as well. Lately in several tourist resorts in Greece tourist business have been subject to local taxes in an effort on the part of local authorities to raise funds for waste management following more or less the basic idea behind the 'polluters pay' principle. Of some interest is the use of a tourist eco-tax in the Balearic Island Region. The Balearic Island Region (Spain) has introduced a tourist tax (Ecotax) in order to raise funds so as to resolve some of the crucial environmental problems (for example over-exploitation of aquifers; increasing demand for electricity). The ecotourist tax will provide the financial resources for the Tourist Areas Restoration Fund. It is, therefore, a tool to improve tourism, the major source of wealth and employment in the Balearic Islands. On the other hand, the ecotourist tax is a way to shift part of the cost for the restoration, improvement and conservation of the natural and cultural heritage of the islands to tourists. It is believed that it can strengthen solidarity between visitors and residents. The funds collected are expected to finance actions that guarantee the improvement of tourism, the preservation of the environment and the maintenance of the natural and agricultural landscape of the Balearic Islands and, specifically contribute to:

- Redesign and restore tourist areas
- Upgrade natural resources, open and rural spaces
- Revalidate heritage resources of social, cultural and tourist relevance
- Revitalize agriculture as an economic and competitive activity.

The tax will involve a small amount per tourist, around 1 Euro per day (around 2 per cent of a tourist's average daily expenditure). The tax would be imposed on visitors and not on enterprises. Children under 12 and adults who come within a social programme would not pay the tax (Ajuntament de Calvià Mallorca, 1999).

At the time of conducting the study on 'Defining, Measuring and Implementing Tourism Carrying Capacity in European Destinations' the tax had not been imposed due to an appeal of the Spanish Central Government to the Constitutional High Court.

Several other tools such as the *cost-benefit analysis* (it has been applied to determine the investment return expected from an area in order to properly employ financial capacities, Wang, 1996) can be applicable, most of them reflecting some fundamental principles such as the *polluter pays principle, compensation principle* (in cases of traditional settlements it can be implemented by shifting some of the fiscal burden of the residents that do not depend on tourism onto those who depend and to the tourists, van der Borg et al., 1993) *or the user pays principle* (heritage managers hesitate in applying the user pays principle since they:

...have tended to associate the pricing of access to heritage with its commodification
...A second possible reason ...is that they find the notion difficult to reconcile with their

ideological beliefs about the wider mission of the heritage sector (Garrod and Fyall, 2000, p. 685).

Organizational-Management Tools

Queuing (Shelby and Heberlein, 1986): it follows the principle 'first come-first served'. In this case, as opposed to pricing, it is time and not money that is traded for the desired commodity. Among its advantages one may recognize that it is time and not money being requested, implying in this way a more or less equitable treatment of all visitors. However time for some visitors is more precious than for others, while some have less available time for waiting than others. Of most importance however may be the fact that time spent waiting is a loss for everyone, both visitors and managers.

Reservation and booking system: They facilitate management of both tourist and excursionist flows. In Venice, for example, the promotion of the Venice Card, which corresponds to a package of services, facilitates management of tourists' flows (van der Borg et al., 1996). In this case it is also possible to introduce taxes in a more equitable way, because the Venice Card is available to everyone. People who use this card can also benefit from discounts on local transportation, and entry fees to museums and other facilities. The only condition is advance booking.

The system of advanced booking has been successfully applied also in ecologically sensitive areas, ensuring a proper balance between conservation and tourism. The system had been applied for example to control overnight stays in the Kruger National Park in South Africa as well as the number of day-visitors (Ferreira and Harmse, 1999).

Overall the system favors those who plan ahead. However some problems may arise due to no-shows (which can be managed to a certain extent if deposits or advance payment of fees are requested), and to the cost of establishing such a system (Shelby and Heberlein, 1986).

Information management: The provision of information (for example on the web site) with respect to congestion, peaks, traffic, and so on may discourage tourists from visiting a place and as a result avoid overcrowding, while encouraging visiting during off-peak periods. Information (in the form of brochures, and so on) regarding zoning in natural marine parks can assist public understanding regarding zoning provisions (Day, 2002).

Education: The education of the local community as well as of tourists and other stakeholders in order to gain their support for implementing TCC, is essential. Educational programs may include interpretive centres, trackside signs, guided activities, and so forth. 'Education and regulation may be linked if leaflets or videos are followed by a test, which must be passed to obtain a permit for access or a particular activity' (Buckley, 1998, p. 209). It is suggested that hard visitor management strategies need to be combined with soft visitor strategies (provision of information, education) if they are to be effective in the long run (Kuo, 2002).

Another tool, which could help visitor management in a resource-sensitive tourism destination, is *environmental interpretation*. It could encourage the adoption of more appropriate behavior on the tourist's part, which could no doubt contribute to both the conservation of the area and the continuation of tourism development (Kuo, 2002). Three types of interpretive information are mentioned: directorial (facilitates channeling of traffic flow), behavioral (guides' behavior towards desirable patterns; codes are more and more often used) and educational (facilitates more enjoyable and memorable visitor experience) (ibid).

Market control and targeting of visitors: At present there is little coordination between management, planning and tourism marketing. Sophisticated marketing and communication allow marketers to pursue particular market segments and to undertake promotions for periods in which there is available carrying capacity (Curtis, 1998). Tour operators could play an important role in managing environmental impacts and maintaining the sustainability of tourism through promoting activities and other actions.

Targeting of visitors on those segments of tourist demand that are more attractive, that is they are expected to provide increased benefits and impose less costs for the area, may be another strategy for pursuing limits in an area (Glasson et al., 1995). The case of Venice presents such a case since the measurement of carrying capacity was based on the preference of overnight visitors against excursionists (van der Borg and Costa, 1995). On the basis of this expressed preference for a particular segment of the market, strategies can be elaborated so as to succeed in maximizing profits, while respecting capacity limits.

Incentive schemes: These should be applied in both public and private sectors in order to spread tourism demand over time and space thus optimizing the use of accommodation, to encourage rational consumption of resources, proper behavior towards local communities, and so forth. *Eco-labels* is one example. Business is asked to comply with accepted environmentally sound practices and for this is granted a certification. The incentive is increased demand for its product and services. The use of eco-labels in tourist accommodation and other public establishments is not widely spread and it may be for this reason that effects on resource consumption and waste production are still limited. However if properly promoted and combined with other initiatives it may have some positive results. *Best environmental practices and codes of practice* are another tool that can be implemented by the various tourism businesses. Guidance is given on conducting the various activities and providing the various services in an environmentally responsible manner. This approach can contribute in applying some capacity limits (for example regarding water consumption).

Information Technology Tools

Information technology tools such as *geographical information systems* and *decision support systems* taking advantage of various models, can assist the implementation of tourism carrying capacity, particularly at the monitoring stage. With the help of these tools both the spatial as well as the temporal dimension are introduced in measuring and in implementing carrying capacity.

Computer simulation modeling can be used as a tool to help implement carrying capacity frameworks in a proactive manner, which can be less risky and costly than on-the-ground experimentation of management actions (Lawson et al., 2003). Simulation modeling can be a useful tool in studying hospitality businesses under many different capacity-management scenarios (Pullman and Thompson, 2002, p. 27). The method has been applied in several national parks to track visitor travel patterns. It has been also used to evaluate the effects of shifting part of the weekend skiers to the weekdays (ibid). It can assist managers in monitoring and managing social carrying capacity (by reducing the resources needed for actual monitoring, by providing information regarding various social indicators), while it can provide information regarding spatio-temporal distribution of visitor use (Lawson et al., 2003).

Implementing the Tools in Tourism Carrying Capacity

Some General Factors to be Considered

In most cases the implementation of tourism carrying capacity requires an integrated approach where managers would be using a scheme of the various tools depending on both local particularities (characteristics of the area and its tourism development) and broader factors (for example the ratification of an international convention or the approval of a new law for the management of coastal areas may facilitate the implementation of conservation measures and the imposition of various limits) as well as on the demands arising from the defined tourism carrying capacity limit(s), the availability of resources (financial, organizational), of time and of technical capacity, the expression of political willingness and commitment, and so on.

However in implementing tourism carrying capacity some other factors, besides those above-mentioned may also need to be considered.

Among the first is the *changing role of the state*. Gradually responsibilities are distributed among more agencies while some of them are shifted from the national to the regional or local level, new forms of cooperation between the public, the private sector and the citizens are being promoted, while the hierarchical and bureaucratic organizational structures are slowly being replaced by other structures with a preventive and interactive character. Local governments are slowly being transformed from supply agencies into agencies with a preventive and supportive role that are expected to create the environment within which all other agencies like voluntary groups, private firms will provide services (Commission of the European Communities, 2001; Healey, 1997).

In the case of tourism the situation and probably the tendency is for less government intervention and regulations, particularly for destinations where resources and infrastructure are on private land (Butler, 1997). These kinds of changes are expected to affect management of tourist resorts, such as coastal and mountain, as well as management of areas with ecological and cultural significance, while they need to be taken into consideration when selecting tools for applying tourism carrying capacity limits (for example there may be a tendency to use tools such as voluntary agreements or other management tools in combination with 'command and control' tools).

In relation to the above is the *increasing role of the private sector*. The private sector is gaining increasing responsibility in respect to land use planning and in general of spatial development (Levy, 1992). Furthermore in a market economy, the private sector is expected to undertake increasingly the responsibility or initiative of nature and environmental protection or local identity enhancement. In some countries, for example forests are privatized. This may lead to increased pressure, since recreational activities may grow and expand in order to increase profits. This change may also have implications not only for the measurement of TCC but also for its implementation. Institutional tools may not be so effective or preferable in comparison for example to economic instruments, or other more flexible mechanisms such as agreements on a voluntary base. The selection of a strategy so as to conform to carrying capacity limits (provided that these have been accepted) will be defined probably on the basis of different criteria than those if the area had not been privatized. This should not necessarily be considered as a negative development, since this new regime may encourage the utilization of innovative approaches and tools, given certain conditions (for example satisfactory availability of resources).

In addition to the above it has been recognized that some capacity limits will no doubt be hard to manage since *coordination of action at various levels* (local, regional, national) may be requested for this purpose. Action is generally encouraged at local and national level while several *environmental problems are transnational.* Managing pressures at the local level often requires policies at a higher level. The utilization of institutional tools presents the mainstream in most of the cases of regional or global environmental problems. The Barcelona Convention adopted for the protection of the Mediterranean Sea and its coastal region presents such a case.

Furthermore a critical issue to be considered when applying tourism carrying capacity is the *existence of synergies*. Synergies are often overlooked as a result of fragmentation of responsibilities. Within this context an integrated approach in planning and management could provide a good basis, while *coordination of actions* will appear as a critical issue in implementing tourism carrying capacity.

Related to the above is the *accumulation of impacts*. Accumulative effects management for coastal areas:

...involves defining minimum thresholds for a region's coastal habitat functions below which the cumulative effects from anthropogenic adverse impacts are unacceptable. These thresholds can be based on the local community's expectations for the provision of goods and services...(Gilman, 2002, p. 381).

The *increasing demand on the part of the citizens for participation in decision-making and planning processes* is a development that need also not be overlooked (Levy, 1992). Planning is perceived more and more as a process of dialog that can support cooperation, facilitate negotiation among the various stakeholders so as to achieve consensus and promote coordination of actions (Hatem, 1992; Meck, 1993). The role of experts is slowly changing as they are asked to work together with the public (Filion, 1993). The benefits from stakeholder participation so as to build a consensus about tourism policies are also noted (Bramwell and Sharman, 1999). These developments will effect the application of tourism carrying capacity since both the identification as well as the implementation of limits needs to incorporate the aspirations, the interests and so on of several participants and not only those of tourists. Expert judgements will retain their fundamental significance for determining capacity limits, while they could provide input in the stakeholder dialogue, thus facilitating effective participation.

The Context of Using Tools

Tools can be employed in various contexts, for example a single management plan for a specific site or in a broader planning framework or an ad hoc basis of pilot actions.

Land use/spatial planning is a process par excellence to implement carrying capacity assessment for certain types of tourist destinations as in the case of islands and coastal areas. It defines zones appropriate for tourism development, taking into account local characteristics, particularities and constraints. Land use planning may not however be sufficient since it does not necessarily take into account prospects for future tourism development, potential impacts, and so on.

Careful *planning for tourism development* may be the key to more rational tourism resort development in the future (Priestley and Mundet, 1998, p. 108). As such it can provide an appropriate context for applying tourism carrying capacity assessment. Unfortunately so far the management of tourist areas focuses almost entirely on marketing; planning proposals are rarely implemented, the majority are simply management proposals (ibid). Most resorts do not adopt a proactive approach but an ad hoc incremental approach following more or less the direction the tourist area takes. Strategic planning is not widely promoted; short-term tactical decisions prevail (Knowles and Curtis, 1999, p. 88). This will inevitably lead to many problems, including uncontrolled growth with detrimental effects on the capacity of the system to assimilate changes and anticipate impacts.

Recently other approaches such as *Integrated Coastal Zone Management* are also being promoted. Integrated Coastal Zone Management (ICZM), as a:

...dynamic and continuous process of administering the use, development and protection of the coastal zone and its resources towards common objectives of national and local authorities and the aspiration of different resource user groups...(Knecht and Archer, 1993)

can provide a proper framework for organizing action for several coastal areas in a broader framework of a strategy towards sustainable development. ICZM starts with an awareness of issues, which facilitates dialog among interested parties, which supports cooperation, which is the basis for the coordination of actions, thus fostering integration of management. ICZM includes information collection, planning, decision-making, monitoring and implementation (EC, 1999). Since tourism is in several cases one of the major activities in a coastal area ICZM can help to anticipate possible environmental impacts from existing development, resolve the various conflicts between activities, etc. Planners and managers need to care for the tourist flows throughout the whole area and at particular sites (for example beaches). Beyond this ICZM takes care of the land development of the area, which is usually responsible for a significant part of the impacts appearing in an area (loss of agricultural land, loss of biodiversity, deterioration of landscape aesthetics, and so on). It is evident that defining tourism carrying capacity ('how many tourists', 'how much development') is at the core of this process; ICZM may provide an appropriate framework for applying tourism carrying capacity (PAP/RAC, 1997). Tools can be also employed on an ad hoc basis of pilot actions. Taking advantage of the various programs, mainly at European level, can help in implementing TCC. However as tourism carrying capacity is not a one shot activity but rather a long-term process it is recommended that it is integrated into the management and planning process of the resort.

Initiatives like the Agenda 21 provide significant opportunities for promoting the basic concept of tourism carrying capacity, that of imposing limits on development; in the case of Agenda 21 for Calvià imposing limits on the bed capacity of the resort was a priority.

The integration of tourism carrying capacity in such ad hoc initiatives may have both positive and negative implications.

In the case of the Agenda 21 initiatives participation and cooperation of local authorities is a determining factor in achieving sustainable development (Leitmann, 1998). The need to follow a consultative process so as to develop a local Agenda 21 can provide significant opportunities for determining and implementing TCC. On the other hand it is hard to assure follow up of initiatives through such programs.

Focus on Both Resource and Visitor Management

In all cases during the implementation stage it is necessary to address requirements arising from the various components of the carrying capacity: requirements related to the capacity of local resources (environmental, social-cultural, and so on), to the physical capacity, to the tourists themselves (satisfaction level, profile, and so forth). Within this context the adoption of tools to facilitate the control spatial-temporal flows, maximum number of overnight visitors, monitoring of the state of the resources and the impacts, and so on will be needed.

'Successful tourism development requires management attention to be focused not only on *tourism resources* but also *visitors'* (Kuo, 2002, p. 87-88). Visitor management includes the development and implementation of rules and regulations with respect to visitor activity and is an integral part of tourism management for both natural and heritage tourism destinations. It aims at the elimination of inappropriate use, at the enhancement of the visitor experience and last but not least at securing the quality of tourism resources. There are various visitor management strategies some of which are targeted at visitor activities, others to visitor enjoyment, understanding and knowledge of the resources (ibid).

Integrating Tools

In applying tourism carrying capacity it is quite probable that managers will not have to pursue a single goal, that is the fulfilment of one single capacity limit, but they will be asked to cope with more than one limit, some of which will no doubt be more critical than others. This will probably confirm the need for an integrated approach in implementing tourism carrying capacity limits based on the utilization of various tools capable to address the requirements arising from each one of the TCC components.

It is gradually recognized that the use of regulatory tools, no doubt of great value, need to be complemented with other tools. As Cope et al. (2000, p.59) note:

...planning for recreation and access is becoming less of an exercise in restriction and prohibition, as policy is becoming more liberal with the improved understanding of the nature of recreation. Planning for recreation requires more and more understanding of usage trends, demand, visitor's desires, expectations and values.

Integration of tools will be encouraged by other factors, besides the multidimensional character of tourism carrying capacity (various goals, factors and limits). The need for example to address pressures and related impacts at various spatial scales will no doubt require managers to focus not only on a micro-scale but also on a larger area; this will respectively require appropriate tools.

Taking Account of the Type of Tourist Destinations

There are no specific rules as to what kind of strategies and what kinds of specific tools managers need to apply so as to promote the implementation of tourism carrying capacity. Several factors will influence the final selection, the most decisive however stemming from the characteristics of the destination to be managed and its tourism development.

In the case of areas which are ecologically vulnerable and protected through a specific regime (for example Natural Parks), as well as of cultural/heritage sites (for example specific monuments, castles, churches), concerns are mainly focused in the spatial-temporal management of visitors flows so as to minimize potential impacts on resources while securing, if not enhancing, tourist experience. In the case of coastal resorts, islands, rural areas and mountain resorts, managers are obliged not only to cope with site specific problems (increased visitation in specific sites of cultural, natural and recreational interest) but furthermore to manage tourism development in a wider area by far (for example the coastal zone) and therefore anticipate the various impacts due not only to visitor flows and their recreational activities but more to the frequently intensive development of tourist and technical infrastructure (hotel units, apartments, restaurants, roads, and so on) and the resulting conflicts between tourism and other traditional or emerging economic activities, competing with tourism for the exploitation of resources.

The type of tourist destination will determine to a great extent the selection of the various tools to be utilized (for example the imposition of entrance fee is possible in well confined areas such as cultural sites and nature reserves).

It seems that the application of tourism carrying capacity for the areas of ecological or cultural value, where recreational activities prevail, may be easier in comparison to other types of tourist destinations (for example coastal areas, islands) given the existence of some institutional provisions that will facilitate the application of limits. What may facilitate the promotion of TCC is the recognition that the other types of tourism destination, which are the ones that traditionally host tourism, confront severe pressure from human activities which poses increasing threats to their ecological but also socio-economic value, in several cases aggravating the quality of resources and ecosystems. This wide recognition may encourage the adoption of a more integrated management and planning approach as well as the approval of new institutional provisions.

Ensuring an Equitable Distribution of Costs and Benefits

It should be recognized that the selection of the various tools that could assist the implementation of tourism carrying capacity needs to fulfil some criteria and not to be made either on an ad hoc basis or more frequently by keeping to the 'beaten track' choosing therefore what is familiar independently of its appropriateness for the specific case. There are some major issues that need to be carefully considered including among others whether the application of a certain tool would promote equitable distribution of costs and benefits, arising from implementing tourism carrying capacity. If not, compensation measures need to be anticipated and adopted by the managers.

'Establishing carrying capacity may lead to an allocation problem: if demand consistently exceeds supply, then some sort of rationing system will be necessary'

(Shelby and Heberlein, 1986, p. 111). Allocation distributes this limited number of opportunities among potential users when demand exceeds capacity, although it is recognized that it is better to set capacities or make allocation decisions before acceptable limits have been reached. Within this context four underlying goals or principles which form the basis for these systems were identified: *equality, equity* (refers to fairness, since equality may not always be fair), *social efficiency* (it is maximized when a resource is put to its highly valued use) and recognition of the *needs of particular user groups* (ibid).

It seems appropriate that tourists who make use of an area take the burden (or part of it) of the costs for applying some limits, which aim at ensuring environmental quality as well as enhancing visitor satisfaction. This is relatively understandable in the case of ecologically significant areas or cultural sites, which are often publicly owned. In a coastal resort however the imposition of limits (which will provide with some costs and benefits) needs to be carefully distributed between visitors/tourists, local community/ties, local entrepreneurs (for example owners of hotel units, local businessmen), local authorities, other participants in the tourism system (for example tour operators). The distribution of the costs and benefits will consolidate the feeling of shared responsibility and will increase the effectiveness of implementing capacity limits. It will no doubt require extensive participation and consultation with all relevant stakeholders.

It should be noted however that even in the cases of areas of natural or cultural significance several other actors, influenced directly or indirectly by the imposition of the various limits, need to participate in the management process (for example residents of neighborhood villages).

Monitoring the Use of Tools

Capacity limits are expected to be changeable over time, as the system itself is expected to change either as a result of management initiatives, or due to changes in the type of tourists, or other internal or external developments. This suggests that the tools utilized will have to be the proper ones on the basis of prevailing conditions. A periodic evaluation would be necessary not only in order to re-examine the capacity limits but also in order to judge the appropriateness of the applied tools and the possibility to consider using new tools. This could be assisted through monitoring. Effective monitoring and review can help managers make informed decisions (Cope et al., 2000).

Conclusions

Some tools may be more or less appropriate than others for recreational activities and for certain types of tourism development. After all the application of limits is not willingly accepted so much in tourist destinations compared to other leisure destinations and facilities (Butler, 1997). The utilization of regulatory tools is more common in the case of areas with ecological and cultural significance. It is in this case that several other techniques related to the management of visitor flows, with the aim to control the number of visitors and to manage the various activities are applied. As far as historical centres, where the pressure is not so much from land development, flow management could prove to be a more suitable way to go. However, attention needs to be placed on the changes of the functions and uses within the cities. In other cases, like tourism development in the coastal areas, other approaches may be more appropriate, such as land use planning and Integrated Coastal Zone Management.

An integrated approach is necessary when using tools for applying TCC. Gradually it has been recognized that command and control approach presented certain shortcomings and for this a number of economic incentives were developed (Leitmann, 1998). A combination of regulatory instruments and incentive measures may therefore be preferable.

Capacity building will be necessary in using tools for applying TCC limits. It is therefore necessary to promote training of existing staff, to establish educational programs, to inform decision-makers and planners, and so on. The utilization of sophisticated systems for measuring carrying capacity or the provision of a final number may not prove to be always useful and the confusion over alternative measures might discourage managers and policy makers.

In addition it is necessary to promote wider implementation of TCC and along with this 'test' of the various available tools. This implies the necessity to promote the practical/pilot implementation of TCC as a way to learn more about not only its measurement but furthermore of its actual implementation and the corresponding opportunities and constraints of the various tools utilized for implementing tourism carrying capacity. On the basis of lessons learnt managers may proceed to appropriate adjustments. The promotion of more *pilot projects* at European level is therefore necessary including the dissemination of experiences over the use of TCC or its components in managing tourism.

Last but not least it should be noted that as tourism carrying capacity approach may confront several methodological weaknesses, similar weaknesses may be encountered in most of the tools utilized. There are various limitations in each case, which however should not serve as an 'alibi' for not implementing capacity limits. In discussing the use of zoning Kelleher and Kenchington (in Day, 2002) note that it is better to create a zoning system which may not be ideal in ecological terms but which achieves in a way its purposes than to try to create first the theoretically ideal zoning system.

References

Ajuntament de Calvià Mallorca (1999), 'Calvià Agenda 21. The Sustainability of a Tourist Municipality. Plan of Action. 10 Strategic Lines of Action and 40 Initiatives', Calvià.

Borg, J. van der, Costa, P., Manente, M. (1993), *Traditional Tourism Cities: Problems and Perspectives*, International Centre of Studies on the Tourist Economy, Venice.

Borg, J. van der and Costa, P. (1995), 'Tourism and Cities of Art: Venice', in Coccossis, H., and Nijkamp, P. (eds), *Planning for our Cultural Heritage*, Avebury, Aldershot, pp. 191-202.

Borg, J. van der, Costa, P., Gotti G. (1996), 'Tourism in European Heritage Cities', *Annals of Tourism Research*, Vol. 23, No. 2, pp. 306-321.

Bramwell, B. and Sharman, A. (1999), 'Collaboration in Local Tourism Policy Making', *Annals of Tourism Research*, Vol. 26, No. 2, pp. 392-415.

Buckley, R. (1998), 'Tools and Indicators for Managing Tourism in Parks', *Annals of Tourism Research*, Vol. 25, No. 4, pp. 208-210.

Butler, R. (1997), 'The Concept of Carrying Capacity for Tourism Destinations: Dead or Merely Buried?' in Cooper, C. and Wanhill, S. (eds), *Tourism Development: Environmental and Community Issues*, Wiley, Chichester, pp.11-21.

Coccossis, H. and Mexa, A. (1995), 'Tourism and the Conservation of Heritage: the Medieval Town of Rhodes', in Coccossis, H. and Nijkamp, P. (eds), *Planning for our Cultural Heritage*, Avebury, Aldershot, pp. 107-121.

Coccossis, H. and Mexa, A. (1997), *Coastal Management in Greece*, Hellenic Ministry for the Environment, Physical Planning and Public Works, Athens.

Coccossis, H. and Mexa, A. (2002), 'The Coastal Zone', in Coccossis H. (ed), *Man and the Environment in Greece*, Ministry for the Environment, Spatial Planning and Public Works, Athens, pp. 74-81.

Collins, A. (1999), 'Tourism Development and Natural Capital', *Annals of Tourism Research*, Vol. 26, No. 1, pp. 98-109.

Commission of the European Communities (2001), *European Governance: A White Paper*, Brussels, 25.7.(COM) 428.

Cope, A., Doxford, D., Probert, C. (2000), 'Monitoring Visitors to UK Countryside Resources. The Approaches of Land and Recreation Resource Management Organizations to Visitor Management', *Land Use Policy*, Vol. 17, pp. 59-66.

Curtis, S. (1998), 'Visitor Management in Small Historic Cities', *Travel and Tourism Analyst*, No. 3, pp. 75-89.

Day, J. (2002), 'Zoning Lessons from the Great Barrier Reef Marine Park', *Ocean and Coastal Management*, Vol. 45, No. 2-3, pp. 139-156.

European Commission (EC) (2000), *Communication from the Commission to the Council and the European Parliament on Integrated Coastal Zone Management: a Strategy for Europe (COM/2000/547)*, Brussels.

European Commission (EC) (1999), *Towards a European Integrated Coastal Zone Management Strategy: General Principles and Policy Options*, Luxembourg.

Ferreira, S. and Harmse, A. (1999), 'The Social Carrying Capacity of Kruger National Park, South Africa: Policy and Practice', *Tourism Geographies*, Vol. 1, No. 3, pp. 325-342.

Filion, P. (1993), 'Factors of Evolution in the Context of Planning Documents: Downtown Planning in a Canadian City 1962-1992', *Environment and Planning B: Planning and Design*, Vol. 20, pp. 459-478.

Garrod, B. and Fyall, A. (2000), 'Managing Heritage Tourism', *Annals of Tourism Research*, Vol. 27, No. 3, pp. 682-708.

German Federal Agency for Nature Conservation (ed) (1997), *Biodiversity and Tourism: Conflicts on the World's Seacoasts and Strategies for Their Solution*, Springer, Berlin.

Gilman, E. (2002), 'Guidelines for Coastal and Marine Site-Planning and Examples of Planning and Management Intervention Tools', *Ocean and Coastal Management*, Vol. 45, No. 6-7, pp. 377-404.

Glasson, J., Godfrey, K. and Goodey, B., with Absalom, H., Borg, J. van der (1995), *Towards Visitor Impact Management*, Avebury, Aldershot.

Hatem, F. (1992), 'Changes in Attitudes and Approaches to the Philosophy of Planning', *Futures*, Vol. 24, No. 4, pp. 320-335.

Healey, P. (1997), 'The Revival of Strategic Spatial Planning in Europe', in *Making Strategic Spatial Plans, Innovation in Europe*, Healey, P., Khakee, A., Motte, A., Needham, B. (eds), UCL Press, London, pp. 3-19.

Knecht, R. and Archer, J. (1993), 'Integration in the US Coastal Management Program', *Ocean and Coastal Management*, Vol. 21, No. 1-3, pp. 183-200.

Knowles, T. and Curtis, S. (1999), 'The Market Viability of European Mass Tourist Destinations. A Post-Stagnation Life-Cycle Analysis', *International Journal of Tourism Research*, Vol. 1, pp. 87-96.

Kuo, I-L. (2002), 'The Effectiveness of Environmental Interpretation at Resource-Sensitive Tourism Destinations', *International Journal of Tourism Research*, Vol. 4, pp. 87-101.

Laarman, J. and Gregersen, H. (1996), 'Pricing Policy in Nature-Based Tourism', *Tourism Management*, Vol. 17, No. 4, pp. 247-254.

Lawson, S., Manning, R., Valliere, W., Wang, B. (2003), 'Proactive Monitoring and Adaptive Management of Social Carrying Capacity in Arches National Park: An Application of Computer Simulation Modelling', *Journal of Environmental Management*, Vol. 68, pp. 305-313.

Leitmann, J. (1998), 'Policy and Practice. Options for Managing Protected Areas: Lessons from International Experience', *Journal of Environmental Planning and Management*, Vol. 41, No. 1, pp. 129-143.

Levy, J. (1992), 'What has happened to Planning?', *Journal of the American Planning Association*, Vol. 58, No. 1, pp. 81-84.

Meck, S. (1993), 'Themes from Thymos', *Journal of American Planning Association*, Vol. 59, No. 2, pp. 147-149.

PAP/RAC (1997), *Guidelines for Carrying Capacity Assessment for Tourism in Mediterranean Coastal Areas*, Priority Actions Programme Regional Activity Centre, Split.

Priestley, G. and Mundet, L. (1998), 'The Post-Stagnation Phase of the Resort Cycle', *Annals of Tourism Research*, Vol. 25, No. 1, pp. 85-111.

Pullman, M. and Thompson, G. (2002), 'Evaluating Capacity- and Demand-Management Decisions at a Ski Resort', *Cornell Hotel and Restaurant Administration Quarterly*, Vol. 43, No. 6, pp. 25-36.

Shelby, B. and Heberlein, T. (1986), *Carrying Capacity in Recreation Settings*, Oregon State University Press, Corvallis, OR.

University of the Aegean, Laboratory of Environmental Planning (2000*), Problems of Development and Environmental Protection,* Final Report for the Programme on Integrated Coastal Zone Management: the Case of Cyclades, Athens, (in greek).

Wang, H. (1996), 'A Systematic Approach to Natural Recreational Resource Management', *Socio-Economic Planning Science,* Vol. 30, No.1, pp. 39-49.

Chapter 6

The Implementation of Tourism Carrying Capacity: Policy Instruments at the European Union Level

Jan van der Straaten

Introduction

The ongoing industrialization of Europe in the second half of the twentieth century was accompanied by increasing environmental pollution and the destruction of nature. During the 1960s and 1970s, environmental groups generated environmental awareness among the general public and public authorities; this resulted in the implementation of environmental laws in the 1970s and 1980s. When this process began, pollution from industry was seen as the main problem. From this perspective, environmental pollution was mainly a result of heavy industry, transport, intensive agriculture, and urban sprawl. Authorities concentrated on the reduction of environmental pollution in these sectors. It can be said that they were quite successful in reducing this type of pollution and environmental disruption (Stanners and Bourdeau, 1995). Generally speaking, this was achieved via the implementation of strict environmental standards within the framework of environmental laws, the introduction of catalytic converters in cars, and better planning procedures in urban planning. Of course, this does not imply that all environmental problems have been solved. However, it is a fact that the emissions of many important polluting substances have been substantially reduced in most European countries (Downing et al., 1993).

Throughout this period of time, the tourism industry was not considered relevant in the debate on environmental pollution and disruption. This situation changed at the beginning of the 1990s, when the concept of sustainable development, as propagated by the World Commission on Environment and Development (1987), became more and more accepted by public authorities as a guideline for public policy.

As sustainable development became the new and generally accepted concept for policy development, the tourism sector could no longer keep out of the environmental debate. Furthermore, with the ongoing acceptance of the necessity to abate environmental pollution, nature was increasingly being seen as a relevant issue. Membership of organizations such as the World Wide Fund for Nature,

Greenpeace, and national nature organizations became very popular in many European countries. In this climate, the concept of nature acquired a positive meaning. The tourism sector became aware of this change and took many initiatives to encourage the adoption of environmental friendly practices in an effort to demonstrate an environmental profile. Thus, in 1993 the World Tourism Organization published a guide for sustainable development for local planners (WTO, 1993); in 1995 the European Commission published its Green Paper on Tourism; and many authors published articles and books about the relationship between the tourism industry on the one hand, and nature and the environment on the other (Goodall, 1995; Hawkes and Williams, 1993; Cronin, 1990; Eber 1992; Butler, 1991; Hunter and Green, 1992, etc.). The concept of carrying capacity is an old one and is quite similar to the underlying ideas of sustainability. In this period, Coccossis and Parpairis (2000) paid special attention to the meaning and the possible implementation of this concept.

None of these publications can give a satisfactory answer, based on scientific conclusions, to the question of whether it is possible or advisable to define a certain level of sustainability or to determine the carrying capacity of a certain ecosystem. Of course, it cannot be denied that the concept of sustainable development and the concept of carrying capacity in principle provide good guidelines for bringing economic activities into line with the yields and the absorption capacity of the ecosystems of the world. It is becoming clear that this is not an ethical issue, but a necessity to guarantee the continuation of the world's production and consumption capabilities for future generations.

The concept of carrying capacity will be discussed in this paper. Firstly, the development of tourism and the pressure it exerts on nature and the environment will be outlined. Secondly, an overview will be given of the possibilities and limitations of the development of this concept as a management tool. Thirdly, some case studies of carrying capacity will be analysed, and finally the possibilities for implementing the concept in the policy field will be discussed.

Tourism Development in European Countries

Figures provided by the World Tourism Organization and other statistical sources make it clear that the number of tourists continues to grow. In most years, this growth is higher than the increase in income in the different countries of Europe. This implies that tourism has a high-income elasticity. In the second part of the twentieth century the increase in labour productivity was partly used to generate higher incomes, but there has also been a strong tendency to use this increase in productivity to create more leisure time. More leisure time and higher incomes have resulted in a high-income elasticity. It should not be overlooked that, as a result of higher levels of education, people are more inclined to visit destinations other than sun and beach resorts.

Richards (1994) came to the conclusion that the following holiday types can be recognized in Europe during the first part of the 1990s: sun and sea 37 per cent, adventure holiday 18 per cent, skiing 6 per cent, city tour 21 per cent, special cultural holiday 19 per cent. From these figures it can be concluded that approximately 60 per cent of tourist activities are based on the availability of nature in the broadest sense, while approximately 40 per cent are based on urban or cultural elements. There is a general tendency among consumers in Europe to shift from the traditional sun and beach destinations towards more active and more culturally oriented leisure activities (see for example, Gratton and van der Straaten, 1994, and Richards, 1994). The vast majority of European tourists (91 per cent) visited a location in Europe in the 1990s. We can therefore conclude that European tourism is a European issue. This implies that, as far as non-European destinations are concerned, the discussion about ecotourism is not relevant for the European debate.

Although more attention has been given to environmental and nature issues recently, the increasing number of tourists generate an increasing pressure on nature and the environment. In certain respects, there is no difference between tourists who visit the countryside and those who visit urban and cultural events. All have to travel to their point of destination. Travelling is generally done by car, train, touring car or aeroplane. In doing so, fossil fuels are used with the accompanying emissions of greenhouse gases and acidifying substances. Greenhouse gases generate the problem of global climate change, while the emissions of nitrogen oxide cause acid rain, which is a regional problem. The mode of transport chosen by tourists plays a significant role in these environmental problems, as the use of fossil fuels per passenger-kilometre can vary substantially. The most polluting mode of transport is the aeroplane, followed by the private car, the touring car and the train. Obviously, biking and walking are the best modes of transport from an environmental perspective.

Figure 6.1 attempts to provide a framework for the analysis of the delicate and complex relationship between the ecosystem and the tourism sector. On the one hand the ecosystem is used as an input in the production process, and on the other hand nature and the environment are polluted by tourist activities.

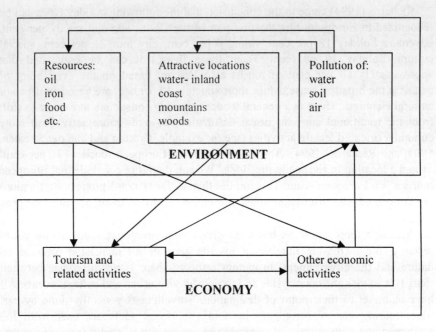

Figure 6.1 The relationship between the tourism sector and the ecosystem

We will apply this analytical framework to the most important tourist areas of Europe, namely the Mediterranean basin and mountain areas, in particular the Alps. This implication is outlined in Figure 6.2.

The Mediterranean Basin

In this region, water pollution is obviously the most important threat to tourist activities. The algal growth along the eastern coast of Italy clearly demonstrates how polluted these waters are. The tourism sector cannot be neglected as a source of water pollution, but the sewerage from industries, residential areas, and the run off of nutrients from arable land are much more important.

The most important threat to the environment from tourist activities in this area is the ribbon development along many coastlines, such as in eastern Spain, on the northern coast of Crete, on the northern coast of the Sea of Marmara, and on many parts of the southern coast of France. Especially in areas where the hotels, buildings, roads, and marinas are unattractive, the tourism value is decreasing rapidly. This is particularly true when the beaches are full of litter. One could conclude that these areas are no longer attractive to tourists, as has been demonstrated on many parts of the Mediterranean coast of Spain. A restructuring of tourist infrastructure, organizing tourist development in such a way that it is more compatible with the hinterland, and reducing seasonal overcrowding are the only ways to realize sustainable tourist development.

	Area 1	Area 2
Erosion	xx	xxxx
Use of fossil energy	xxx	xxx
Use of land and infrastructure	xxxx	xxxx
Disturbance of ecocycles by organic materials	xxx	x
Acid rain	x	xxxx
Greenhouse effect	xxx	xxxx
Disruption of habitats for plants and animals	xxxx	xx
Area 1 is the Mediterranean		
Area 2 includes mountain areas, in particular the Alps		

Figure 6.2 The scale of environmental disruption in the most important tourist areas of Europe

Williams (1992) indicates the potential future scale of the problem:

> Tourism development in the northern Mediterranean is regarded to be amongst the most extensive and intensive in the world. It is estimated that by the year 2050, 95 per cent of that coastline will be urbanized. Under such a situation, the Mediterranean basin may have to support more than 500 million inhabitants and 200 million tourists with 150 million cars.

The Alps

The Alps are of great importance for tourists in summer as well as in winter. Over the last decades, there has been a sharp increase in the number of winter visitors. This has resulted in an increase in the total number of skiing facilities, leading to erosion of mountain slopes as a result of the cutting down of forests and the levelling of steep slopes. The use of artificial snow also provides skiing facilities. As an ideal ski run has to have a certain angle of inclination, mountains that are too steep are remodelled using bulldozers and dynamite. In certain French ski resorts it is normal for more than 30 metres of ground and rocks to be blasted in order to achieve the desired angle of inclination.

Where vast mountain forests cover the slopes, these are partly cut down to make ski runs from the mountaintop to the valley, from where the skier can be transported back high up the mountain with the help of lifts, which use substantial amounts of electricity. Many skiing resorts in France and Italy are surrounded by ski lifts and ski runs, which are cut into the landscape as if by the knives of giants.

The results for vegetation are disastrous. The ski runs are heavily affected by erosion, which transports the fertile humus down to the valleys and subsequently out to sea.

From the previous description one may conclude that in the Alps the carrying capacity of the ecosystem has been considerably surpassed. The negative effects of acid rain, which has caused considerable deterioration in the condition of the mountain forest, are also a problem.

General Problems

As mentioned above, acid rain is an important threat to the role of mountain forests in the protection of mountain valleys against erosion. The dying off of these forests will have significant effects on the inhabitation of these valleys. The main source of the emission of acidifying substances in the Alps is traffic. This implies that tourist traffic generates problems for the tourism sector itself. Tourism is not the only source of acid rain, but in mountain areas its importance cannot be ignored.

Recently, more attention has been given to the greenhouse effect. Tourists using private cars and planes for transport use a considerable amount of fossil energy and hence contribute to global warming. The warming up of the earth, caused by an increase in levels of CO_2, will cause a rise in the level of the sea which will in turn affect beaches. This will have significant effects on the possibilities of using some Mediterranean beaches for tourism purposes.

Finally, in many cases, destruction of nature results from the construction of certain types of infrastructure. This is the case when hotels and other buildings are constructed in vulnerable and valuable nature areas. For example, the new beach resort Matalascañas was actually constructed within the boundaries of the Coto Doñana National Park in south-western Spain. The development of such a tourist resort is always accompanied by the construction of roads, car parks, camping sites, petrol stations, banks, real estate companies, rent-a-car companies, supermarkets, tennis courts, golf courses, etc.

Methodological Development of Tourism Carrying Capacity Assessment

The Debate of Environmental Economists

Pigou was the first neoclassical economist who paid serious attention to environmental problems by introducing the concept of the external diseconomy. In order to indicate the significance of this concept, Pigou distinguished the social product from the private product. Between these two, a divergence may occur *'out of a service or disservice rendered to persons other than the contracting parties'* (Pigou, 1920/1952, p. 192). In other words, the actions of market parties influence the welfare of non-market parties.

In Pigou's view, externalities create a difference between the social and the private cost prices of goods and services. For example, when a firm discharges processing water containing heavy metals into a river, it transfers part of its production costs to society (in this case the costs of restoring the quality of the river water). Under sufficient competitive pressure, the consumer price will be too low, that is, the costs of the purification of the river water are not incorporated in the market price of the produced goods and services. In such a situation, market prices do not reflect the actual relations of scarcity, as the increased scarcity of clean river water is kept outside consumer decisions. In other words, the factors of production are not optimally allocated.

According to Pigou (1920/1952, p. 192) it is the task of the government to pass external diseconomies onto the buyers of polluting products. He proposes imposing a levy on activities causing external diseconomies, such as the discharge of polluted wastewater. The externality will therefore be given a shadow price, which economic agents take into account. External diseconomies are no longer transferred onto society; the optimal allocation of production factors has been restored.

When environmental problems became increasingly a common phenomenon in the course of the 1960s, many economists propagated the Pigovian approach of implementing environmental taxes to reduce pollution. However, there are many pitfalls and barriers in the Pigovian approach (Dietz and van der Straaten, 1988). Although the shortcomings of this approach are becoming more recognized, many economists are still strongly inclined to give a high profile to economic instruments. A good overview of this discussion is provided by Hanley and Spash (1993). Others tried to develop new instruments to handle environmental problems. The Contingent Valuation Method (CVM) in particular became very popular in the policy field in the USA and the UK. If there is no market price for an environmental asset, respondents are asked how much they are willing to pay to protect that asset. The outcome is seen as the result of a revealed preference, which means that the CVM approach is in line with neoclassical thinking. In the beginning, the CVM was developed to deal with tourism problems in particular (Mitchel and Carsson, 1989). Pearce and Moran (1994) for example, give a complete overview of all known CVM studies leading to the calculation of the economic value of tropical forests, wetlands, rangelands, and marine systems. Garrod and Willis (1999) provide a good overview of the various methods that have been developed recently to calculate the economic value of nature and the environment with new instruments. Other environmental economists have their doubts regarding the possibility of giving economic value to nature and the environment (van der Straaten, 2000).

In this problematic field it should not be forgotten that in normal everyday life we are often confronted with economic goods that do not have a price and where there are no fundamental problems regarding the decision-making process. For example, the San Marco Square in Venice would be a marvellous location for a skyscraper. It is certain that many large companies would be willing to pay very high prices for an office in such a location. Therefore, from an economic point of view one could argue that using the San Marco Square differently in the future could bring great benefits. However, nobody has the slightest intention of translating the existing value of San Marco Square into monetary terms vis-à-vis its use as a location for prestigious offices. Moral, ethical, and cultural ideas form, in fact, a complete barrier to the use of the square for any other purpose.

Of course economists can argue that the square, in its current use, has a higher economic value than could be obtained through any other use. However, many others would argue that these considerations have nothing to do with economic value. They would argue that the San Marco Square cannot be used differently on the basis of any other economic bid. The use of the San Marco Square falls outside the realm of economics. The same ideas can be put forward when dealing with the existence of an army, a monarchy, a Rubens painting, a Shakespeare poem, a piece of music by Mozart, the sight of migrating raptors and storks on Gibraltar, an attractive partner, the Amsterdam canals, a Marquez novel, the Matterhorn, Delphi, the Atlantic coast of Portugal, a nation, human rights, or an educational system. These goods have no price and that, in this view, is the best option. Few economists would claim that it would be better to calculate prices for these goods in one way or another. Of course, the counter argument could be presented that people are willing to pay money to see these assets and to read these books, etc. This is true, but that is different from saying that the price people are willing to pay to visit the Amsterdam canals, the Matterhorn, or the Van Gogh Museum is the economic value of these assets.

The Concept of Carrying Capacity

The concept of Carrying Capacity was developed in the context of the economic debate on the relevance and possibilities of using economic instruments. The point cannot be overlooked that in environmental policy the principle of the Pigovian approach, namely, that it makes sense to monetize environmental disruption in one way or another, is barely accepted. For many environmental problems, authorities define acceptable levels of environmental disruption. This is, for example, the case with water pollution in the rivers Rhine, Meuse, Scheldt, and Thames. After extensive debate authorities came to the conclusion that good functioning of the ecosystem of these rivers should be the starting-point of all environmental policy.

In the debate on acid rain policies, many countries concluded that the only way to solve this environmental problem was to accept so-called critical loads, which implies that the buffering capacity of the ecosystem is taken as the aim of all policies. Countries need to reduce their emissions to a particular level. It took many years before these conclusions were accepted by all countries. The concept of Carrying Capacity takes the same position: the ability of the ecosystem to withstand pollution is taken as the starting-point for all policies.

Approaches of Carrying Capacity Assessment

There are many similarities between the concept of carrying capacity and that of sustainable development. In the case of carrying capacity, the sound functioning of the ecosystem is seen as a guideline for the development of environmental and economic policies. The starting-point is that the level of economic activities should not and cannot exceed the level 'permitted' by the ecosystem. In the case of sustainable development, the ecosystem should not be damaged by economic activities in such a way that production and consumption possibilities of future generations are jeopardized. In both cases, the crucial question to answer is what the maximum stress on the ecosystem could be.

In the case of sustainable development this has been an ongoing debate, which started after the publication of the Brundtland Report. An overview of this debate is given in the following publications: van den Bergh, and van der Straaten, 1994; Tylecote and van der Straaten, 1997; Faucheux et al.,1998; Köhn et al., 1999; Requier-Desjardins, et al., 1999; Briassoulis, 2001. It is very difficult, and perhaps impossible, to define exactly what sustainable development is. It is easier to conclude ex post facto certain types of behaviour or policy are *un*sustainable.

In the case of carrying capacity, a similar debate exists. Coccossis and Parpairis (2000) argue that already in the beginning of the debate it was stated that carrying capacity 'must be considered as a means to an end and not as an absolutely definite limit that is unalterable for each type of environment under discussion.' Elements from outside the realm of ecology entered into the debate, such as the amount of use and user satisfaction (Nielsen, 1977; Stankey, 1982), social-psychological characteristics (Kreimer, 1977), cultural issues and urban environmental problems. All these approaches are discussed by Coccossis and Parpairis (2000). At the end of their paper they argue that 'At present, the possibility of establishing quantitative limits through carrying capacity expressions as absolute figures seems rather remote. In any case, the concept of tourist carrying capacity is not the panacea it may seem to be.' We are of the opinion that more can be concluded about the implementation of the concept of carrying capacity. In this contribution, another type of approach, is presented based on the following considerations:

- Of course, Coccossis and Parpairis are correct in arguing that carrying capacity can never be an absolute figure. However, it is questionable whether these figures need to be absolute. Perhaps it could be possible to achieve more, if it is accepted that it is necessary to look for more general approaches and figures. The best way to do this is to study certain cases and to learn which issues prove to be relevant. After the presentation of the case studies, it can be concluded which elements play a main role in many of these case studies and should therefore be given special attention.
- Much can be learned from the debate on acid rain. This debate started at the UN conference in Stockholm in 1972. Sweden, negatively affected by acid

rain depositions caused by emissions in adjacent countries, put this issue on the international agenda. Most countries were not willing to reduce their emissions and claimed that it was not certain that they were responsible for the depositions in Sweden. The Economic Commission for Europe set up research groups with the aim of describing and analysing the then current emissions and depositions. It took a relatively long time before these groups were able to publish their research reports. The first official result was the signing of the Helsinki Protocol in 1985, through which many countries agreed to reduce their SO_2 emissions by 30 per cent. Later on, a wider range of acidifying emissions was also taken into account. After lengthy negotiations, a protocol regarding all relevant emissions was signed in Göteborg in 1999. A full description and analysis of this issue is provided by Alcamo et al., 1990, and Castells, 1999.

The main issue in this debate was the carrying capacity of the ecosystem to handle acidity. This capacity is not the same in all parts of Europe. Therefore, some countries benefited more from the reduction of emissions than others. Nevertheless, all European countries agreed on the premise of taking the suggested carrying capacity as a guideline for their policies. In this case no absolute figures could be given. Nevertheless, a result was achieved.

- Institutional and political issues are not given high profile in many studies on the topic of carrying capacity. These influences are very important in many cases. Full attention is discussed to these elements in the case studies.
- In the acid rain debate, the protection of nature is taken as a serious aim of environmental and economic policies. At the beginning of the debate, certain countries were inclined to emphasise cost-benefit analyses. They tried to calculate the costs resulting from acid rain, as well as the costs of abating it. By comparing these figures, conclusions could be drawn concerning the level to which emissions had to be reduced. However, these estimations failed owing to a lack of economic data. It is extremely difficult to calculate the economic losses occurring as a result of a certain type of environmental disruption. Countries were forced to look for other approaches. Eventually, they accepted the carrying capacity of the ecosystem as an approach. No part of Europe should have a deposition level exceeding the critical load of its ecosystem.

Nature differs from the (physical and chemical) environment in that it is easier to determine a critical load in the case of environmental disruption. The level to which ecosystems can be degraded, disrupted and eroded is, however, difficult to estimate and solutions are therefore complex. Still, current European policies in the field of nature protection can help us in this matter. The Habitat Directive and Natura 2000 of the European Union are generally accepted policy frameworks and can perhaps help to determine what is considered worth protecting concerning nature in the European Union.

Case Studies

Free Access to the Dutch Forests

The ecological quality of most forests in the Netherlands is relatively low in comparison to forests in other European countries. Staatsbosbeheer (National State Forest Agency) and Natuurmonumenten (Association of Nature Conservation) are the main owners of these forests. Until the summer of 2001, both organizations had the same strategy regarding visitors and tourists. People were allowed to visit the forests on condition that they kept to the paths in the forests. Walking through the forests beyond the paths was not allowed. The reason for this strategy was the vulnerability of the forest ecosystem.

In the summer of 2001, Staatsbosbeheer changed its strategy. Visitors were allowed to walk in the forest without using the paths. Staatsbosbeheer argued that the experience of walking through the forest is so exciting that the small possibility of ecological damage being caused should be ignored. Natuurmonumenten did not change its strategy. They argued, as before, that the ecological damage is too great when people do not keep to the paths. Again, the carrying capacity of the ecosystem was used as an argument. It can be concluded that these two organizations have different views regarding the carrying capacity of the forest ecosystem. However, both aim at nature protection. SOVON, the most important organization of bird watchers in the Netherlands, entered the debate with the argument that particularly in the breeding season visitors should keep to the paths, as breeding birds of prey can easily be disturbed by walkers in the forests (Saris, 28 June 2001).

One may get the impression that there is only a difference in opinion regarding the precise definition of the carrying capacity of the forest ecosystem. This is questionable. Staatsbosbeheer was originally a state organization. A few years ago, it became an independent private organization although the aims remained unchanged. In this process, Staatsbosbeheer was forced to give market forces and recreation activities a higher profile than before. It is not surprising that the organization would then change its strategies. Therefore, it can be concluded that it has a different view regarding carrying capacity. Furthermore, one cannot overlook the point that changing the regime is expected to influence resources management and that privatization imposes – at least in the first place – a strong pressure for increasing financial benefits. Therefore there is an increasing danger that this will be done at the expense of nature protection.

Vulnerability of Ecosystems

Wetlands, which are important ecosystems in the Netherlands, are often vulnerable. In some wetlands, such as the Nieuwkoopse Plassen and Botshol, visitors are not allowed to enter the main parts of the marshes during the breeding season. Even a single small boat can negatively affect the breeding success of rare birds. The carrying capacity of the ecosystems is taken as a guideline.

In winter, when there is ice, the birds are gone. Skating tours are then organized in these marshes. When the weather is good, some 10,000 skaters per day visit the wetlands. No serious ecological damage is likely in winter, because the behaviour of animals varies during the year.

This makes it clear that the carrying capacity argument is not a fixed argument. What could cause an ecological disaster in a certain period of the year can be done without any problem in another period. Nature organizations use the carrying capacity argument in winter and summer. However, the impact of tourist behaviour is different in different seasons.

A similar situation can be recognized regarding the Loggerhead Turtle (*Caretta caretta*). This sea turtle lives in many seas and oceans. However, it breeds only in the Mediterranean Sea. Eggs are laid in the sand of beaches of Greek locations such as Crete, Kiparissia Bay, Lakonikos Gulf, and Kefalonia, with Zakynthos as the most important breeding site. Approximately 2,000 female loggerheads lay their eggs in Mediterranean countries. This sea turtle is in danger of extinction. A large number of turtles are caught during the swordfish season, and even when they are released they often do not survive (Gasc, et al., 1997).

Particularly on the beach of Zakynthos a conflict has arisen between tourists and the sea turtles during their breeding season. The sea turtles come to the beach at night to lay their eggs in the sand, and as soon as the baby turtles leave the eggs they go back to the sea. This beach, like the beaches of most Greek islands, is a popular destination for tourists and the tourists disturb many eggs. This is undesirable for such a vulnerable and rare species, whose main breeding location is Zakynthos. These facts are well known by the authorities of Zakynthos and Greece, nevertheless, it has become extremely difficult for these authorities to take adequate conservation measures. They were, in fact, not at all willing to cooperate with conservation groups on this issue. WWF tried to press the local authorities in this respect and have recently experienced a certain degree of success.

This example shows that the problems are not in the concept of carrying capacity as such as the facts concerning a threatened and protected species make completely clear. The problems lie in the vested economic interests in the tourist sector on Zakynthos beach, and the perceived irrelevance of nature protection to certain Greek authorities. Increased conflicts due to competing interests render the whole situation difficult. The implementation of tourism carrying capacity needs to be carried out along with conflict resolution.

Alpine National Parks and the Planning Process

The Alps are one of the most undisturbed European ecosystems. Switzerland recognized this when early in the twentieth century it established a national park in the south-eastern part of the country. No economic activities are allowed within the boundaries of the park, and some parts of the park are not open to visitors.

France, Italy, and Austria also intended to establish national parks. Only Italy was able to realize this in the same period with Grand Paradiso, which was given to the Italian state by the Italian king at the beginning of the twentieth century. The other countries experienced difficulties in the designation process. The Alpine societies of Austria, for example, argued that the central part of the Austrian Alps, the Tauern-Glockner mountains, should become a national park. However, vested economic interests in the tourist sector were able to neutralize these plans to a considerable extent. Eventually national parks were established in the peripheral parts of the Austrian Alps, where the economic interests of the tourist sector were relatively low, and a relatively small park was located in the Tauern mountains.

A comparable situation can be seen in France. In mountain areas, national parks have been established in the massifs of the Écrins, the Central Pyrenees, the Mercantour, and the Oisans. The boundaries of these parks are defined in such a way that the economic interests of the tourist sector in the French Alps are not negatively affected by their existence. All significant ski resorts in France, such as Les Deux Alps, Alp d'Huez, Tigne, Val d'Isère, Les Quatre Vallées, Chamonix, and Les Ménuirs are outside the parks and, therefore, it remains possible to build cable cars, ski runs, and car parks, and to blast rocks in one of the most important and vulnerable ecosystems of Europe.

If the carrying capacity and the importance of the ecosystem would have been taken as a starting-point, the locations and the boundaries of the Alpine national parks would have been completely different from where they are now. The Mont Blanc would have become the cornerstone of a huge national park, covering areas of France, Switzerland, and Italy. Another park would have been located in the centre of the Berner Oberland and in the Alps around the Matterhorn, covering areas of Italy and Switzerland. In the Eastern Alps, the Ortler, the Bernina, and the Dolomites would have been eastern counterparts. However, such national parks do not exist in reality, as the interests of tourist and ski resorts such as Saas Fee, Zermatt, Chamonix, Courmayeur, Breuil-Cervinia, St. Moritz, Pontresina, Bad Gastein, and Cortina d'Ampezzo are sufficiently powerful to nullify such plans. These resorts take no account of the concept of carrying capacity. The level and the type of tourist activities in these resorts far exceed the carrying capacity of the mountain ecosystem. However, vested economic interests are not interested in this type of information, as long as the future revenue from tourist activities is not in danger.

Conflicts between Different Users of Ecosystems

When ecosystems are scarce, conflicts can easily arise between different groups of users. The more groups that use an ecosystem, the more likely it is that such a situation will occur. A traditional point of conflict in the Alps, for example, is the use of mountain slopes by skiers and mountaineers. These two groups use the mountains at different times of the year so the conflict is not a result of shared use at the same time. Downhill skiing, however, is in many cases accompanied by a massive development of infrastructure, in particular ski runs and cable cars. As long as there is snow, this infrastructure can be overlooked, however, in summer when the snow is gone, the eroded ski runs become visible.

Many typical ski resorts look ugly and eroded in summer. This is particularly the case in French and Italian ski resorts, where winter tourism is very popular. Such ski resorts are rarely visited by mountaineers in summer. In this situation, the carrying capacity of the mountain ecosystem is not surpassed in the view of skiers. However, the vast majority of mountain climbers will argue that insufficient attention is given to the carrying capacity of the ecosystem.

The coastal dunes in the Netherlands are a very important area for recreational activities in summer and winter. Biking and walking in particular are very popular in the dunes, which are located close to the major cities in the western part of the country. Biking however, is not a one-dimensional activity in this country, some people cycle on 'normal' bikes but other groups of bikers use racing bikes with the sole intention of going as fast as possible. This gives the 'normal' bikers and walkers a feeling of being unsafe, and quite often leads to serious conflicts between these different groups of users of the dunes. In fact, the main problem here is congestion. Similar conflicts occur in overcrowded parts of the Alps in summer, where walkers, mountain bikers, rafters, hang gliders, etc. use the same space. These problems can only be overcome by strict regulations. The carrying capacity of the ecosystem has been socially surpassed.

The Coto Doñana National Park in Spain

This national park is one of the most important European wetlands. It is located along the Atlantic coast of Spain, in the province of Huelva. Its surface area is approximately 600 km^2 and no people live in the park. Approximately 25 years ago farmers and developers of beach resorts wanted to 'develop' the region. Spanish nature conservationists were strongly against these plans and WWF took the initiative to buy this wetland and to transform it into a nature reserve. In the course of time, WWF was able to get the support of some Spanish authorities. However the developers of beach resorts were strongly against the establishment of a nature reserve along these beaches. The current boundaries were established as a result of these different views and options. The developers were able to keep a certain stretch of coast outside the boundary of the park which became the current beach resort of Matalascañas.

The wetlands outside the national park are used in such a way, in particular for horticulture, that their ecological value is declining year by year. Of course, this has nothing to do with the concept of carrying capacity. This concept was never applied in the debate concerning the use of this wetland, which was a struggle between economic interests of agriculture and the tourist sector on the one hand, and the interests of the ecosystem on the other.

This can be clearly demonstrated by the current situation regarding access to the park. The park is not open to the public and only minor parts on the periphery can be accessed via a few short trails. It is possible to visit the park itself only by booking a trip organized by a private company, which is entitled to conduct tours through the park. The demand for these trips is so high that it is necessary to book several months in advance. So, the strategy of the park authorities is in fact to minimize the number of visitors as much as possible. This limited access is a result of the carrying capacity of the vulnerable wetland for visitors, which according to the national park authorities is limited.

However, in the month of May, which is the breeding season of nearly all birds living in the wetland, there is a traditional Maria festival in the village of El Rocío. It is visited by more than 500,000 people coming from the regions around the park. These people travel to El Rocío in horse-drawn carriages traditionally, passing through the wetlands. The national park authorities have never been willing to stop this massive influx, resulting in a huge disturbance of breeding birds. This is in contradiction to their own claims to respect the concept of carrying capacity, as the visit of more than 100,000 people in the breeding season substantially surpasses the carrying capacity. Unfortunately, the park authorities regard the visit of 'normal' visitors to the park differently to that of the people who visit the Maria festival.

From the previous description it can be concluded that a concrete definition of Carrying Capacity in a certain area is always influenced by many societal developments. In a country like Spain where the Roman Catholic feasts are a part of everyday life, it is hardly possible to define carrying capacity in contradiction with these types of interests. Furthermore, the farmers around the national park have, generally speaking, more political influence and power than nature protectors from a ministry far away from the area in question.

Ribbon Development Along the Coast

Beaches are highly attractive tourist destinations. Tourists visiting a beach resort want to stay in a hotel or apartment as near to the coast as possible. This often leads to ribbon development along the coastline. Such development can be seen along the northern coast of Crete, the eastern coast of Spain, and the southern coast of France. The effect is that unspoiled coastlines are becoming increasingly rare in Europe. This type of development often poses a threat to the marine ecosystem and carrying capacity is surpassed in many locations.

The coastlines of the Netherlands and Belgium are quite similar as the same geological processes formed the dunes all along the North Sea. However, the spatial planning processes in the two countries were very different. The Netherlands protected the natural value of its dune coastline, while Belgium completely destroyed the beauty and natural value of this ecosystem by building a ribbon development along the coast. In fact, the Belgian coastline is a 60 kilometres long boulevard with car parks, houses, apartments, etc. It goes without saying that the carrying capacity of the Belgian coast is completely surpassed.

Such differences between these two adjacent countries are strange as the carrying capacity argument is the same in both countries. The difference can only be explained by pointing to the public decision making process. Traditionally, public policy and common properties such as nature have always been given a high profile in the Netherlands. The Dutch government has always stressed that the value of the dune and coast ecosystem should be maintained. Thus, the carrying capacity argument has been used by Dutch authorities in spatial planning. Additionally, the Netherlands uses its dunes to protect the land from the sea, and as a source of drinking water but these functions are not equally important in Belgium. Furthermore, private interests play a more significant role in the Belgian political system than in the Netherlands. This implies that people who want to build a house on the dunes will not find substantial administrative barriers in their way, where as in the Netherlands, it is impossible for a person to build a private house on the dunes.

It is therefore concluded that the political decision making process is the decisive factor in this case. The concept of carrying capacity has not played any role in decision making in Belgium while in the Netherlands nature protection was based on the carrying capacity principle and planning authorities have been able to give nature protection a vital position. This is only possible when and if nature protection has a strong support in society itself, otherwise it will be nullified as in the Belgian case.

Conclusions on Policy Instruments

From these case studies, one can conclude that in the political debate on the use of common resources such as ecosystems, the concept of carrying capacity has often been overruled by vested economic interests. Hardin (1968) argues that common resources will always be overused because individual users can make a high profit by overusing them. As this applies to all users of a common resource, overexploitation is always the result. This has become known as 'The Tragedy of the Commons'.

In Hardin's approach, common property resources will be overexploited and overused until the resource is exhausted. However, in the case of common pasturelands historical evidence contradicts his view. In many countries of the world, common property pasturelands exist. In the Alps, for example, common pasture lands (the Alps) were numerous for many centuries. However, common property can only exist if a common property regime is defined. Without a definition of common property, this type of property does not exist, as was clearly demonstrated by Bromley (1991). This is to say that common property is not freely accessible to everybody, as is the case in Hardin's example. The most typical characteristic of common property right is that certain persons (in most cases, people from one village) are allowed to use the pastureland, to the exclusion of others. If everyone is allowed to use the resource, there is no clear definition of property rights, and a situation arises where the property belongs to nobody, and is therefore accessible to everybody. In all cases of traditional common property, there are regulations stating what is permitted to the users of the resource and what is not. One may, therefore conclude that Hardin did not take into account the difference between common property and open access (van der Straaten, 1997).

Hardin's article is often misused to argue that common property rights lead to overuse of the resource, so the solution to environmental problems is privatizing common property. This is not, however, the point of Hardin's article. Furthermore, this frustrates the real possibilities, namely using public policies to limit the use of common resources and to protect the environment.

In the case studies, the common property right is often not so well articulated and is sometimes not maintained, as was the case with the Belgian dunes. It can be concluded that the crux of the problem is not a weak definition of the carrying capacity principle, nor the impossibility of defining it, but the relative irrelevance of the argument itself in many public debates on the use of natural resources.

Can we conclude that it is next to impossible to implement the carrying capacity concept? Is it also true that we do not have sufficient instruments to do so? In our view, this is conclusion is not correct. The following instruments should be given full attention.

1. Nature protection plays a significant role in EU legislation. In particular, Natura 2000 and the Habitat Directive have proven to be very important instruments. They can function in the same way as the critical load concept in many environmental policies. As noted previously, the critical load concept has played a very important role in the debate on environmental policies. It is not true that there were no vested interests in these cases, trying to nullify the implementation of strict norms. On the contrary, in the acid rain debate the interests of the car industry, heavy industry, electric power plants, and oil refineries were clearly recognized. They tried to neutralize the effects of strict environmental policies. Nevertheless, it can be argued that generally speaking they were not successful.

    Natura 2000 and the Habitat Directive can function in the same way. EU countries can be forced to include these standards in their national legislations. This future process will bring forward a renewed interest in the carrying capacity concept. For example, Dutch nature organizations recently went to court to argue that certain developments, such as the construction of houses in vulnerable areas, were in violation of the Habitat Directive. They won these cases.

2. In most EU countries, the so-called compensation principle is standard practice. This implies that the construction of infrastructure, houses, or industries is possible only on the condition that the disruption of nature as a result of these activities is compensated by the creation of 'new' nature. For example, 1 million trees were cut down to build the new TGV railway between Lyon and Marseille; SNCF, the French railway company, was forced to plant the same number of trees elsewhere.

The compensation principle has various effects. In the first place many planned new developments, which would lead to a massive destruction of nature, become too expensive. If, for example, the project developers in the Matalascañas case had been forced by a decision of the court to reconstruct another wetland ecosystem with the same ecological value as the one that was destroyed by the construction of the beach resort, the project would probably have become too expensive to complete.

Another effect is that the destruction of nature is no longer considered 'normal' in society. Environmental groups can use EU legislation to stop the destruction of nature of high ecological value. The carrying capacity concept can play a significant role in this debate. The carrying capacity is the primary principle to be adhered to when deciding whether or not nature should be protected.

References

Alcamo, J., Shaw R., Hordijk L. (eds) (1990), *The RAINS Model of Acidification*, Kluwer Academic Publishers, Dordrecht.

Bergh, J.C.J.M. van den and Straaten, J. van der (eds) (1994), *Toward Sustainable Development, Concept Methods and Policy*, Island Press, Washington.

Briassoulis, H. (2001), 'Sustainable Development and its Indicators: through a (Planner's) Glass Darkly', *Journal of Environmental Planning and Management*, Vol. 44 (3), pp. 409-427.

Bromley, D. W. (1991), *Environment and Economy; Property Rights and Public Policy*, Basil Blackwell, Oxford.

Butler, R.W. (1991), 'Tourism, Environment, and Sustainable Development', *Environmental Conservation*, Vol. 18, 3, pp. 201-209.

Castells, N. (1999), *International Environmental Agreements, Institutional Innovation in European Transboundary Air Pollution Policies*, European Commission Joint Research Centre, Ispra, S.P.I. 99.182.

Coccossis, H. and Parpairis A. (2000), 'Tourism and the Environment: some Observations on the Concept of Carrying Capacity', in Briassoulis, H. and Straaten, J. van der (eds),

Tourism and the Environment, Regional, Economic, Cultural and Policy Issues, revised second edition, Kluwer Academic Publishers, Dordrecht, pp. 91-106.

Cronin, L. (1990), 'A Strategy for Tourism and Sustainable Development', *World Leisure and Recreation*, Vol. 32, 3, pp. 12-18.

Dietz, F.J. and Straaten, J. van der (1988), 'The Problem of Optimal Exploitation of Natural Resources', *International Journal of Social Economics*, Vol. 15 (3/4), pp. 71-79.

Downing, R.J., Hettelingh, J.P., Smet, P.A.M. de (eds.) (1993), *Calculation and Mapping of Critical Loads in Europe*, Status Report 1993, National Institute of Public Health and Environmental Protection, Bilthoven, The Netherlands.

Eber, S. (ed.) (1992), *Beyond the Green Horizon: Principles for Sustainable Tourism*, World Wide Fund for Nature, Godalming, UK.

European Commission, DG XXIII (1995), *Green Paper on Tourism*, EU, Brussels.

Faucheux, S., Connor M. O., Straaten, J. van der (eds) (1998), *Sustainable Development: Concepts, Rationalities and Strategies*, Kluwer Academic Publishers, Dordrecht.

Garrod, G. and Willis, K. G. (1999), *Economic Valuation of the Environment*, Edward Elgar, Cheltenham.

Gasc, J.P., Cabela, A., Crnobrnja-Isailovic, J., Dolmen, D., Grossenbacher, K., Haffner, P., Lescure, J., Martens, H., Martinez Rica, J.P., Maurin, H., Oliveira, M.E., Sofianidou, T.S., Veith, M., Zuiderwijk, A. (eds) (1997), *Atlas of Amphibians and Reptiles in Europe*, Societas Europaea Herpetelogica and Muséum National d'Histoire Naturelle, Paris.

Goodall, B. (1995), 'Environmental Auditing: a Tool for Assessing the Environmental Performance of Tourism Firms', *The Geographical Journal*, Vol. 161, 1, pp. 29-37.

Gratton, C. and Straaten, J. van der (1994), 'The Environmental Impact of Tourism in Europe', in Cooper, C. P. and Lockwood, A. (eds), *Progress in Tourism, Recreation and Hospitality Management*, John Wiley and Sons, Chichester, pp. 147-162.

Hanley, N. and Spash, C.L. (1993), *Cost-Benefit Analysis and the Environment*, Edward Elgar, Aldershot.

Hardin, G. (1968), The Tragedy of the Commons, *Science*, Vol. 162, pp. 1243-1248.

Hawkes, S. and Williams, P. (eds) (1993), *From Principles to Practice. A Casebook of Best Environmental Practice in Tourism*, Center for Tourism Policy and Research, Simon Fraser University, Burnaby, B.C., Canada.

Hunter, C. and Green, H. (1995), *Tourism and the Environment: a Sustainable Relationship?*, Routledge, London.

Köhn, F., Hinterberger, F., Gowdy, J., Straaten, J. van der (eds) (1999), *Sustainability in Question – The Search for a Conceptual Framework*, Edwar Elgar, Cheltenham.

Kreimer, A. (1977), 'Environmental Preferences: a Critical Analysis of some Research Methodologies', *Journal of Leisure Research*, pp. 88-98.

Mitchel, R.C. and Carson, R.T. (1989), *Using Surveys to Value Public Goods; the Contingent Method*, Resources for the Future, Washington D.C.

Nielsen, J. (1977), 'Sociological Carrying Capacity and the Last Settler Syndrome', *Pacific Sociological Review*, Vol. 20, No. 4.

Pearce, D. and Moran, D. (1994), *The Economic Value of Biodiversity*, Earthscan, London.

Pigou, A. C. (1920/1952), *The Economics of Welfare*, Macmillan, London.

Requier-Desjardins, D., Spash, C., Straaten, J. van der (eds) (1999), *Environmental Policy and Societal Aims*, Kluwer Academic Publishers, Dordrecht.

Richards, G. (1994), 'Cultural Tourism in Europe', in Cooper, C. P. and Lockwood, A. (eds), *Progress in Tourism Recreation and Hospitality Management*, John Wiley and Sons, Chichester, pp. 99-115.

Saris, Frank (28 June 2001), 'Staatsbosbeheer kan maar beter op de paden blijven (It is better if Staatsbosbeheer will take the paths)', *de Volkskrant*, 28 June 2001, p. 7.

Stankey, G.H. (1982), 'Recreational Carrying Capacity Research Review', *Ontario Geography*, pp. 57-72.

Stanners, D. and Bourdeau, P. (eds) (1995), *Europe's Environment, The Dobris Assessment*, European Environment Agency, Copenhagen.

Straaten, J. van der (1997), 'The Revival, Introduction', in Nelissen, N., Straaten, J. van der and Klinkers, L. (eds), *Classics in Environmental Studies*, International Books, Utrecht, pp. 77-94.

Straaten, J. van der (2000), 'The Economic Value of Nature', in Briassoulis, H. and Straaten, J. van der (eds), *Tourism and the Environment; Regional, Economic, Cultural and Policy Issues*, Kluwer Academic Publishers, Dordrecht, pp. 123-132.

Tylecote, A. and Straaten, J. van der (eds) (1997), *Environment, Technology and Economic Growth, the Challenge to Sustainable Development*, Edward Elgar, Cheltenham.

Williams, P.W. (1992). 'Tourism and the Environment: No Place to Hide', *World Leisure and Recreation*, Vol. 34 (2), pp. 13-17.

World Commission on Environment and Development (1987), *Our Common Future (Brundland Report)*, Oxford University Press, Oxford.

World Tourism Organization (1993), *Sustainable Tourism Development: Guide for Local Planners*, WTO, Madrid.

PART II
DEFINING AND IMPLEMENTING TOURISM CARRYING CAPACITY IN SELECTED TYPES OF TOURIST DESTINATIONS

Chapter 7

Issues in Applying Carrying Capacity Concepts: Examples from the United Kingdom

Richard W. Butler

Introduction

Over the past four decades ever-increasing numbers of visitors to recreation and tourist areas have created concerns among many planners, managers, owners and users of destinations about resulting problems of overuse and unwanted impacts. Such feelings are still not universal, there are many involved in the promotion and development aspects of recreation and tourism facilities who are keen to continue to attract even more visitors; however even bodies such as the World Tourism Organization (WTO) have begun to recognise that the sheer volume of tourism has negative as well as positive impacts on destination environments and populations (WTO 1999). With the exception of 1991 (Gulf War) and 2001 (September 11 World Trade Center attack) international tourist numbers have increased every year since statistics have been collected (WTO 2001). There is little to indicate that this trend will end unless a global catastrophe occurs, although of course individual areas and destinations are likely to increase and decrease in popularity depending on their attractions, management and local conditions. The problems which increasing numbers bring to recreation and tourist areas have been recognised for many years (see for example, Darling and Eichorn 1967; and Young 1973).

Figures for domestic tourism are much more unreliable, as no borders are crossed and thus most figures are based on sample surveys and it is clear that levels of accuracy are not always high. However, there is little doubt that numbers of domestic tourists are increasing also, perhaps at an even faster rate than international tourist numbers, as people are more likely to take their first holidays within their home country rather than abroad. As countries with large populations such as China and India reach an economic level that allows increasing numbers of their citizens to take vacations for the first time, potentially vast additional numbers of people are becoming tourists. It is reasonable to assume, therefore, that overall tourist numbers will continue to increase globally and that pressure on resources, populations, environments and destinations generally will continue to increase with every greater severity.

Trends in leisure, recreation and tourism have been such that the boundaries between these phenomena, if they every really existed, have become less and less perceptible (Jackson and Burton 1999). It is more realistic to think of *visitors* to destinations rather than attempting to categorise people into leisure visitors, recreationists or tourists, and for much of the discussion which follows, the term visitor will be used. It is recognised that there may be differences in behaviour, and particularly in time spent at destinations depending on whether a visitor is there for a short visit (leisure visitor), a day trip (recreationist), or a holiday (tourist), but it is their cumulative impacts on the destination which are the primary cause for concern rather than inter-category differences.

The Case for the Concept of Carrying Capacity

The primary focus of this paper is a short review of the application of actions to limit overuse and negative impacts on protected areas in the United Kingdom, but before this it seems appropriate to briefly make the case for continuing to utilise the concept of carrying capacity. It has become common in recent decades to downplay the validity of the carrying capacity concept in the management of recreation and tourist areas, most recently by McCool and Lime (2001). This paper, like many written by present and former members of the US Forest Service, bears excellent witness to the splendid research undertaken in wildland management by that organisation. To this author, it is disappointing, although all too frequent, to see the scholars who, along with their colleagues, have been instrumental in undertaking so much valid and important work on carrying capacity, now being prepared to abandon the concept as 'Tempting Fantasy' rather than 'Useful Reality' (McCool and Lime 2001). The study of carrying capacity research in a recreation (and tourism context) has been discussed by a good many authors (Getz 1982, 1983; Manning, Lime and Hof 1996; Johnson and Thomas 1994; O'Reilly 1986; Shelby and Heberlein 1986; and Williams and Gill 1999a, b) and there is little point in attempting to repeat such reviews.

Suffice to say that the concept had its origin in rangeland ecology and since the seminal works of Lucas (1964) and Wagar (1964) has been a central if controversial feature of recreation resource research, and a more limited area of research in tourism. Over the decades since the early efforts in the 1960s, attention has shifted more heavily to the social side of carrying capacity and the application of norms in attempts to determine maximum acceptable levels of use (see for example, Brouwer et al. 2001; Bultena et al. 1981; Ditton et al. 1983; Hall and Shelby 1996; Hammitt and Rutlin 1995; and Shelby et al. 1988). With the focus increasingly on social aspects of overuse and crowding, and management implications, attention and support began to focus on management approaches such as the Limits of Acceptable Change (Stankey and Cole 1985) and the Recreation

Opportunity Spectrum (Clark and Stankey 1979). The acceptance of these concepts and their application meant a shift in emphasis from determining maximum acceptable levels of use and visitor numbers to determining acceptable and desired quality of environment and experience, matching appropriate activities with environmental and social constraints. Appropriate though these techniques may be in many outdoor and wilderness settings, this author has already argued (Butler 1996) that they are not acceptable substitutes for determining carrying capacity of all areas.

The seminal work of Hardin (1969) on common resources, and the application of some of his ideas in a tourism context (Healey 1994) note the importance of limits on use if environments are to be preserved. While change in many areas may be acceptable, there are areas in which permanent change caused by intrusive activities (such as recreation and tourist use) is not acceptable, and in such situations, there is, in effect, no acceptable change. In order to maintain an environment or perhaps, more appropriately, allow an environment to maintain itself, there are situations in which limits on the amount of use must be imposed, and such limits almost inevitably have to involve limits on the numbers of visitors. In recent years there has been much less attention paid to the ecological element of carrying capacity (Brown and Turner 1997; Buckley 1999) but this aspect of the problem is the most important one in the context of protected areas which are normally protected on environmental grounds.

It is widely accepted that a single magic number can rarely be found as the answer to the question of what is the carrying capacity of an area, unless it has a homogenous environment and a single set of homogenous users. Even in densely used recreation areas such as beaches, however, which may have an extremely high resistance to impact, ultimately there is a maximum number of people who can be accommodated, although some users may not be able to tolerate such high levels of density (Brougham 1982; McConnell 1977). It is also clear that there is more than one type of capacity of an area, relating at the very least to ecological, social, perceptual, safety and spatial limitations. To identify all of such limits for all potential uses at all times by all sorts of users would be impossible and pointless. What is possible and needed, it is argued, is to identify the lowest limit in terms of level of use and utilise that limit as the effective management carrying capacity for that area. As an area is developed, some aspects of that capacity may change (Butler 1980; Martin and Usyal 1990) and a different element emerge as the critical and defining one. Thus development may change the market and hence the social carrying capacity, or expand the spatial limits, and the new defining limit may become the ecological component of an area. When this occurs, if the area is a protected area being maintained because of specific ecological values, it is surely vital that the critical level of use be determined and used as a limit.

It is accepted that this is not easy, and it is accepted that there will often be arguments that what this generation regards as important is not necessarily appropriate for all time, as values change. Mountains once were not regarded as worth preserving but were viewed as barriers to be scaled and cut through, and wildlife species were made extinct because they were not valued at the time. These mistakes and changes in tastes should convince us that we should err on the side of protection and maintenance of some areas, and that this will inevitably require limits on numbers. We need to find those numbers sooner rather than later. If we accept that ultimately there will be too many users, however we manage them and whatever uses they engage in, then we have to accept the concept of carrying capacity. It need not be a fixed number and it may change, there can be more bird watchers than bird hunters permissible in a set area, and if the mix of uses change, then numbers can change also. We accept hunting and fishing limits because we can see and measure what is taken and we can calculate (not always very well) what is a sustainable yield. We simply have not learned or been willing to learn what is an acceptable if less tangible take relating to other uses of natural areas. There is rarely a simple direct correlation between numbers and impacts (and change) but there is a relationship and at some point numbers count, and therefore there is a carrying capacity.

In-the-field managers of a wide variety of recreation and tourist destinations face the problem of excessive numbers and overuse on a regular basis. They find ways to deal with this problem, most often in ad hoc and pragmatic ways, very often limiting use in some form in order to limit impacts. They are applying carrying capacity principles because they have to and applying them in the way they do because there is little information available on how to calculate or establish what appropriate limits might be. The problem which managers of protected areas face is both simpler and more serious than that faced by managers of other visitor destinations. They have a charge to protect all or some elements of the ecosystem under their control, and overuse threatens this. They, above all, if the world is serious about sustainability, need assistance, advice, and management tools to deal with issues of capacity.

The United Kingdom Context

Many of the above points are particularly true in the case of the United Kingdom, where the patterns of leisure excursionists, day recreationists and holiday-making tourists are closely intertwined and often almost indistinguishable. The countryside of the United Kingdom is a primary attraction, as are many of the cities, particularly London, for all who wish to spend leisure time away from home. Britain, like many European countries, has a large population, a small land area, (and thus a high population density), a dense pattern of communications, high car ownership, and a long history of settlement and established patterns of behaviour. It is also characterised by an absence of true 'wilderness', and although there are significant areas of unsettled or very thinly populated areas, particularly in Scotland, Wales and some of the other upland areas, no area is more than 20 miles from some permanent population and thus all parts of the country are potentially exposed to pressure from visitation.

Visitation to the coast, to urban centres, to upland areas, and to specific sites such as heritage properties and designated natural areas is extremely high, with estimates of 100 million visits a year to the countryside alone probably being conservative (Countryside Commission 1996). The problems that result from such heavy and continuous use have been apparent for many years (Tivy 1973) and management agencies have tried a number of approaches to both reduce pressure and to reduce impacts, generally with relatively little success in absolute terms, although considerable success in relative terms. By this it is meant that the absolute increases in pressure and impact have been considerable, because increases in visitor numbers have tended to overwhelm efforts to reduce impact through management, but relative impacts and pressure, for example if measured per capita, have almost certainly been reduced. The only real solution to the problems of overuse and negative impacts lies in reducing both national and international visitor pressure, and individual destinations, or even individual agencies can do little or nothing in this regard. They can only attempt to alleviate some of the problems in respect to their own operations, and this is what this paper focuses on.

Examples from the United Kingdom Experience

Introduction

A major caveat has to be given at the beginning of this discussion. What follows is not meant to be a comprehensive survey or review of everything which has been undertaken in the United Kingdom. The author has not had resources or opportunity to undertake such a study, although a brief survey was undertaken of some specific destinations to explore what has been the management response. A review was made of published material which involved studies of carrying capacity (few though they are) and findings synthesised from these. The discussion which follows is, therefore, an overview and interpretation rather than a definitive statement. It endeavours to summarise approaches and their effectiveness but should not be viewed as complete or all-inclusive.

National or System-Wide Initiatives

The issue of carrying capacity in recreation and tourist areas in the United Kingdom was not seen as one of national importance during the 1950s and 1960s. There is very little reference to the topic in any plans or management documents during those decades. The only well publicised example of carrying capacity guidelines is one produced in the Republic of Ireland (and thus not in the United Kingdom, although within the British Isles) which was published under the auspices of the United Nations in 1966 (An Foras Forbatha 1966). Although innovative in approach at the time, the delimitations of capacity and suggested levels were arbitrary and not based on specific empirical work and, as far as is known, were not applied elsewhere. The first significant study on carrying capacity was done by Tivy (1973) for the Countryside Commission for Scotland (CCS). This was essentially a review of mostly North American work (such as that by Lucas, 1964 and Wagar, 1964), along with some suggestions relating to the allocation of priorities in recreational land uses and limits. There is no evidence that this report was implemented in specific areas, and the role of CCS was such that it had no direct management responsibility for facilities. Nevertheless, the commissioning of this study was an indication that by the 1970s the UK authorities (such as CCS and its then counterpart for England and Wales, the Countryside Commission, along with the Forestry Commission and the National Park Authorities) had recognised the problems resulting from heavy and excessive use of areas under their jurisdiction or for which they had research and advisory responsibility.

The next initiative was less research focused and more an example of applied management and planning. This was the adoption of the 'honeypot' approach to facility provision, and could be regarded as the application of a system-wide management approach. It involved the establishment of so-called 'honeypot' recreation facilities, often country parks (Butler 1969), specifically designed to take pressure off more sensitive and vulnerable sites. It was an important initiative, even though it was ultimately unsuccessful, in that it was a clear acknowledgement that congestion and overcrowding were occurring at a number of important sites and that action was needed to resolve this problem. In one sense the honeypots were successful, in that they did attract large numbers of visitors. There, is however, little or no evidence that visitation to the vulnerable sites decreased as a result of their popularity, but some indictions that their establishment in fact increased overall demand and participation for country park type facilities. (In some respects one might compare the establishment of honeypots to the establishment of development or intensive recreation zones within parks and other designated areas. They were intended to draw off and contain heavy and in some cases inappropriate uses to the more sensitive and significant ecological and heritage sites or areas but, as often happens in parks, demand for such areas increases and requires expansion or creation of additional such zones.)

The decades of the 1980s and 1990s have been marked by an abandonment of such system-wide approaches in general and by the substitution of individual site or park management attempts to deal with capacity problems. Considerable efforts have been made to persuade users to give up the car as a means of access to and within parks and other protected areas, substituting public transport for access to areas and pedestrian access within them. These have succeeded in some areas where public transport has been convenient, reliable and existing (relatively few in the UK today), and in some areas, such as locations in the Peak District National Park, appear to have reduced visitor numbers at peak periods. Downsides have included the imposition of necessary restrictions upon potential users, in some cases increased costs of access, and in some cases demand diverted to other areas. The nature of National Parks in the United Kingdom (Ravenscroft and Parker,

2000) is such that most of the area within their boundaries is privately owned and managed, and national park status is essentially a form of planning control. The application of management policies is essentially through a plan for each park, which is established and managed by a committee with local and national representation and which has to be operated by agreement and consensus, with some funding for management applications. In all UK national parks there are communities engaged in a variety of land uses including farming, forestry, quarrying and mineral extraction, power production, sports, industrial, military, leisure, and residential activities. Reducing or limiting access or activities in such areas is extremely difficult and generally confined, if present at all, to specific sites. In National Forest Parks and National Nature Reserves, where the primary function of the area is not commercial or leisure related (but timber production and nature protection respectively), more stringent management restrictions could be applied. Such is the more limited appeal and less easily accessible locations of these latter two types of areas that the application of such restrictions has not really been necessary on ecological grounds to date, except in a very few locations. A considerable range of other sites and properties exist which are open to the public and which serve some protection function, ranging from individual private houses and gardens to large areas of land owned by bodies such as the National Trusts.

Facility-Level Approaches

A limited review of selected natural and cultural heritage and protected areas produced a mixed set of responses. Virtually all sites seemed to be experiencing what were viewed as incidences of overuse in almost all of the past ten years, with, as would be expected, the most frequent occurrences being on holiday weekends and in the peak summer months. Overfull car parks, long lines at facilities, road congestion, no accommodation vacancies and waiting lists for reserved facilities (for example guided trips and walks) were given as indicators of congestion and overuse. The concept of carrying capacity itself was frequently mentioned but was not incorporated into official plans or management guidelines per se. That is to say, there was general acknowledgement that a facility's carrying capacity (albeit normally undefined) was exceeded on some occasions, but no specific carrying capacity figures were established against which to confirm or judge such statements. In this situation one might conclude that management was still operating along 1960-vintage principles, namely that excessive use on a few occasions was acceptable, because, and this is a key point, there was a strong interest in maintaining or increasing visitor numbers to almost all sites. This issue is returned to below.

The actions taken fell into two distinct categories, neither of them unusual or novel, namely, reducing visitor numbers and increasing the resistance of the feature to use.

The most common response to excessive numbers was to take local and specific action to reduce numbers on a temporary basis. Only in one case was an action taken with what might be defined as a long-term view (beyond two years!). These actions included closing access facilities such as car parks when officially full and diverting later visitors elsewhere, instituting temporary closures of main features, rationing access in a variety of forms, controlling entry on a time basis, requiring entry to be in parties/groups rather than individually, and rotating access to features. This latter approach also relates to increasing resistance to use.

The only example of an action intended to have more than an immediate short-term effect was to delete a specific location from publicity information and maps. This was the case of Steel Riggs, a site on Hadrian's Wall, which was experiencing over 500,000 visits annually, and the action was taken not only to reduce visitation at this site but to spread use over other sites (Butler 1996). This specific site is still not publicised although it remains open for visitation, and visitor numbers have declined, although specific figures were not available.

The closing of car parks when full is a fairly common action, occasioned as much, it would appear, by practical issues (avoidance of accidents, safety, and police requirement) as by any desire to reduce visitation. The effects are not always desirable as visitors often park elsewhere rather than not visit the site. Such alternative locations sometimes may be in more hazardous or inappropriate locations, or they may be annoying and inconvenient to local residents. On some occasions visitors may simply wait at an entrance until the car park is opened, thus not reducing visitation at all. Closing car parks, even with advance warning (for example so that visitors do not arrive to discover a car park full), is rarely successful, especially in situations where there are few alternative sites and visitors may have travelled considerable distances. Denying access in such a way works more effectively if early announcements can be made on a regular basis, for example, the Ontario Provincial Parks system makes announcements on local radio and television stations when campsites at specific parks are full for upcoming dates to avoid people being disappointed on arrival at full parks.

The temporary closure of main features is similar to that of closing car parks and tends to have similar effects. If done suddenly and without warning, it is generally only effective in deterring small numbers of visitors and results in considerable discontent and complaints. Visitors will wait until the facility re-opens, and thus at best, numbers are moved from the busiest time of the day to quieter times, but overall visitation may not decrease appreciably. Visitor enjoyment may increase as crowding at peak times may be decreased. Controlling access by limiting entry to groups is quite common and allows for easier management and control of behaviour, but requires interpretive or other staff and an awareness and acceptance of such management, which may not always be present among visitors. If some benefits can be seen from such management, then acceptance is likely to be higher than if it seems arbitrarily imposed.

Limiting attendance through pre-booking and through allocation of entry times is increasing in popularity. The new Queen's Gallery which opened at Buckingham Palace in the summer of 2002 has adopted this technique to manage anticipated large numbers. Visitors are limited, with 50 being admitted every fifteen minutes, although no maximum time within the Gallery has been imposed. Various other institutions, including galleries in other European cities such as Florence, have adopted this method to reduce line ups and congestion. Adoption of such a technique in natural areas is very limited, although a similar approach has been used on occasion at one rare bird observation site, where visitors have to utilise a relatively small building to observe the birds.

In the second category, increasing resistance to use, actions include replacing natural paths with stone, tarmac, wood and other surfaces, confining access to such specific paths rather than allowing universal access, denying access to specific features, supporting or hardening features with artificial elements, substituting re-creations for original artefacts, using honeypots to relieve pressure on the most sensitive features, stocking and breeding of species, and using exotic vegetation that is hardier than indigenous species. The use of a specific technique varied with the nature and primary function of the facility; in a nature reserve the use of exotics would not take place, while this might be quite acceptable in a country park or historic property, where other exotics are already present.

The use of hardening materials for paths and other access points is well established and generally well accepted in many areas. The use of local stone or wood chips makes such an action less aesthetically jarring than the use of concrete or tarmac, but at entry points or hazardous situations such as waterfalls or lookouts, more extreme measures may have to be taken. In most cases visitor acceptance is high as the benefits are obvious. The channelling of visitors to specific paths is also common; sand dune areas in particular are highly prone to lateral as well as vertical erosion and whole dune systems can be threatened by uncontrolled erosion through unofficial footpath development.

Denying access to specific features because of visitor impact is not always popular, but has occurred in extreme situations. Two well known examples are Stonehenge and the Major Oak in Sherwood Forest. Stonehenge has had direct access to the stones prohibited for several years, and visitors are required to keep on a perimeter path to avoid further ground compression and the stones loosening. While visitors are often disappointed the interpretation makes the reason for the ban clear. Occasional promotional tourist advertisements showing visitors climbing over the stones however does not help this situation. Long-term proposals for dealing with overuse at Stonehenge include building an artificial set of stones on a nearby site, an approach not generally possible, although a precursor of this approach exists at Lascaux Caves in France (and perhaps in all Disney theme parks). The second example is a long-standing ban on access to the Major Oak in Sherwood Forest, a very old tree supposedly associated with Robin Hood, and which visitors used to be able to climb and enter (it is hollow). Again, ground compression and overuse over many years caused immediate access to be prohibited over twenty years ago, and interpretive signage explains the reasons. The tree has also been subjected to considerable support over the years including the use of iron and concrete to keep it standing, again without appearing to diminish its appeal to visitors. Such a step can probably only be taken for very specific features which are well known and irreplaceable.

Substitution of natural features by artificial ones was not found, although this practice does occur in the context of cultural heritage, often unannounced for security as much as overuse reasons. The average visitor has to assume that heritage artefacts such as the Mona Lisa, the Elgin Marbles, the Vatican Chapel ceiling, and the British Crown Jewels, are the originals, as most visitors would be unable to differentiate a good copy from the original, particularly at times of excessive visitation and hurried short opportunities for viewing. The use of honeypots, as noted above in the discussion of system-wide actions, is not common but has been used in a few situations. Promotion of less visited features to draw people away from vulnerable popular sites is one example. In the context of natural features, the publicity given to the original nesting site at Loch Garten of the first breeding ospreys in Scotland this century attracts casual visitors to the interpretive centre there and obviates the need for people to search for the other nesting pairs of the birds elsewhere in Scotland. Excellent management and interpretation at this site has so far prevented any signs of overuse or disturbance to the birds themselves, although parking in the vicinity can be a problem on some occasions. As the site has increased in popularity over the four decades that the birds have nested there, the need for more comprehensive and extensive site management has become apparent. A supportive local landowner, absence of immediate local population, little local traffic, and a specific form of visitor, along with close hands-on management have so far succeeded in avoiding any major problems, despite heavy visitation over a short period.

Implications

While a variety of methods have been used to deal with the problems of overuse, congestion, over-capacity and unwanted impacts, there is little evidence of consistent application or overall planning for these problems. This is not intended to be critical of management of these areas; many are managed to a very high standard and visitor satisfaction appears to be high and is expressed in increased visitor numbers in most locations (see below). What is clear is that the solutions or attempted solutions to capacity-related problems are mostly ad hoc, un researched and of limited success. They may succeed in resolving a specific problem, loosening of stones at Stonehenge for example, but rarely deal with the cause of the problem, which in most cases is excessive numbers of visitors. Actions which tackle this specific problem simply tend to move visitors to different times or to other parts of a site. Only in a very few cases do they move visitors to other areas.

Protected areas in the United Kingdom face considerable problems in dealing with visitation. There is a high population with a considerable degree of mobility and a reasonably high standard of living. There are several million foreign visitors who wish to visit the more visible and well known sites, compounding the problem of domestic visitation. Few sites are inaccessible and awareness is relatively high.

In many cases, especially in the case of historic properties, which may have natural features associated with them, reliance on visitor expenditure and admissions is key to their survival, given the expense of upkeep and management. Reduction of visitor numbers is not something which is desired in many cases unless the problem of overuse is extremely severe. Rather the concerns are with dealing with short-term excessive use on a limited number of occasions. Perhaps fortunately, some of the most vulnerable and important sites are less well known and less accessible, and therefore less visited. One has to conclude, however, that such a situation is likely to change in the future as almost all of the factors influencing participation in leisure seem to indicate increased rather than decreased future use.

Problems resulting from the probability of increased visitation are likely to be compounded by what appears to be a widespread belief among facility operators and managers that constant or increased visitation is desirable. For those operating commercial leisure facilities this is rational economic thinking, normally more visitation means greater return on investment and greater profit (although even in facilities such as theme parks it is acknowledged that there is a maximum number of guests who can be comfortably and in some cases safely accommodated, particularly on rides). For those operating venues which have public access as their primary objective, increasing numbers is also rational, as the greater the public access, the more they are achieving their goals, again within safety and comfort limits. For those operating and managing sites where the primary function is preservation of natural or cultural heritage (nature reserves, some areas within national parks, historic properties and ancient monuments), then accepting or pursuing ever-increasing numbers up to safety and comfort limits is both irrational and could be contrary to their primary purpose for existing. Yet even within some of these establishments, constant or increasing visitor numbers are still seen as desirable, even when overuse is admitted. The reason behind this is almost entirely political (in the broad sense). Job security depends in many cases on doing what is seen as a satisfactory job, and this is measured most often, if at all, in relation to visitation. Declining visitor numbers is generally perceived by those in central headquarters as a sign of decreasing public interest, thus meaning there is little to be gained politically by keeping the facility open or by investing additional funds. Increased visitation, on the other hand, is taken as indicative of increased public interest; 'voting with their feet' was one expression used, and therefore financial and moral support could be justified. Deliberately decreasing visitor numbers, even to safeguard a specific feature, was rare and only undertaken after extensive investigation and approval from a higher level. As long as this mindset remains, tackling overuse and capacity-related issues is unlikely to be widely or enthusiastically practised, except in extreme cases.

Conclusion

This paper has attempted to review the issue of carrying capacity in some protected areas and to its application in general. The argument put forward for maintaining the concept and application of carrying capacity principles should not be seen as denying the validity of visitor management approaches such as those discussed above. This author has also proposed an approach (Butler and Waldbrook, 1991) based on the Recreation Opportunity Spectrum model and certainly does not deny that LAC, VIMP and other approaches have considerable validity in their application in many natural areas. The research and effort needed to implement such techniques is often considerable, however, and the necessary data and knowledge may not always be available, thus the application of these approaches may not be practical in poorly funded sites with little opportunity for research, particularly where public and political support for such sites is limited and may not be supported by legislation and where centrally based expertise and support may also be lacking or minimal. In such situations the protection of the site and its elements may end up as a simple choice between unlimited or limited use, with little scope for the application of opportunity spectrums, management of visitors or visitor preference surveys, let alone the determination of realistic carrying capacity levels, if these exist. In such situations, most managers seem to resort to 'seat of the pants' management, relying on gut feelings in the absence of alternatives. In these cases, more often than not, they resort to applying the principles of carrying capacity, limiting numbers or access in order to preserve the features they are charged with protecting.

McCool and Lime (2001: p. 385) argue that 'It is now time to bury the concept of a numerical tourism and recreation carrying capacity' because the variables involved are too numerous, the assumptions and tests which need to be met do not occur in reality and that it is an illusion that it is a scientific question not a moral choice. It is precisely because carrying capacity is partly a moral choice as well as partly a scientific question that it is important that it be studied and acceptable maximum levels of use (and perhaps visitation) be established on a site-specific basis. If society does not accept that it has a moral as well as a scientific obligation to protect and maintain some specific sites and features for future generations, then it is abrogating all responsibility for the future. The Canadian National Parks system used to have as its definitive objective 'To preserve unimpaired for the benefit, education and enjoyment of future generations' the parks within its charge (Indian Affairs and Northern Development 1956: i). Difficult, if not impossible, though this noble aspiration may have been to achieve, it was at least definitive and clear, much more so than managing for change, when what is acceptable obviously changes from generation to generation. Surely some things are worth protecting so that they can continue to exist in as natural a state as possible, rather than being managed subject to changes in fashion and taste? If this is believed, and it is reasonable to assume that this is why protected areas exist, then society must be prepared to protect such areas from excessive overuse/overvisitation. This implies that society believes there is a limit to the amount of use such areas can withstand and, ipso facto, that there is a carrying capacity. The fact that researchers have still not determined how this can be measured effectively or accurately is a feeble excuse for replacing the idea of limits to use with something else. To twist de Bono's analogy, society and researchers would be substituting questions which need to be answered with questions which can be answered. Future generations may not be content that such a step was taken, particularly at a time when sustainable development concepts are widely supported in principle.

References

An Foras Forbatha (1966), *Planning for Amenity and Tourism*, Bord Failte, Dublin.

Brougham, J.E. (1982), 'Patterns on the Beach', *Ontario Geography*, 19, pp. 79-91.

Brouwer, R., Turner, R.K., Voisey, H. (2001), 'Public Perception of Overcrowding and Management Alternatives in a Multi-purpose Open Access Resource', *Journal Of Sustainable Tourism*, 9 (6), pp. 471-490.

Brown, K. and Turner, H.K. (1997), 'Environmental Carrying Capacity and Tourism Development in the Maldives and Nepal', *Environmental Conservation*, 24, pp .316-325.

Buckley, R. (1999), 'An Ecological Perspective on Carrying Capacity', *Annals of Tourism Research*, 26 (3), pp. 705-708.

Bultena, G.L., Field, D.R., Womble, P., Albrecht, D. (1981), 'Closing the Gates: A Study of Backcountry Use-limitation at Mount McKinley National Park', *Leisure Sciences*, 9 (3), pp. 174-187.

Butler, R.W. (1969), 'Parks in Britain', Parts 1 and 2, *Bulletin of the Conservation Council of Ontario*, Conservation Council, Toronto.

Butler, R.W. (1980), 'The Concept of a Tourist Area Cycle of Evolution: Implications for the Management of Resources', *The Canadian Geographer*, 24 (1), pp. 5-12.

Butler, R.W. (1996), 'The Concept of Carrying Capacity for Tourist Destinations: Dead or Merely Buried?', *Progress in Tourism and Hospitality Research*, 2 (3), pp. 283-292.

Butler, R.W. and Waldbrook, L.A. (1991), 'A New Planning Tool: The Tourism Opportunity Spectrum', *Journal of Tourism Studies*, 2 (1), pp. 2-14.

Clark, R., and Stankey, G.H. (1979), *The Recreational Opportunity Spectrum: A Framework for Planning, Management and Research*, General Technical Report PNW-98 USDA Forest Service, Pacific North West Forest and Range Experimental Station, Seattle.

Countryside Commission (1996), *Visits to National Parks*, Countryside Commission, Cheltenham.

Darling, F.F. and Eichorn, N. (1966), *Man and Nature in the National Parks*, Conservation Foundation, Washington, D.C.

Ditton, R.B., Fedler, A.J., Graefe, A.R. (1983), 'Factors Contributing to Perceptions of Recreational Crowding', *Leisure Sciences*, 5 (4), pp. 273-288.

Getz, D. (1983), 'A Rationale and Methodology for Assessing Capacity to Absorb Tourism', *Ontario Geography*, 19, pp.92-101.

Getz, D. (1983), 'Capacity to Absorb Tourism: Concepts and Implications for Strategic Planning', *Annals of Tourism Research*, 10 (2), pp. 239-263.

Graefe, A.R., Kuss, F.R., Vaske, J.J. (1990), *Visitor Impact Management: The Planning Framework*, National Parks and Conservation Association, Washington, D.C.

Hall, T. and Shelby, B. (1996), 'Who Cares about Encounters? Differences Between Those With and Without Norms', *Leisure Sciences*, 18 (1), pp. 7-22.

Hammitt, W.E. and Rutlin, W. (1995), 'Use Encounter Standards and Curves for Achieved Privacy in Wilderness', *Leisure Sciences*, 17 (3), pp. 245-262.

Hardin, G. (1969), 'The Tragedy of the Commons', *Science*, 162, pp. 1243-1248.

Healey, R.G. (1994), 'The "Common Pool" Problem in Tourism Landscapes', *Annals of Tourism Research*, 21 (3), pp. 596-611.

Indian Affairs and Northern Development (1956), *National Parks Policy*, IAND, Ottawa.

Jackson, E.L. and Burton, T.L. (eds) (1999), *Leisure Studies: Prospects for the Twenty-First Century*, Venture Publishing Inc., State College, Pa.

Johnson, P. and Thomas, B. (1994), 'The Notion of Capacity in Tourism: A Review of the Issues', in Cooper, C.P. and Lockwood, A. (eds), *Progress in Tourism, Recreation and Hospitality Management*, Wiley, Chichester, Vol. 5, pp. 112-120.

Kuss, F.R., Graefe, A.R., Vaske, J.J. (1990), *Visitor Impact Management: A Review of Research*, National Parks and Conservation Association, Washington, D.C.

Lucas, R.C. (1964), *The Recreational Carrying Capacity of Quetico-Superior Area*, Research Paper LS-8, USDA Forest Service Lake States Forest Experimentation Station, St. Paul, Mn.

Manning, R.E., Lime, D., Hof, M. (1996), 'Social Carrying Capacity of Natural Areas: Theory and Application in the National Parks', *National Areas Journal*, 16 (2), pp. 118-127.

Martin, B.S. and Uysal, M. (1990), 'An Examination of the Relationship Between Carrying Capacity and the Tourism Lifecycle: Management and Policy Implications', *Journal of Environmental Management*, 31, pp. 327-333.

McConnell, K.E. (1977), 'Congestion and Willingness to Pay: A Study of Beach Use', *Land Economics*, 53, pp 185-195.

McCool, S.F. and Lime, D.W. (2001), 'Tourism Carrying Capacity: Tempting Fantasy or Useful Reality?', *Journal of Sustainable Tourism*, 9 (5), pp. 372-388.

O'Reilly, A.M. (1986), 'Tourism Carrying Capacity', *Tourism Management*, 7 (4), pp. 254-258.

Ravenscroft, N. and Parker, G. (2000), 'Tourism, "National Parks" and Private Lands', in Butler, R.W. and Boyd, S.W. (eds), *Tourism and National Parks*, Wiley, Chichester, pp. 95-106.

Shelby, B, Vaske, J.J. and Harris, R. (1988), 'User Standards for Ecological Impacts at Wilderness Campsites', *Journal of Leisure Research*, 20 (3), pp. 245-256.

Shelby, B. and Herberlein, T.A. (1986), *Carrying Capacity in Recreation Settings*, Oregon State University Press, Corvallis, Ore.

Stankey, G.H. and Baden, J. (1977), *Rationing Wilderness Use: Methods, Problems, and Guidelines*, USDA Forest Service, Intermountain Research Station, Ogden, Ut.

Stankey, G.H. and Cole, D.N. (1985), *The Limits of Acceptable Change (LAC) System for Wilderness Planning*, USDA Forest Service Intermountain Research Station, Ogden, Ut.

Tivy, J. (1973), *Carrying Capacity*, Countryside Commission for Scotland, Battelby.

Wagar, J.A. (1964), *The Carrying Capacity of Wild Lands for Recreation* (Forest Service Monograph 7), Society of American Forests:Washington, D.C.

Williams, P.W. and Gill, A. (1999a), 'Tourism Carrying Capacity Management Issues', in Theobald, W.F. (ed), *Global Touris*, Butterworth Heinemann, Oxford, pp. 231-246.

Williams, P.W. and Gill, A. (1999b), 'A Workable Alternative to the Concept of Carrying Capacity: Growth Management Planning', in Singh, T.V. and Singh. S. (eds), *Tourism Development in Critical Environments*, Cognizant Communication Corporation, New York. pp. 51-64

World Tourism Organization (WTO) (1999), *Sustainable Development of Tourism*, World Tourism Organization, Madrid.

World Tourism Organization (WTO) (2001), *Summary of Statistics*, World Tourism Organization, Madrid.

Young, G. (1973), *Tourism - Blessing or Blight*, Penguin, Harmondsworth.

Chapter 8

Tourism Carrying Capacity in Areas of Ecological Importance

Thymio Papayannis

Introduction

The increasing public interest in nature and landscapes is today considered a major positive factor in the process of conservation and wise use of ecologically sensitive and important areas. These areas may be defined as large or small sites with a very high biodiversity, providing habitats for threatened, or endangered or endemic species of fauna and flora, and maintaining a unique beauty as landscapes, the most important of which are legally protected under international agreements or conventions and/or national legislation.

On the other hand, the growing influx of visitors may exert strong pressures on fragile ecosystems and lead to their degradation with a consequent loss of biodiversity. Such problems have already appeared in some of the most popular national parks in the United States of America (Everglades, Yellowstone, Yosemite) and are also being recognized in Europe. It becomes advisable, therefore, to examine the relationship between tourism and sensitive areas and to propose a balanced approach that might be of benefit to both sides. The carrying capacity of these areas, and measures to avoid exceeding it, must be considered within the framework of such a balanced approach, based on a theoretical and practical understanding of the issues involved.

The proposals included are based on the experience gained mainly in the Mediterranean Region.

Trends of the Tourism Sector

The increasing leisure time for most working persons throughout the world results both in the intensification and the diversification of tourism demand. As to the latter, the availability of more free periods of time – among other reasons – encourages a shifting from traditional tourism demand to more activity-oriented choices (WTO, 2001a).

A considerable part of this demand is now being directed towards activities that depend on ecologically sensitive, and often important, natural areas in which the condition of the natural environment plays a major role (Benyahia and Zein, 2003). The list of such activities is endless, but some of the most popular ones can be highlighted.

Table 8.1 Tourism activities depending on natural areas

Activities with moderate impact	Activities with serious impact
Canoeing	4-wheel drive racing
Hiking	Hunting
Horse riding	Motocross racing
Mountain climbing	Motorboat tourism
Rafting	Mountain biking
Sailing	Skiing
Sport fishing	Underwater fishing
Underwater diving	

The degree of impact on the natural environment of each activity depends on both the resources used and on the intensity of use. The intensity in turn depends to a large extent on the number of individuals participating within a given period of time. As demand grows, the tourism sector encourages further activities, some of them quite extreme, and develops infrastructure in new areas to receive them. Thus the pressure exerted is constantly being increased and the trends indicate that it will continue unabated (Buckley and Sommer, 2001).

On the positive side, one should note the growing realization from the side of the tourism industry of the need to protect the resources – both natural and cultural – on which it depends. Thus the emergence of 'green' or sustainable tourism, strongly encouraged by the World Tourism Organization, represents a trend that will certainly play an increasing role in the first part of the 21st century (WTO, 2001b).

New Realities Concerning Sensitive Areas

During the last decades of the 20th century, some positive developments have appeared concerning ecologically sensitive areas. Perhaps the primary one has been the recognition of the dramatic losses that have occurred mainly during the past 50 years, due to overexploitation of resources, land use changes, urbanization and other anthropic-induced changes. These losses have been credibly documented and confirmed. Thus the Mediterranean Region has lost more than 50 per cent of its wetlands during that period, while many of those remaining are heavily degraded.[1] This has led to various efforts at both national and international levels for their conservation.

Most of them have focused on the establishment of protected areas within various legal frameworks. National parks for example have been designated in most countries, covering a significant part of extremely valuable natural territories. In addition, international conventions – such as the Conventions on Biological Diversity, on Wetlands (Ramsar, 1971) and on the Protection of World Cultural and Natural Heritage – have attempted to encourage multilateral collaboration and concern, especially on transboundary sites, and to provide a protection status of broader recognition.[2] Within the territory of the European Union, the 'Natura 2000' network was instituted to provide effective protection to characteristic ecosystem types, and is being extended to neighbouring countries.

It soon became apparent that such protection status designations were not sufficient to ensure actual implementation and to safeguard these areas against threats that usually originating from greed and ignorance. Thus integrated management and planning was adopted as a major conservation approach, and this in turn resulted in the establishment of specialized multidisciplinary bodies for its preparation and implementation. Such bodies have now been established at many of the larger protected sites throughout the world, and have been instrumental in their rational and sustainable management.

Management bodies have also been catalytic in the recognition of the crucial role played by local communities and especially by indigenous people (Beltran, 2000). Based on millennia of intimate contact with the natural environment, local people have developed a profound traditional knowledge of the functions and values of ecosystems. In many cases, their survival and well-being depends on natural resources. As a consequence, they maintain a strong sense of ownership which cannot be disregarded without serious negative results. Thus it has become accepted that the conservation of ecologically sensitive areas must be inextricably combined with a care for the legitimate needs of local communities, through the wise use of available natural resources. This has extended the mandate of management bodies in dealing not only with ecological aspects, but also with social, cultural and economic ones (Epler Wood, 2002).

The adoption of the concept of sustainability at both the global and the national level has provided an additional boost to such a balanced, integrated and inclusive approach to sensitive areas, which aims at both the use of their resources for the benefit of current and future generations and to the conservation of their biodiversity, through the maintenance – and at times restoration – of their natural functions and values (Eagles et al., 2002).

Very recently, this has led to the understanding that the relation of human communities to nature has traditionally created culture in its many forms, and that preserving and enhancing cultural expression related to nature can become a powerful tool in strengthening the links of contemporary people with their natural environment (Hall and McArthur, 1998).[3]

Interface between Tourism and Nature

Before attempting to outline a balanced approach to tourism in sensitive areas, it is useful to investigate the interface between the two.

Tourism Requirements

Most tourist activities, even those not focusing directly on nature, require an attractive natural environment, to be used with various degrees of frequency. Thus the pleasure of rafting is greatly enhanced by the existence of untouched landscapes along the river banks (as in the case of the Voidomatis River in north western Greece), in opposition to an urbanized milieu.

In addition, there is a growing tourism interest in sites with particular natural features, such as rare and exciting animal and plant species, or in unique landscapes. Thus the Greater Flamingo nesting island at Salins du Midi in the Camargue in France or the Dalmatian Pelican colonies in Mikri Prespa and Amvrakikos Gulf in Greece attract a large – and increasing – number of visitors. The same can be said of the oases in Southern Algeria and Tunisia, the South African national parks, or the Amazon River in Brazil and Peru.

As already noted, demand is growing for areas that combine both natural and cultural interest. Such sites can be found readily throughout south eastern Asia, but also in the Mediterranean, for example Butrint in Albania, combining a rich Greek and Roman archaeological heritage with the natural elements of an important wetland site. Combining the two elements of nature and culture can provide a new tourism interpretative product, which in turn can contribute valuable returns to local populations (Ceballos-Lascuráin, 1996).

A number of tourism activities (such as hunting, kayaking or rock climbing) have specialized environmental requirements, which can be satisfied only at specific locations.

Values

Thus ecologically sensitive areas can provide significant values to tourism. These include intrinsic ones, not only scientific and educational, but also eco-recreational (with opportunities for hiking, bird watching or underwater diving). Exploitation values include the potential for outdoor sports, and the availability of natural resources which can be used or collected (such as game, fish, wild fruit and mushrooms).

On the other hand, tourism can significantly contribute to the conservation of sensitive areas. Just the realization that a particular place attracts visitors is often sufficient to convince local people and decision-makers of its importance and of the need to maintain it. This has been the case in the area of Prespa Lakes in northern Greece, where public attitude towards conservation has improved dramatically during the last ten years mainly due to increased visitor flow, including large numbers of schoolchildren.

In addition, visitors provide significant economic benefits to the local communities and thus contribute to the establishments of new services and the increase of employment and family income (Lindberg, 1991). They also break the isolation and neglect of remote areas and create links with the rest of the world, reducing the need for emigration and the resulting demographic attrition.

Tourism Pressures

However like most other anthropic activities, tourism – especially in its mass form – may exert serious pressures on ecologically sensitive areas in three principal ways.

The first is through the construction of facilities within the area itself, mainly hotels and resort housing, but also leisure installations. This is the case in most of the very sensitive coastal zones of the Mediterranean, and especially in large parts of the islands of Crete, Cyprus, Malta and Rhodes, as well as the Costa Brava in Spain.

The second is through the construction of the infrastructure necessary for tourism, especially in the transport sector, such as road arteries, airports, harbours and marinas, often built in valuable natural areas.[4] Islands and the coastal zones are heavily affected by such public works.

The third is through the use of the area itself by motorized or pedestrian traffic and the practice of various harassing activities. Uncontrolled mooring of pleasure boats for example causes extensive damage to *Posidonia* beds and to coral reefs.

In addition, tourists compete with local inhabitants and with nature for the use – often excessive – of water, space and energy and produce large quantities of solid and liquid wastes, which must be properly disposed of. Their impact upon local societies is often quite dramatic, with loss of identity and local traditions, ethical problems and a weakening of social and family structures.

The combined result of all these pressures upon ecologically sensitive areas subjected to a large tourist influx has been dramatic environmental and social degradation, which in turn has undermined the tourist activity itself. Corfu Island in the Ionian Sea in Greece is a typical case of such abusive development, while Zakynthos located in the same region – famous for its *Caretta caretta* nesting beaches – is well on its way to a similar fate. Even for the areas that have been protected up to now from mass tourism, and receive only limited numbers of visitors, the impacts can be degrading depending on their sensitivity, as in the case of sand dunes, rare forests or bird nesting colonies.

Criteria for a Balanced Approach

Simplistic methods to address similar highly problematic situations have never borne positive results. The first reaction of tour operators is to abandon the degraded area and move to a virgin one. Soon, however, such untouched areas are no longer available. Attempting to mitigate the impacts by extensive restoration efforts is very costly, time-consuming and not always feasible, especially in cases of heavy artificialization. The example of demolition in Mallorca in Spain of old hotels built too close to the beaches is a positive one, but cannot be considered as an indication of an emerging trend. Large-scale demolition of resort housing has taken place in the Faro wetland in southern Portugal, but was not attempted however, due to political timidity in the core of the Messolonghi Ramsar site in western Greece.

Setting limits – usually arbitrary – on the construction of tourism facilities and on tourist arrivals is difficult to implement and is often circumvented, or simply ignored (Wolters, 1991). In this context, efforts to calculate the carrying capacity of specific areas are interesting theoretical exercises, because they usually attempt to analyse probable impacts of tourism pressures upon the natural environment, using various simulation tools, and attempt to determine an optimization level. In this way they may help to sensitize decision-makers and the public by providing an apparently objective and scientific method of identifying probable environmental degradation, if the optimum capacity is exceeded. However, they have debatable practical relevance, as their implementation requires consistent, long-term public-level efforts to provide adequate filter mechanisms, enforcement and monitoring. In this context, the use of visitor fees has been proposed as a tool to limit access and to finance relevant infrastructure, but it faces serious ideological challenges and difficulties in its application (Lindberg, 2001).

Thus it becomes important – particularly for ecologically important areas – to experiment with new concepts, with a novel approach that would integrate all various aspects, reconcile conflicting interests and attempt to create a 'win-win' situation. The European Charter for Sustainable Tourism in Protected Areas[5] provides useful guidelines for this. Such an approach should satisfy the following criteria:

- conservation and enhancement of the ecological and cultural values of each sensitive area;
- sustainable use of resources by the tourism sector, especially natural ones;
- significant contribution to the socio-economic development and quality of life of local communities;
- wider economic benefits, fully compatible with the above three criteria, equitably distributed.

It is obvious that all four of these criteria cannot be satisfied completely and simultaneously, and must be considered more as goals, rather than *sine qua non* conditions.

Towards a New Approach

The approach proposed is based on the premise that systematic management is necessary to ensure the sustainable use of space and resources, and especially in the most sensitive or conflictive cases. The approach consists of a series of steps that must be planned and implemented in a consistent way through close collaboration among the management body of each sensitive area, the local authorities and the representatives of the tourism sector. It is not necessary to carry out the steps proposed below in a linear, sequential manner; some of them can be launched in parallel, although constant co-ordination is required.

Determination of Ecological Values

Unless credible scientific information is already available, as is the case with some of the better known natural sites, the work should start with the determination of the ecological values of each area, through systematic inventories of habitats and species. There are already sophisticated methods for producing such inventories[6] through a combination of remote sensing methods, global information systems (GIS) and fieldwork.

The desirability and feasibility of restoring certain degraded habitats must be evaluated at that time and resources for it must be earmarked.[7] A factor to be taken into account is the desirability of such restoration actions from the visitor point of view. In the Camargue in France, for example, the restoration of the Marais du Vigueirat was guided to a large extent by visitor planning considerations.

The results of the inventories must be evaluated on the basis of national and international criteria and in comparison to other similar sites, so that an objective assessment of the overall ecological value of each area can be obtained.

Inventory of Tourism Attraction Resources

In parallel, a similar systematic analysis must be carried out to evaluate the tourism attraction potential of the area. This should include not only the identification of characteristics that may satisfy general or specific tourism requirements, but also the determination of existing or predictable land use conflicts or constraints.

All these in turn must be prioritized, so that necessary interventions for the use of the area and the resolution of conflicts can be planned, after suitable environmental impact (EIA) and cost-benefit analyses (Viñals Blasco, 2002).

Integrated Management and Planning

The results of the previous two analytical steps must be integrated in the management planning of the sensitive area, which should consider tourism development in a balanced form versus other economic activities. This should be the task of the management body of the area, if one exists. Of course wide participation of all stakeholders in the process should be ensured, including international and national tourism operators, as well as local enterprises and individuals concerned with or related to tourist activities.

The consensus of the local communities on the proposals and measures of the management plan, which is a prerequisite for its adoption and implementation, should be cultivated through public awareness activities and the dialogue with elected representatives and non-governmental organizations (NGOs).

Zoning Patterns

A key aspect of the management planning is the zoning of the sensitive area on the basis of ecological criteria and permissible anthropic uses. Such a model has been devised and practised successfully at the Abruzzo National Park of Central Italy, with very satisfactory results, and has been duplicated in other sensitive areas (such as the Doñana National Park in Andalusia, Spain) in one way or another. It includes the following four zones, clearly demarcated.

Zone A, most valuable from the ecological point of view and of high vulnerability: In it access is authorized only to scientific teams for research purposes, with written permission.

Zone B, highly sensitive: Visits in predetermined itineraries are limited to small groups (not exceeding 20 persons), led by well-trained guides. The visits can be either on foot or with special vehicles driven by the guides. In the case of some of the Croatian wetlands, such visits are carried out in silent electrically-propelled boats.

Zone C, with considerable natural interest: Some traditional primary sector and tourism activities are allowed, and visitor access is free though private automobile use is limited.

Zone D, buffer area, mainly agricultural, of mild development: Tourism and visitor facilities are located here, with car access and extensive parking. Traditional villages are often included. Experience indicates that the large majority of visitors remain in this fourth zone, if the facilities provided are satisfactory, and only a small percentage show an interest in exploring Zones C and B. Naturally, significant income is produced within Zone D through commercial activities.

Infrastructure, Services and Organization

Visitor attraction to ecologically sensitive areas in turn creates serious obligations from the managers of the area for the provision of the necessary services. Adequate infrastructure must be provided for transport (including public means of transport where private vehicles are not allowed), sanitation, health and security. Commercial facilities for overnight stays, dining and leisure of visitors must be constructed. But also information and educational opportunities must be available in properly designed and operated visitor centres, which should take into account the different age and interest groups.

In addition, a visitor management and control system, discreet but effective, must be instituted, so that the zoning regulations will be respected. Currently there are a number of proposals for such systems – some of them with very ambitious goals – which need testing and comparative evaluation.[8]

Monitoring

The organization responsible for the management of the sensitive area must institute a permanent monitoring scheme. Through it the impacts of tourist activities on ecosystem processes and functions will be assessed in a systematic way and indications of environmental degradation will be identified at a very early stage. Such a system, at least in the beginning, would make the efforts to calculate the carrying capacity of the area, and the attempt to implement access and exploitation controls unnecessary.

In parallel, surveys of tourism demand and modes will provide useful information about the attractiveness of the area. This would be combined with an assessment of the economic and social benefits provided through tourist activities, if any.

Feedback and Remedial Measures

On the basis of such monitoring it will be possible to plan and carry out remedial actions, wherever required. In more serious cases, the management plan of the area will have to be modified in order to address negative tourist impacts and their root causes. In extreme cases, and only if other milder methods prove inadequate, strict regulatory measures may become necessary, including limits to the provision of tourist facilities and to visitor access, which would then take into account both carrying capacity calculations and a pragmatic assessment of local experience.

Principal Conclusions

From the above reflections, a number of conclusions can be drawn, which may have broader implications.

In spite of past negative experience, there are strong indications that sustainable tourism can be compatible with the conservation of ecologically important and sensitive areas, and may even contribute significantly to it.

However, integrated management planning, which must incorporate tourism activities and prescribe clear zoning of land uses, is an absolute prerequisite.

The tourism carrying capacity of sensitive areas depends on many factors, both physical and social, and is highly site-specific. However a key factor remains, the existence of appropriate reception planning and infrastructure, integrated into the management mechanisms for each area. If these do not exist, tourist activities will prove highly destructive.

In each case, an operational determination of the carrying capacity based on a careful and on-going monitoring of physical and social parameters may prove more useful than the application of theoretical models. However, integrating the two approaches may provide valid results.

Finally, through tourist activities in ecologically sensitive areas, there must be concrete benefits to local populations in order to offset social, economic and environmental pressures received through such activities.

Notes

[1]   See Finlayson, C.M., G.E. Hollis and T.J. Davis (eds) (1992), *Managing Mediterranean Wetlands and Their Birds*, Proc. Symp., Grado, Italy, 1991, IWRB Spec. Publ. No. 20, Slimbridge, UK.

[2]   Such as Ramsar Sites of International Importance or World Heritage Sites.

[3]   Thus in November 2002 the Conference of the Contracting Parties of the Convention on Wetlands adopted Resolution VIII.19 on 'Guiding principles for taking into account the cultural values of wetlands for the effective management of sites'.

[4]   Most of the airports in the Mediterranean – such as Corfu, Larnaca, Marseille and Tunis – are built on parts of drained wetlands.

[5]   Developed recently with the support of the European Commission and the EUROPARK Federation. The PAN Parks initiative by the Worldwide Fund for Nature (WWF) has proposed similar guidelines.

[6]   One could mention the MedWet Inventory System, extensively used for Mediterranean-type wetlands in various parts of the world.

[7]   See Zalidis, G.C., T.L. Crisman and P.A. Gerakis (eds) (2002), *Restoration of Mediterranean Wetlands*, Hellenic Ministry of the Environment, Physical Planning and Public Works, EKBY, MedWet, Thermi and Athens, Greece.

[8]   Some of the better known ones are: Limits of Acceptable Change (LAC), Visitor Impact Management (VIM), Visitor Experience and Resource Protection (VERP), Visitor Activity Management Process (VAMP) and the Recreation Opportunity Spectrum (ROS).

References

Beltran, J. (2000), *Indigenous and Traditional Peoples and Protected Areas: Principles, Guidelines and Case Studies*, IUCN, Gland, Switzerland.

Benyahia, N. and Zein, K. (2003), *L'Ecotourisme dans une Perspective de Développement Durable*, Sustainable Business Associates, Lausanne, Switzerland.

Buckley, R. and Sommer M. (2001), *Tourism and Protected Areas: Partnerships in Principle and Practice*, CRC for Sustainable Tourism Pty Ltd. and Tourism Council of Australia, Sydney.

Ceballos-Lascuráin, H. (1996), *Tourism, Ecotourism and Protected Areas: The State of Nature-based Tourism Around the World and Guidelines for its Development*, IUCN, Gland, Switzerland.

Eagles, P.F.J, McCool, S.F. Haynes, C.D. (2002), *Sustainable Tourism in Protected Areas: Guidelines for Planning and Management*, IUCN, Gland, Switzerland.

Epler Wood, M. (2002), *Ecotourism: Principles, Practices and Policies for Sustainability*, UNEP, Nairobi, Kenya.

Hall, C.M. and McArthur, S. (1998), *Integrated Heritage Management: Principles and Practice*, The Stationery Office, London.

Lindberg, K. (1991), *Policies for Maximizing Nature Tourism's Ecological and Economic Benefits*, World Resources Institute, Washington DC.

Lindberg, K. (2001), *Protected Area Visitor Fees: Overview*, Cooperative Research Centre for Sustainable Tourism, Griffith University, August.

Viñals Blasco. M.J. (2002), *Herramientas para la Gestión del Turismo Sostenible en Humedales*, Ministerio de Medio Ambiente, Spain.

Wolters, T.M. (1991), *Tourism Carrying Capacity*, WTO/UNEP.

World Tourism Organization (WTO) (2001a), *Tourism Market Trends: The World*, WTO, Madrid.

World Tourism Organization (WTO) (2001b), *Sustainable Development of Tourism: A Compilation of Good Practice*, WTO, Madrid.

Chapter 9

Tourism Management and Carrying Capacity in Heritage Cities and Sites

Jan van der Borg

Introduction

The objective of this chapter is to discuss the relevance of the concept of the tourism carrying capacity for both heritage cities and heritage sites. The starting point of the chapter is the notion that the concept of the carrying capacity is strictly related to the sustainability of tourism development. In fact, tourism is not always beneficial for destinations. There may either be too few (hence, the destination loses the development opportunities it possesses) or too many people (in this case tourism damages the environment in the broader sense) visiting a destination. In other words, the tourism carrying capacity indicates where the upper limit to tourism development finds itself.

Heritage sites and art cities are visited yearly by millions of tourists. The continuous expansion of the tourism market in general, notwithstanding occasional setbacks due to, for example, wars (Iraq) or epidemics (SARS), and more specifically the recent boom in cultural tourism have raised the awareness that historical settlements and art cities may be subject to excessive tourism pressure just as much (and in some cases even more) as some natural environments are.

Heritage cities are particularly sensitive to excess tourism demand. They are socially, economically and environmentally complex. The conflicts that may arise between the normal functioning of the heritage city and its tourism may threaten both the continuity of the settlement itself and in the end even the local tourism industry. The management of these conflicts therefore becomes of the utmost importance, first of all to ensure that heritage cities will be conserved for humanity; secondly to make sure that tourism remains one of the engines of social and economic development rather than an obstacle to it. This explains why this paper focuses on heritage cities more than on heritage sites. However, most of the issues that are discussed hereafter are relevant to both art cities and heritage sites.

The structure of the paper is as follows: Section 2 is dedicated to a description of the different issues regarding tourism development in heritage cities, principally citing evidence from seven European art cities that was gathered between 1992 and 1999 in the context of the 'Art Cities and Visitor Flows' project commissioned by UNESCO to the University of Venice. Section 3 introduces the reader to the concepts of sustainable tourism development and the carrying capacity and proposes a quantitative methodology that helps to establish the maximum number of visitors a destination may support. Section 4 discusses the consequences of this limit on tourism development for the management of tourism in heritage cities, both in general as well as with reference to the case of Venice, Italy. Special attention will be paid to a particular instrument of visitor flow management, the so-called Venice Card.

Tourism in Heritage Cities: The Issues

Having Venice in mind as an emblematic example of what can happen to any heritage city when tourism pressure exceeds the carrying capacity, the University of Venice has been involved since the early nineties in a UNESCO project that has been investigating the role of tourism in heritage cities. Seven important art cities have been analysed: Aix-en-Provence, Amsterdam, Bruges, Florence, Oxford, Salzburg and Venice (see among others van der Borg, Costa and Gotti (1996) for a full description of the research).

Although some time has passed since the start of the project, the principal results of this research are still of relevance today and may therefore be used here to identify the main issues that concern tourism development in heritage cities.

At the time of the research, Florence and Amsterdam, the two largest cities in the group, are also those that have the most tourist stays: more than 4 million nights in 1995. Venice follows with 2.6 million overnight stays. In Oxford and Salzburg, the number was lower and Bruges and Aix-en-Provence registered less than a million overnight stays per year. The picture was similar for the number of tourist arrivals.

The average duration of the tourists' stay varied significantly amongst the different art cities. The longest duration was observed in Aix-en-Provence taking into consideration not only hotels, but also other types of tourist accommodation were included in the figure. In general, the length of stay in the latter was slightly longer, consequently raising the average. The figures for the other heritage cities were more comparable. Oxford had the longest average duration of stay (three nights), while for Salzburg the average duration of stay was only 1.8 nights. Amsterdam, Florence and Venice had averages that are similar to those registered for most other European heritage cities.

In almost all the heritage cities considered during the period between 1990 and 1995 a tendency towards an increasing demand for accommodation was observed. Moreover, the average duration of stay in the cities did not fluctuate much in this period. However, the occupancy rate of hotels remained constant or dropped due to the entry of new structures into the market. An increasing demand for urban-based cultural tourism justifies a growing economic investment in the accommodation sector, investments that reflect the growing economic significance of the tourist function in all of the analysed destinations.

Also there has been a gradual marginalisation of the establishments less capable of meeting the requirements of a more sophisticated market, typically one and two-star hotels. In fact, an upward shift was and probably still is taking place between the clients of various hotel categories, from 2 to 3-star and from 3 to 4-star and 5-star. The tourists' growing tendency to patronise high-quality hotels occurred even during periods of unfavourable economic conditions. This has meant that there is a high level of demand for superior qualitative standards. Change was both quantitative and qualitative. Strangely, the supply of very simple forms of accommodation has been growing (hostels, bed-and-breakfast) as well. Demand became and remains therefore highly polarised.

In the majority of destinations, official statistics did not display crucial information on overall tourism demand, in other words on the total number of visitors. The subdivision between overnight visitors and day visitors or excursionists has become a focal point of the analysis of tourism in many heritage cities, especially since the growing interest in cultural tourism, combined with increased mobility, usually manifests in an explosive increase in the number of day trips and much less in terms of overnight stays (see for example Costa and van der Borg 1992). Therefore, in order to better understand the relevance of tourism in these cultural destinations, it is always essential to include excursionists in tourist demand and observe the composition of the visitor flow.

Excursionists are most often blamed for problems related to the excess in tourism demand and to carrying capacity issues, since they bring the destination more costs and less benefits than traditional tourists. The cities, given the relatively high share of excursionists in total tourist demand, found themselves in advanced stages of the tourism life cycle that has been discussed in Costa and van der Borg (1992) and will also be used in Section 3.

Of the seven cities on which the study has been concentrated, Amsterdam and Florence catered to the most varied demand ranging from leisure tourism to congress tourism, with a significant business-related sector. Furthermore, the Dutch capital city, by far the largest city included in the study, was the only one that in 1995 played a role as an international destination directly linked to its function as a transportation hub, a role that it continues to play. Furthermore Amsterdam was and is a notable venue for international congresses, it benefits from being the cultural heart of the Netherlands and it takes profit from the image of its historical centre.

Even in Florence, the second largest city in the study and a cultural destination with a global reputation, many tourist visits were based on reasons other than culture. In fact, Florence is a very important business and congress venue. In 1995, it ranked third in Italy, after Rome and Milan, as a congress venue for nationals. Nevertheless, all of the seven cities were leisure-dominated tourist destinations. With the exception of Salzburg, the seasonal pattern of the heritage cities did not show a marked peak in the summer months. However, for all cities, the first trimester of the year was the one less frequented by tourists.

Salzburg was the only destination with a particularly heavy concentration of tourists in the summer months, which formed a serious threat to its socio-economic structure. In fact, the fragile equilibrium of the urban environment in a city such as Salzburg was imperilled by an excessive concentration of visitors. In general, such a situation generates an increase in the level of pollution, an augmentation of real estate prices, a forced transfer of small artisan workshops to peripheral zones and a deterioration of historical heritage.

Amsterdam, Bruges and Salzburg hosted predominantly non-national tourism. They also enjoyed a significant proportion of overseas tourists who are certainly very aware of the cities' cultural and artistic reputations. Among the nationals, those living in the nearby regions were the most numerous. Of course, even for the foreigners, distance played a major role, but these cities of culture benefited from an established world-wide reputation that made and still makes them key destinations in overseas visitors' European tours.

American and Japanese tourists are often the most desired from an economic perspective; the Italian cities Florence and Venice benefited in particular from their presence. The seasonal pattern differed in the different segments of the market. Generally speaking, the further away the origin country was, the more the demand was concentrated in the summer months. Surprisingly, overseas tourists on a leisure-motivated vacation stayed the same length of time (two days) as the Europeans.

Tourists on an educational trip (ten days to three weeks) had a significantly longer length of stay and are a relevant segment of the market in places like Florence, Oxford and Aix-en-Provence. More generally, on the basis of the results of the UNESCO project it became clear that the motivations for an urban visit can be classified as follows: business tourism, expressing merely the social-economic vitality of a city; congress tourism and leisure tourism. Business and congress tourism merely reflect the economic rank of a city while leisure tourism reflects the quality of life it provides.

Glasson, Godfrey and Goodey (1995) have shown that the impact of tourism on a destination can be measured at various levels, such as the level of the individual attraction and that of the destination as a whole. The character of the city determines which of the levels is the most relevant. For those heritage cities that are attractions themselves (Bruges and Venice are good examples of cities where the ambience as such attracts most of the visitors) the destination level dominates; for cities with a particularly attractive urban site (for example the castle of Salzburg and the university colleges of Oxford) the attraction level is the most suitable. Furthermore, the impact has various dimensions. For most heritage cities, the social-economic dimension, which expresses the conflict between tourism and the social and economic dynamism of the city, will be of particular concern. For others it may be the environmental or the anthropological dimension. These facts were confirmed by the UNESCO study.

It is not easy to establish exactly what the tourist pressure is on a society or a city. One way of quantifying the pressure is by calculating the visitors/residents ratios for the seven case studies; it is thus possible to perceive how the different cities bear varying dimensions of visitor impact. With more than 89 visitors per inhabitant (Russo 2002), Venice's historical core seemed in 1995 by far the most 'mature' of the seven destinations. It is the city that most clearly represented what the term 'touristification' means for an urban area. Salzburg and Bruges followed at a distance. Amsterdam and, to a lesser extent, Aix-en-Provence and Florence did not seem to be under extreme pressure from tourism.

If the more homogenous indexes at the municipality scale are observed, then Venice's 27.6 visitors per inhabitant came much closer to Bruges and Salzburg, with 23 and 36 visitors per inhabitant respectively. All cities exhibited the same phenomenon due to the fact that their well-preserved historical centres became 'cultural resorts' attracting a significant proportion of excursionists. The lower ratio observed in Aix-en-Provence and Oxford was merely due to the fact that the total number of visitors (tourists and excursionists) is not yet as important as in the other cities.

Despite their reputations as cities of art, the tourist function of Florence and Amsterdam are relatively minor in respect to their political, administrative, educational, economic and of course residential roles. In fact, although they benefited from large numbers of visitors, their vast resident populations numerically offset the social impact of tourism on the urban area. Being cities with a large, diversified economy, they were and still are less vulnerable than the smaller heritage cities.

No reliable data was available for a more precise analysis of residents/visitors ratios for specific zones of the urban centres. Even in cities such as Florence and Amsterdam, specific areas around concentrations of attractions (respectively Ponte Vecchio and Museumplein) could be found where pressure seemed excessive. However, considering the intensity of the supply of accommodation, it was shown by Costa, Gotti and van der Borg (1996) that in Florence and Venice the role of the tourist function in the historical centre was clearly evident. The historical centre of Florence had the highest tourist function index: more than fifteen hotel beds per inhabitant of the inner city. The hotels that were constructed many years ago in Venice's suburbs to host commuting tourists (van der Borg 1991; van der Borg 1998) caused it to score very high for the inner city and also for the municipality as a whole.

Of course, these indices were all mere indicators of the relative weight of tourism on the heritage cities. In fact they symbolised a whole range of problems, of negative externalities. Most of them are impossible to quantify. The following is but a tentative list of problems observed in the cities included in the UNESCO investigation:

- Aix-en-Provence tended to be overcrowded in the summer months.
- The centre of Amsterdam had serious parking problems.
- Bruges had problems with traffic all year around, but especially during weekends and holidays. Its centre was rapidly losing inhabitants and economic activities. Hotels and souvenir shops are taking their place;
- Florence lost many opportunities offered by tourism offered due to poor urban management.
- Oxford's most famous university colleges were threatened by huge visitor flows. Its inner city was congested with tourist buses.

- Salzburg, like Bruges, had a serious traffic problem, caused by the huge number of tourist buses transporting excursionists during the summer months. The centre of the Austrian town suffered from crowding-out of residents and businesses.
- The historical centre of Venice was becoming a monoculture. Congestion suffocated and continues to suffocate economic activities and therefore negatively affects the quality of life of inhabitants.

The people's interest in heritage cities and sites is still growing. This not only causes an increase in the number of traditional tourists, but also in the number of excursionists. The share of excursionists in tourism demand was already considerable in the seven cities studied and has certainly worsened since 1995. Moreover, the continuous expansion in the number of hotel beds has led to diminishing occupancy rates, explaining the ongoing intensification of promotional activities.

This has all led to excessive pressure on the more vulnerable heritage cities, threatening the vitality of the local economies, the integrity of the heritage and the quality of life of residents at the same time. The problems the cities under study were faced with were either caused or aggravated by tourism. They can be summarised as follows: traffic and parking problems, pollution, crowding-out, occasional irritation of the local population and 'wear and tear' of heritage.

The answer to the above-mentioned problems has always been that of forsaking the 'laissez faire' principle that often dominates the attitudes of policy makers and entrepreneurs towards tourism development and adopting an explicit tourism management policy that goes much further than promotion alone. In Section 4 some of the main ingredients of such a policy will be extensively discussed. The next section attempts to link the problems described to the concepts of sustainable development and carrying capacity.

Tourism in Heritage Sites and Cities and their Carrying Capacity

Sustainability of Tourism in Heritage Cities and Sites

Sustainability has become a central issue in much of today's tourism development literature. However, the practical application of the concept of sustainable tourism development has traditionally been limited to non-urban or rural areas. Only recently has it been fully recognised as applicable to urban environments in general and to historical settlements of different dimensions in particular.

But what is actually meant by sustainable tourism development? Wall (1994) has stated that tourism permanently changes a local society subject to tourism flows and that sustainability is very much connected with the acceptability of such changes or, more precisely, with 'acceptable' change. If change is acceptable, tourism development that generates this change is sustainable.

But not only does the local society continuously undergo heavy alterations, tourism in the destination itself tends to change over time. The development process of any tourist location may be represented cyclically. Butler's 'life-cycle theory' of tourist destinations is an elaboration of the product life-cycle used by business economists to describe the fluctuations in the sales volume of a product. Instead of the quantity of products sold, the life-cycle theory of tourist locations uses the number of visitors as the indicator of the level of destination development.

In its most elementary formulation (see for example Butler 1980; Mill and Morrison 1985), the life-cycle theory of tourist locations tells us that, in the absence of drastic external interventions, the total number of visitors changes cyclically. Initially, the locality that stimulates tourism experiences a very slow rise in the number of visitors. In the second stage, tourism is booming, while in the third stage growth stagnates and eventually turns into decline, entering the fourth stage. In van der Borg (1991), it was argued that not only the volume of the visitor flow changes over the cycle, but also its composition (for example the mix of tourists and excursionists).

Since different types of visitors generate different positive and negative impacts, costs and benefits vary over the different stages of the cycle. Growth in tourism demand will positively affect income and employment levels of a relevant part of the population. At the same time, increasing numbers of visitors will generate negative effects, or 'costs' borne by the physical and cultural environment, the local population and the visitors themselves. By comparing benefits and costs in each heritage city, it is possible to determine whether tourist flows are either insufficiently voluminous or excessive. In reality, the assessment of the benefits and the costs of tourism proves to be difficult because there are several 'parties' involved, which perceive benefits and costs in a different manner.

The concept of sustainability – in terms of desirable or acceptable change, as Wall suggested – and the cyclical development of the tourist destination are closely related. If tourism development gets stuck in the initial stage, investments are unable to trigger the social and economic change desired. There are too few visitors, and the opportunities that tourism offers are not fully used. Opportunity costs are high. If growth in tourism demand is such that the quality and accessibility of attractions are compromised, the society and eventually even tourism suffer. Change is no longer acceptable. In this case, tourism demand has become excessive, and, instead of providing growth, it threatens the continuity of the local society.

Tourism management strategies for cities that face the problem of overcoming the minimum limit to sustainability have been described by both Law (1993) and van den Berg, van der Borg and van der Meer (1995). As far as the author of this chapter knows, no serious attempts have been made to quantify the minimum level of sustainable tourism development.

In the case of mature heritage sites and cities, Costa and van der Borg (1992) suggested that most relevant is the maximum limit to tourism development, very much related to what is more generally known as the carrying capacity.

Carrying Capacity: Some Economics

Developing tourism in a sustainable manner means trying to use the scarce resources that a destination possesses in an optimal manner for tourism purposes, safeguarding not only the interests of today's tourists and tourism industry, but also of tomorrow's (see also Coccosis and Nijkamp 1995 and Fossati and Panella 2000). An optimal use of these resources implies that the net impact of tourism development on the local society is being maximised over the different stages of tourism development.

Using Butler's life-cycle model, van der Borg (1991) has clearly shown that a development process of the destination contains both sustainable and unsustainable stages. Van der Borg, Costa and Gotti (1996) developed this approach further with the help of cost-benefit analysis. Typically, the first stage of tourism is hardly profitable: investment costs are huge and benefits meagre. Therefore, developing tourism only makes sense if one may expect that after having invested in attractions and facilities the number of visitors will increase sufficiently. The saturation stage tends to generate a net loss for the local society: benefits no longer compensate for negative externalities, such as congestion and pollution.

In general, negative externalities appear when a limit to development has been surpassed. As already pointed out, the limit to tourism development is called the tourism carrying capacity – that is the maximum number of visitors a destination can host. Notwithstanding the criticism to which the carrying capacity as a planning instrument has frequently been exposed (see for example Lindberg, McCool and Stanley 1997), it is very difficult to deny that an upper limit to tourism development actually exists; in fact, the concept has proven its value for visitor management in Venice.

It has already been shown by Glasson, Godfrey and Goodey (1995) that the carrying capacity of a tourist destination is a complex and a dynamic instrument to work with. It was mentioned previously that the carrying capacity may be measured on various territorial and functional levels, including the level of individual attractions and of the destination as a whole. In practice, local peculiarities determine the most relevant level of analysis. For example, interviews with attraction managers in Venice have taught us that, since the majority of visitors do not visit any of Venice's attractions but just wander around in the centre, the attraction level does not seem of much relevance to Venice. A similar situation exists in well-conserved and well-restored heritage cities such as Bruges, Rothenburg and Salzburg, which are attractions in themselves. And since the attitudes and behaviour of inhabitants, tourists and the tourism industry changes over time, the negative and positive effects generated by tourism will be valued differently over time. Hence, time is an important factor.

Moreover, as was pointed out earlier the tourism carrying capacity has a multitude of dimensions. The number of visitors may be limited because the physical structure of a destination is compromised (corresponding to what is usually called the physical carrying capacity), because the local society loses its character (corresponding to what is normally called the social-anthropological carrying capacity) or because the local economy gets frustrated (corresponding to what is usually called the social-economic carrying capacity). Two different dimensions that have always worried Venetians are briefly discussed below: the social-anthropological and the social-economic carrying capacity.

Residents are an important part of the tourism system. Indeed, inhabitants are a fundamental ingredient of the 'hospitality' of all destinations. The reaction of the inhabitants of a tourism city to tourism in general, and to tourists and excursionists in particular, determines the social impact of tourism on the local society and thus the social-anthropological carrying capacity of the destination.

Following a survey among inhabitants of Oxford (for more details on the methodology see Glasson, Godfrey and Goodey 1995), the University of Venice organised in 1993 a survey among the inhabitants of Venice. The results of this survey were quite surprising. It showed among others that Venetians did not have a negative perception of tourism in their city as might have been expected. The respondents were nevertheless very well informed about tourism development in general. They perceived the 'massification' of tourism and the diminishing quality and especially the growing weight of excursionists in total demand. However, the decreasing quality of life in the city is not so much blamed on excessive tourism demand but also on the poor management of the local government as a whole.

The social-economic tourism carrying capacity may be defined as the total number of visitors that can be allowed into a city without hindering the other functions that the city performs. This dimension is closely linked to the phenomenon of 'crowding out', described for the first time by Prud'homme (1986). Tourism in cities like Venice or Bruges tends to dominate if not to suffocate the urban societies; they push other activities or functions from the centre to the outskirts. The price of centrally located land and the diminished attractiveness of a city for families and firms due to congestion and pollution explain the process of crowding out.

The problem of determining the social-economic carrying capacity for the centre of Venice has been formalised in Costa and van der Borg (1988) and in Canestrelli and Costa (1991). They translated the conflict between tourism and other functions into a fuzzy linear programming model that maximises the income from tourism under several capacity restrictions. Formally:

MAX Income from tourism = (average expenditure of a tourist) x number of tourists + (average expenditure of an excursionist) x number of excursionists
Subject to:
(average use of facility i by an excursionist) x number of excursionists + (average use of facility i by a tourist) x number of tourists < net availability of facility i
with i = 1, 2, 3, ...

These restrictions take into account, for example, the availability of accommodation, catering facilities, parking facilities, intra-urban transportation, waste disposal services and the space available in Saint Mark's Cathedral. The philosophy of the linear programming model is very close to the sustainability approach, namely that of the quest for the optimal use of resources. As far as the author is aware of, until now the model has been successfully applied by students in their dissertations on different mature tourist resorts such as Cambridge (urban environment), Rhodes and Capri (islands) and Cortina d'Ampezzo (mountain resort).

Costa and van der Borg found that in the case of Venice, the historical centre can support about 25,000 visitors in one day, of which about 15,000 are tourists (60 per cent of tourism demand) and 10,000 are excursionists (the remaining 40 per cent of the total number of visitors). Among the active restrictions are: the number of beds for tourists (the model tends to fill Venice first of all with tourists and then begins to look if there is still space available for excursionists); the availability of local water transport (which determines the number of excursionists); and, relaxing this last restriction, Saint Mark's Cathedral.

Although the model lacks an explicit temporal dimension, its results are of great interest for visitor management. It teaches us first of all that the 'optimal' visitor mix differs from the actual one. In fact, instead of an optimal weight of 60 per cent, tourists represented in 2002 amounted to slightly more than 30 per cent of the actual total tourism demand. The total carrying capacity of Venice is slightly less than 10 million visitors per year. In reality, the historical centre of Venice is visited nowadays by approximately 12 million people. Therefore, a second conclusion should be that at present the overall pressure from tourism seems close to reaching – at least in absence of seasonal fluctuations in demand – the total stress the social-economic texture of the city is able to support.

Compared to a few years ago, tourism demand is now structurally conflicting with the most restrictive dimension of the carrying capacity. Nevertheless, an analysis of the distribution of demand over the year 2002 shows that demand continues to be concentrated at weekends and in the spring, autumn and particularly summer months. During ten days of the year, total demand amounts to more than 100,000 persons. Peaks of 200,000 visitors on special occasions are no exception. But what is worse, on two-thirds of the days in a year, the number of visitors easily surpasses the social-economic carrying capacity.

Thus, at present, sustainability of tourism development in Venice depends on one hand on the mix of the visitor flow, or in other words the weight of excursionists in total demand, and on the other on the seasonal fluctuations in tourism demand. In effect, the number of excursionists should be reduced, while that of tourists increased. At the same time, peaks in demand need to be smoothed out and the low season utilised more intensively. Furthermore, a better distribution of demand over space would be welcomed. These then become the two priorities of the visitor management strategy of Venice and of any other heritage city and site that is confronted with excess tourism demand during peak seasons.

Tourism Management in Heritage Cities and Sites

Tourism in heritage sites is relatively easy to manage. ICOMOS has produced a very useful set of guidelines, as far as the author knows unfortunately never officially published, that allows site managers to deal with all the problems that the exposure of a heritage site to tourism may bring. The suggestions found in a draft version of this manual have been adapted by van der Borg and Russo (1999) so that one can take care of complex heritage sites, such as Pompei in Italy or the Acropolis in Athens, as well. For our purposes, it is sufficient to remember that the access to a heritage site may easily be controlled, not only through a system of queuing but also by setting the entrance fee at a level that tends to cut out excess demand.

Tourism in heritage cities is much more difficult to manage. Cities are built to receive visitors and need to be accessible for many types of city users and asking an entrance fee for visiting a city is against most constitutions. Moreover, cities that have started to experiment with price discrimination for public facilities, making tourists pay more and therefore discourage their use, are being taken to the European Court of Justice by private citizens.

On the other hand, the number of heritage cities where pressure on the local society and economy is becoming unbearable and where tourism management should therefore be an integral part of urban policies is rising rapidly. Bruges, Florence, Salzburg and Venice are examples of such destinations. Also recently in Amsterdam the negative effects that tourism may produce when developed excessively are being felt and countermeasures may be expected.

Although the UNESCO study cited previously led to more awareness of the range of problems caused by visitor flows and have also specified potential tactics to overcome or reduce them, it has been hard to find any municipality involved in the investigation taking decisive political decisions regarding tourism issues.

The issue most frequently being confronted by the city councils' urban policy, an issue that in some way concerns visitor management, relates to traffic and parking. In most cities, a policy to manage traffic congestion has been implemented in the form of a park and ride system on the edge of town, often in combination with a new traffic plan. In the cities of Bruges, Oxford and Salzburg, the pressure from day-visitors has been eased by means of control of incoming excursionist buses, which are easy to spot and thus to divert. Similar schemes are being developed in other countries, for example in the smaller Spanish art cities like Toledo, Granada and Segovia.

However, more direct interventions to improve the visitors' experience and to ease the conflict among tourism and other urban activities are now sorely needed. More than traffic control, it is management of the tourism function that should be the central focus in controlling the flows of visitors, in particular the excursionists, which is the real threat to a more balanced and profitable urban tourism system in all of the analysed destinations.

In theory, there are two procedures available: enlarging tourism supply in time and space; and acting on the demand by rationing the use of the city. The actions can be divided in two distinct options:

1. The control of the flows through an increase in the costs of the visit, some type of booking policy or a restrictive traffic policy.
2. The invitation to visitors to make use of alternative attractions.

The measures intended to control tourism demand in the heritage cities studied are in most cases taken by public bodies that are not directly involved in tourism development, such as traffic departments and planning agencies. The measures are not part of the tourism policy of the city as such. Hence, the probability that these measures are co-ordinated with other, usually direct, interventions regarding tourism is low. The measures that are supposed to stimulate dispersion of tourism demand in time (initiatives to render the low season more attractive, for example) or in space (alternative routes) tend to be implemented by public and private bodies together. However, their promotional aspect is still dominant.

Of course, the implementation of strategies and policies affecting visitors in a city of art is not independent from other issues and policies for the management of that urban area. Thus, a clear, comprehensive, action plan is necessary to meet goals for sustainable tourism development in delicate urban environments.

The numerous components of the tourism product make it necessary to co-ordinate the decisions and the actions taken by all of the entities operating within the sector. In order to conduct a marketing campaign in the most efficient manner, the tourism offer should be the fruit of a comprehensive agreement between all of the operators of the city, public and private. This is especially relevant for those places characterised by an historical core area and by an active urban life. Due to their physical structure and their social functions, these cities require a public body capable of more than passively controlling the private sector but of assuming a pro-active role.

For this reason, heritage cities ought to have a public body powerful enough to manage tourism in all its facets. As stated earlier, in order to do so, public administrators need to know how tourism is developing and how the changes can be managed. There are several other reasons why tourism should be an integral part of the political decision process in all of the art cities that were examined in the context of the UNESCO project and briefly analysed in this paper. First, both at the city and attraction levels, tourism can be a strongly disturbing factor. Secondly, tourism in cities affects the entire urban community, and services that were originally provided for residents must be extended to satisfy the visitors' requirements. Last but not least, competition has been intensified by an increasing number of new urban destinations.

Having recognised the social and economic forces of tourism and its critical impact on urban systems, it is surprising to note that, even in these highly reputed international destinations, tourism is still treated as a self-maintainable activity and is thus left to itself. The real problem is that the cities' policy makers are unable to respond properly because they do not appreciate the 'soft' sphere of tourism issues. They are generally effective on 'hard' issues such as parking lots and congress centres. However, they are not equipped to handle the management of the multiple variables associated with tourism in heritage cities.

On the other hand, the private sector, pursuing its proper interests, has insufficient vision to ensure that limits to tourism development are respected. A good example of the consequences of this is the continuous flow of promotional material produced on the heritage cities. Since the increase in the supply of hotel beds has by far exceeded the growth in demand, operators insist in promoting the cities, stimulating however, principally due to a limited supply of hotel beds, mainly excursionist demand. The lack of overall organisational capacity has a devastating effect on the development of tourism in these sensitive urban environments.

The city of Venice may in this respect become a benchmark. It is ready to implement a 'softer' and probably more efficient way of avoiding excess demand, both from the city's and from the visitor's point of view, introducing a series of incentives that guide tourism demand. These incentives recognise the fact that the destination is an asset with a limited capacity, the use of which should be rationalised also for the sake of visitor experience. Of course, this should be communicated in advance to the market, either directly to the potential visitors or indirectly to the travel agents and tour operators.

This type of rationalisation policies asks for an advanced booking system. Through the reservation of service packages, which could include for example meal vouchers, tickets for exhibitions and museums and discounts in souvenir shops, visitors may be stimulated to visit Venice during specific periods. The booking of such a package could be mandatory (a sort of entrance ticket) or optional. In the last case the potential user must be convinced of the advantages the package offers, and hence accept advanced booking. The package could be stored on a 'City Currency Card', serving in all effects as a credit card, valid for the length of the visit, and with which goods and services in the city can be paid for. The card can be issued in different forms to different types of visitors, in numbers that are fixed in advance. The personal credit card furthermore allows for price discrimination according to the hour or the day that the card is used, i.e. it is the visitor's behaviour that triggers the differentiation of the price not the card's characteristics.

Both the city service package and the city currency cards can be seen as surrogates for the core service the tourist uses, the hotel bed. It thus helps to convince excursionists to plan their visit instead of improvising. Their reservation could be organised in the context of any telecommunication network that permits long-distance sales in real time, an immediate update of the availability, and the emitting of relevant receipts, such as the systems developed by various consortia of airlines.

In this context, the Internet has some promising characteristics that offer very interesting possibilities when it forms the core of such a reservation system. In principle, the Internet reaches the potential visitors at home before their trip, it is interactive and therefore allows for an eventual booking, it operates in real time, it is cheap, and, last but not least, it is selective in the sense that search engines guide only interested surfers to the site.

Venice is currently implementing a system that offers the possibility of asking tourists to book their visits to the city in advance, both on the Internet and at call centres. The first step has been the creation of a specific site with the name www.venicecard.it. For the time being the potential visitor receives a voucher that allows him several interesting advantages. The subsequent introduction of the smart card version of the Venice Card might offer the visitor an incentive strong enough to make him book his visit to the city well in advance.

How does this Venice Card exactly work? Visitors are invited to book their visit to Venice, and receive in exchange the 'Venice Card' which offers them a series of advantages and possibilities that are either inaccessible or less accessible to visitors that do not book (although they still have access to the city). The number of cards issued will be per definition equal to the optimal number of visitors that results from the most restrictive dimension of the different carrying capacities of the centre of Venice, which seems to be the social-economic restriction that has been modelled using the linear programming model described earlier. Visitors spending the night within the Municipal boundaries can receive the card together with the reservation for hotel accommodation.

Implementing the card has not been easy. Two years ago, an agreement was signed between the Municipality and six municipal companies, among them the company managing public transport, the company managing municipal parking and the department managing the museums of the city. The companies agreed, after more than a year of negotiations, to construct a package of their services and 'sell' the package exclusively to a newly erected, non-profit company named Venice Cards SpA. This company was divided up in ownership with 70 per cent owned by the City and the remaining 30 per cent by the companies. The company was given the responsibility for the development of the card for tourists and a slightly different card for the inhabitants.

The Venice Card was launched in January 2002. At the time of the launch, the Venice Card was merely a prepaid ticket for a multitude of services. Efforts were made to render the package more robust, adding a number of interesting discounts to the basic package. By the end of 2002 more than 20 agreements were signed with cultural institutions, shopkeepers' associations and other parts of the tourism system. One advantage of discounted over prepaid services is that the prepaid services require a complex system of financial and fiscal clearing; discounts on the other hand are handled by those offering the discount to the people that show the card. Once the package was definitively formed, the communication campaign took off in the 2003 Carnival. Around the Carnival approximately 6,000 Venice Cards were booked and sold. Although the number of cards sold is as yet far below the number that allows Venice to control the visitor flow, the sales volume continues to grow. The Venice Card is now ready to be promoted and sold to the international tourism industry.

Ermolli and Guidotti (1991) described the conditions that have to be satisfied to guarantee a successful implementation of such a reservation system. They came to the conclusion that from a technical point of view, the monitoring and the control of the tourist flows in real time does not create any problems. What is essential, however, is that all the actors involved in tourism development are convinced that a reservation system brings them specific benefits.

Venice is not only studying ways to improve the spread of visitors over time, but it has been working on improvements of the territorial distribution of the visitors once they are in the city. At present just a few areas of Venice are involved in tourism development. Tourism is concentrated in the area between Rialto Bridge and St. Mark's Square. Alternative routes within the city may be introduced to rationalise the use of the city and its numerous unknown cultural treasures. Alternative routes are attractions linked through a route and sustained by complementary tourism facilities. Since tourism demand concentrates around the 'musts', an alternative tourism route might persuade the visitors to visit attractions that have been less promoted and thus are less known to the public (which certainly does not mean that they are not worth a visit; on the contrary), and thus relieve the already congested attractions and areas. The alternative route may also involve the surroundings of the city. It has already been said that mature destinations do not only suffer from excess demand, but also from an unfavourable mixture of overnight and same day visitors. The route may, therefore, also constitute a strong incentive for the visitor to stay a bit longer in the city.

Not all cities are willing to spread tourism over the municipal territory. In some cases the concentration of tourism is preferable, in order to keep certain areas genuine. Furthermore, there is the danger that by introducing the alternative tourism route the quality of the overall tourism product will increase which may eventually lead to an additional rise in demand. If total demand rises consequently congestion problems after spreading might well remain the same as before, especially if one realises that the 'musts' will be visited anyway. The tourism development strategy should address these issues in particular.

Concluding Remarks

Heritage sites and cities are facing a continuous increase in tourism pressure. The cultural segment of the tourism market still shows signs of expansion, notwithstanding temporary setbacks in economic growth, September 11th and SARS. This growing interest of vacationers in culture translates itself primarily in more city trips and more visits to a limited number of world-famous heritage sites.

Since tourism development generates both benefits and costs, the question of whether some optimal level of development exists has become a crucial one, not only for natural and rural environments, but for urban environments as well. In other words, tourism development must be sustainable, respectful to the host community and to future users of the tourism resources the destination possesses. In Wall's words: tourism should not alter the destination more than its stakeholders would like to see it change.

This paper has illustrated this statement supplying evidence for various art cities that were the subject of a UNESCO project carried out by the University of Venice. The project showed among other things how important the issues related to excessive tourism development had already become for a series of art cities in 1995. The author has the impression that the situation in these cities has not improved; it is more likely to have worsened, also due to the scarceness of adequate tourism management strategies in place at the time of the research.

A fundamental tool for understanding the limits to tourism development, notwithstanding its undeniable shortcomings, is the tourism carrying capacity. A linear programming model has been proposed as a possible means to get a better insight in the concept of the carrying capacity, explaining the working of the model referring to the case of Venice. Once the carrying capacity has been calculated, the tourism strategy may be designed and implemented. Often this means not only reducing the total number of visitors that come to a destination in a year but establishing a more profitable share of residential tourism in total tourism demand and improving the distribution over time and space as well; in short, managing the flows of visitors.

Managing tourism flows in heritage sites is rather easy. It is merely a matter of pricing and routing in a perfectly controllable, mono-functional environment. It is far more difficult to manage tourism flows in heritage cities. Traditional means of offering incentives or disincentives do not seem to function, since many visitors do not use any service and therefore do not perceive the scarcity of the tourism resources that they are using. The City of Venice has initiated an original project, the Venice Card. This card is nothing more than a package of services that can be found on any city card but is available, once sufficiently promoted, only on reservation and in limited numbers. Advantageous only for those willing to book their visit in advance and by booking help make their visit more worthwhile and at the same time respect the needs of the inhabitants and those economic activities in other sectors than the tourism industry. There is still a long way to go, but a reservation system for visitors of heritage cities may very well be the only way to defend the interests of inhabitants, the tourism industry and the visitors alike.

References

Berg, L. van den, Borg, J. van der, Meer, J van der (1995), *Urban Tourism*, Avebury, Aldershot.

Borg, J. van der (1991), *Tourism and Urban Development*, Thesis Publishers, Amsterdam.

Borg, J. van der (1998), 'Tourism in Venice or How to deal with Success', in Tyler, D. Guerrier, Y. and Robertson, M. (eds.), *Managing Tourism in Cities*, Wiley and Sons, London, pp. 125-135.

Borg, J. van der and Russo, P. (1999), 'La Gestione di un Heritage Site', in Collantoni M. (ed.), *Turismo: Una Tappa per la Ricerca*, Patron Editore, Bologna, pp. 455-516.

Borg, J. van der, Costa, P., Gotti, G. (1996), 'Tourism in European Heritage Cities', *Annals of Tourism Research*, 2, Vol. 23, pp. 306-321.

Butler, R. W. (1980), 'The Concept of a Tourist Area Cycle Evolution: Implications for the Management of Resources', *Canadian Geographer*, 24 (1), pp. 5-12.

Canestrelli, E. and Costa, P. (1991), 'Tourist Carrying Capacity: a Fuzzy Approach', *Annals of Tourism Research*, 18 (2), pp. 295-311.

Coccosis, H. and Nijkamp, P. (eds) (1995), *Planning for our Cultural Heritage*, Avebury, Aldershot.

Costa, P. and Borg, J. van der (1988), 'Un Modello Lineare per la Programmazione del Turismo', *CoSES Informazioni* 32/33, pp. 21-26.

Costa, P. and Borg, J. van der (1992), 'The Management of Tourism in Cities of Art', *Vrije Tijd en Samenleving*, 10 (2/3), pp. 45-57.

Ermolli, B. and Guidotti, B. (1991), 'Un'Ipotesi Progettuale per il Monitoraggio e il Governo dei Flussi Turistici a Venezia', *Rivista Veneta*, 38, pp. 103-114.

Fossati A. and Panella G. (2000), *Tourism and Sustainable Tourism Development*, Kluwer, Dordrecht.

Glasson, J., Godfrey, K. Goodey, B. (1995), *Approaches to Carrying Capacity and Visitor Management*, Avebury, Aldershot.

Law, C. M. (1993), *Urban Tourism*, Mansell, London.

Lindberg, K., McCool, S., Stanley, G. (1997), 'Rethinking Carrying Capacity', *Annals of Tourism Research,* 24 (2), pp. 461-465.

Mill, R. C. and Morrison, A.M. (1985), *The Tourism System*, Prentice Hall, Englewood Cliffs.

Russo, A. (2002), *The Sustainable Development of Heritage Cities and their Regions*, Research Series Tinbergen Institute, N. 304, Thela Thesis Publishers, Rotterdam.

Wall, G. (1994), 'Change, Impact and Opportunities: Turning Victims into Victors', *Proceedings of the expert meeting on 'Sustainability in Tourism and Leisure'*, Department of Leisure Studies, Tilburg University, Tilburg, pp. 279-292.

Chapter 10

Tourism Carrying Capacity in Mediterranean Coastal Tourist Destinations

Ivica Trumbic

Introduction

In many countries coastal areas are often considered as the most cherished and/or valuable parts of their territories. This view is based on the fact that coastal areas are either rich in their natural and environmental qualities and, thus, worthy of conservation and protection, or that their potential for economic development is very high. Therefore, it is not surprising that the population has always been attracted to coastal areas. This has often resulted in population densities being much higher in coastal areas than in other parts of many nations, with all the accompanying problems such development brings to coastal ecosystems and resources.

It is estimated that today, more than 65 per cent of the total population lives within 100 kilometres of the coastline, while trends in many parts of the world show that this percentage will only grow in the future. Equally so, a large number of the world largest urban agglomerations is located in coastal areas.

Mediterranean tourism is largely concentrated in its coastal areas, utilizing its coastal natural and man-made resources of high quality. In many areas however, carrying capacity has been exceeded. The excessive number of tourists is undermining the opportunities of the resource base to support sustainable tourism growth. The purpose of this chapter is to present the efforts of Mediterranean tourist destinations to plan for the sustainable future of their tourism by using carrying capacity assessment as a management tool.

Coastal Zones and Coastal Areas

From the perspective of tourism development, it is important to define what 'coastal area' is. In doing so, a distinction has to be made between the 'coastal zone' and the 'coastal area'. This distinction is necessary, because different management guidelines are usually applied to these two spatial entities.

The 'coastal zone' is defined as a relatively narrow stretch of land affected by its proximity to the sea, and that part of the adjacent coastal sea affected by its proximity to the land. The coastal zone has been very attractive for tourism developers in the past. Because of the increase in density of use such development has brought, many coastal problems are concentrated in the coastal zone today. In most cases, the environmental and other limits have been exceeded and coastal zone ecosystems were unable to cope with the resulting pressures. Consequently, the narrow coastal zone has to be managed following very strict rules and regulations.

The 'coastal area' is a geographically broader space than the coastal zone. In most definitions it includes all transitional and terrestrial ecosystems, and the territorial sea up to 12 nm. It usually extends to the nearest mountain range inland, but could also be extended well into the hinterland in order to allow for integrated assessment of all environmental, social, demographic, economic and other processes (UNEP, 1995). The territory relative to the coastal area is much better suited to the implementation of the Tourism Carrying Capacity Assessment (TCCA) than the coastal zone.

The estimation of the number of tourists an area can accommodate without causing environmental damage, or tourism carrying capacity assessment, has recently become an important issue for sustainable tourism development. However, its practical value as a management tool is often under debate. Some embrace TCCA as a panacea for the problems that tourism causes, as if it will provide tourism managers with the exact number of tourists for an area, which will then allow them to plan for sustainable tourism development. The others are critical of TCCA, because they think the concept is not yet mature enough to be used outside its original scope of environmental (agricultural) studies. The fact that there have not yet been so many practical demonstrations that show how a carrying capacity for tourism could be calculated only strengthens this line of thought. However, TCCA should be considered neither as a scientific concept nor a formula for obtaining an exact number of tourists (Saveriades, 2000). It should be considered only as a flexible management tool for sustainable tourism development that allows for optimum level of capacity in a certain area.

Tourism Development in Coastal Areas of Mediterranean Countries

Tourism industry in many regions usually grows annually at 5 per cent or more. A similar situation can be found in the Mediterranean region, indeed the projections are very dynamic for the entire region. According to the Blue Plan scenarios, the number of tourists in the region would increase from 117 million in the mid-1980s to 140-180 million in 2000, and to 175-340 million in 2025 (Grenon and Batisse, 1989).

Tourism is an important contributor to national economies. The share of tourism in GDP of particular countries in the region is relatively high. Thus, for example, in Spain it is 8 per cent, in Tunisia 7.5 per cent, in Greece 7 per cent, in Cyprus 22 per cent, and in Malta it accounts for 24 per cent of the GDP. Foreign currency earnings contribute to reducing trade deficits in a number of countries. Thus, for example, in 1992 tourism covered the foreign trade deficit by 28 per cent in Greece, 102 per cent in Malta, 70 to 80 per cent in Tunisia, and 74 per cent in Cyprus (Chabason, 1999).

Tourism income is unequally distributed among the countries of the region. EU countries create around 80 per cent of the regional tourism income. There are opposing development expectations with regard to future tourism development. Developed countries of the north favour slower growth, while the developing countries of the east and south of the region consider tourism as the major generator of development, and are making efforts towards accelerating its growth.

Positive contribution of tourism to national economies is accompanied by some negative trends in the coastal resource use. Tourism industry is an intensive user of coastal land, while regional tourism capacities are spatially highly unequally distributed. There are coastal regions with high concentrations (the case in EU Mediterranean countries), but also coastal areas where tourism is almost non-existent (several countries in the south of the region).

Tourism development is adding to the already existing pressures in coastal areas. Population densities (resident plus tourist population) increase in the tourist coastal regions during seasonal peaks. In the Mediterranean, the density increase ranges from 765 per cent in Monaco, 383 per cent in Malta and 207 per cent in France, to 157 per cent in Italy. Coastal urban tourist agglomerations are particularly exposed to these pressures. In some cities, the number of beds is very high in relation to the number of resident population. Thus, for example, in Lindos (Greece) the number of beds is 81 per cent of the number of resident population, in Hammamet (Tunisia) it is 70 per cent, in Sliema (Malta) 47 per cent, and in Pafos (Cyprus) 42 per cent. However, the general rule is that the larger the city the lower the percentage. Thus, in Athens and Tunis, the number of beds is only 1 per cent of the number of resident population, although these cities are important tourist destinations (UNEP/MAP/Blue Plan, 1999).

Taking into account the basic needs and characteristics of the tourism sector, it is not surprising that tourism development is being concentrated in the coastal zones/areas of many maritime countries. Coastal areas benefit significantly from tourism through relatively high income rates for the resident population, higher employment and investment rates, infrastructure construction, and so on. Tourism however, is a large consumer of natural resources. Unfortunately, the environmental limits of the coastal ecosystems are often largely exceeded, because the tourism industry tends to consume the best, the most attractive and the most sensitive sites, thus creating constant conflicts with other coastal uses.

Many negative impacts of tourism development are evident in coastal areas. They include: reduction of water resources and their pollution, land pollution caused by inappropriate disposal of solid waste, marine pollution caused by discharges of untreated waste water, loss of space that could be used for other productive activities, biodiversity degradation, loss of habitats, coastal erosion caused by the construction of inappropriate marinas, increased urbanization, and so on (Ministry of the Environment, Physical Planning and Public Works of Greece, 1994). Many negative social impacts are evident too, such as loss of local traditions, abandonment of traditional economic activities creating mono-cultural economic development, breaking up of social structure, excessive immigration, and so forth. All these factors may influence TCCA.

Methodological Development of TCCA as a Management Tool

From Sustainable Tourism to TCCA

Definitions of sustainable tourism are numerous. According to the Committee of Ministers of the Council of Europe (1995), sustainable tourism development pertains to all forms of development and management of tourism activity that respect the environment, protect long-term natural and cultural resources, and are socially and economically acceptable and equitable. Council of Europe (1997) defines sustainable tourism as a development which:

> ...meets the needs of present tourists and host regions while protecting and enhancing opportunity for the future. It is envisaged as leading to management of all resources in such way those economic, social and aesthetic needs can be fulfilled while maintaining cultural integrity, essential ecological processes and life support systems.

A number of other authors have defined sustainable tourism similarly to the above. Representative among them is Blangy (1997) who defines sustainable tourism as:

> ...any form of development, provision of amenities or tourist activity that emphasizes respect for all and long-term preservation of natural, cultural and social resources and makes a positive and equitable contribution to the economic development and fulfillment of people living, working and staying in these areas.

While all of the above definitions are relatively simple 'interpretations' of the Brundtland Commission's definition, Travis (1994) gives a slightly more focused definition that is somewhat more related to the specific issues of tourism. According to him, sustainable tourism is:

> ...all forms of tourism, development, management, and activity which enable a long life for that cultural activity, which we call tourism, involving a sequence of economic

tourism products, that are compatible with keeping in perpetuity the protected heritage resources, be it natural, cultural or built, which give rise to tourism.

Similarly, Middleton and Hawkins (1998) state that sustainable tourism is a:

...means [for] achieving a particular combination of numbers and types of visitors, the cumulative effects of whose activities at a given destination, together with the actions of the servicing business, can continue into the foreseeable future without damaging the quality of the environment on which these activities are based.

The last definition is closer to the idea of carrying capacity for tourist destinations. Applying the concept of sustainable development to sustainable tourism one can say that the idea of carrying capacity is deeply embedded in both concepts. Carrying capacity could thus be considered as a measure or indicator of sustainability because: it could be used in maintaining the balance between development and conservation; it is a threshold beyond which one should go only with careful planning; it is an indicator to measure change; and it is an early warning system for problems resulting from over-capacity in tourist destinations (Chamberlain, 1997).

Integrated Coastal Areas Management (ICAM)

The sectoral coastal activities (urbanization, industry, tourism and recreation, fisheries and aquaculture, energy production and transportation) produce combined environmental impacts resulting in marine pollution, air pollution, loss of marine resources, loss of natural land resources and land degradation, destruction of historic settlements and architectural heritage, loss of public access to the coast, noise and congestion. In the areas designated for tourism, as demand rises, coastal user conflicts increase and greater stress is placed upon the environment on which it depends.

The impacts of tourism and recreation are similar to those of urbanization and settlement, but have some particularly problematic characteristics. Irreversible physical impacts of development may cause damage to the very resources that attract visitors, such as fragile ecosystems, vulnerable visual landscapes and valuable historic and archaeological sites. It is not rare to find that specially valued ecosystems are destroyed to provide sites for tourist development. The generation of effluents is highly seasonal; the provision of treatment facilities adequate for the large influx of tourists for a relatively short season has often been regarded as uneconomic and unjustified by coastal communities.

The evidence in the Mediterranean shows that governmental policies to reduce or stop coastal degradation have produced only limited results (UNEP/MAP/PAP, 2001). Policies have been based on sectoral approach and therefore failed to take into account the overall impact of coastal development on resources. Because of the sectoral approach, preventive policies were difficult to develop and usually ineffective. It is now generally accepted that coastal systems are far too complex to be managed through independent sectoral policies. Rather than being transferred from one sector to another, from one region to another, or from one source to another, the existing as well as potential problems should be viewed and resolved within a comprehensive environmental, social and economic management framework. It is now widely acknowledged that Integrated Coastal Area Management (ICAM) is an efficient tool for sustainable development. If successfully applied, ICAM could help in reducing or eliminating pollution, rectifying other impacts, and preventing these occurring in the future.

ICAM could be defined as a continuous, proactive and adaptive process of resource management for environmentally sustainable development of coastal areas. Fundamental to ICAM is the comprehensive understanding of the relationships between coastal resources, their uses and mutual impacts of development on the economy and the environment. These relationships need to be understood and expressed not only in physical and environmental terms, but also in economic, institutional and legal terms. ICAM is not a substitute for sectoral planning; on the contrary, it focuses on the linkages between sectoral activities to achieve more comprehensive goals. As coastal resources are used simultaneously by the different economic and social sectors, integrated management can only be accomplished when all these uses, users and relationships are clearly known.

ICAM should focus on facilitating horizontal and vertical dialogue, agreements and compromises between all parties involved in the use of coastal and marine resources. It is a participatory process that involves strategic planning that considers local values, traditions, needs and priorities to define overall priorities and objectives for the development and management of coastal areas (Trumbic, 1994; UNEP, 1995). There are several characteristics of ICAM that are essential for understanding the crucial link between coastal planning and management, and sustainable tourism development:

- ICAM is essentially the process of resource management, with a decision making process leading to allocation of natural and cultural resources over time and space (Rees, 1990). The process of integrated resource management does not imply making each activity possible or fulfilling every interest. Doing so, but taking into account the limitations of coastal areas, would certainly result in numerous conflicts.
- ICAM as a resource management process implies that an early definition of priority issues be made. Sustainable tourism planning and management should fit into this framework. This means, *inter alia*, that a certain area, suitable as it may be for tourism development, cannot be utilized entirely for tourism, if that is to be done to the detriment of other activities, particularly if they would find that same area equally as suitable and/or profitable. Integrated management means that an adequate balance among activities should be ensured so as to satisfy various interests of the communities concerned.

- ICAM has a clearly marked spatial component. The land use planning is still one of the most powerful instruments used for the realization of sustainable coastal development objectives. Sustainable tourism development should be regulated through land use planning.

- Since coastal areas are host to numerous ecosystems, it is recommended that these systems be completely included within the boundaries of coastal planning and management units. Since tourism development largely depends upon the protection and conservation of coastal ecosystems and biodiversity, its management should be closely linked to ICAM since it regulates the management of coastal ecosystems. The definition of carrying capacity is highly instrumental in establishing these links.

- Coastal tourism requires large tracts of land for its development, and this land needs to be very close to the coastline. Coastal vegetation, wetlands, lagoons and other environmentally sensitive areas very often create a physical obstacle to coastal tourism development. Construction of tourism facilities very often results in linear coastal development. Policies to mitigate problems that tourism generates in the coastal environment should rise above the traditional physical planning approaches. ICAM, as an approach that is beyond the strictly sectoral realm, could be highly instrumental in providing opportunities for effective integration of tourism in coastal development policies.

Carrying Capacity for Coastal Tourist Destinations

The term 'carrying capacity' is borrowed from the wildlife ecology where it has been used to define the maximal population size of a certain species that an area can support without reducing its ability to support the same species in the future. Planners have enlarged the definition of carrying capacity by including many variables inherent to man-made systems (Hall and Lew, 1998). Subsequently, the concept has been enriched by the evaluative standards being attached to it, meaning that many conflicts over carrying capacity do not revolve around resource (physical) questions but around value questions and many other issues related to the social context.

Consequently, carrying capacity assessment as a precise technique was born in the 1960s as a method of numerical, computerized calculation for prescribing land use limits and development controls (Clark, 1997). Earlier, when it was applied to tourism, many types of tourism stakeholders were looking for 'a number'. Early calculations (late 1960s to early 1970s) were quite simple. They were often based, for example, on the division of the available area of a certain beach by the floor area a person needed to stay, more or less comfortably, on the beach. Today, there are still examples when carrying capacity is being calculated only in this manner.

However, recent development of the concept has meant the enlargement of its earlier perspective. Hall and Lew (1998) for example, state that carrying capacity is increasingly being identified as:

...a management system directed towards maintenance or restoration of ecological and social conditions defined as acceptable and appropriate in area management objectives, not a system directed toward manipulation of use levels *per se*.

The authors seem to be critical towards the opportunities that normally exist for the practical utilization of the concept, because there has been only a limited number of its practical applications. However, they might be right when stressing that carrying capacity analysis is a management tool, and not a control and regulation tool. Tourism carrying capacity, therefore, is frequently being mentioned as a method of controlling the direction and consequences of tourism development. Carrying capacity analysis helps in establishing a development benchmark, which is certainly more important than 100 per cent accuracy. Tourism carrying capacity today should remain a management concept that guides the policy creation and action, and not a technical, precise management tool that produces the number, on which regulatory actions are based.

There have been many other attempts to define the tourism carrying capacity. Middleton and Hawkins (1998) define carrying capacity as a:

...measure of the tolerance a site or building is open to tourist activity and the limit beyond which an area may suffer from the adverse impacts of tourism.

Chamberlain (1997) defines it as:

...the level of human activity an area can accommodate without the area deteriorating, the resident community being adversely affected, or the quality of visitors' experience declining.

Clark (1997) defines tourism carrying capacity as a:

...certain threshold level of tourism activity beyond which there will occur damage to the environment, including natural habitats.

The World Tourism Organization (WTO) proposes the following definition of the carrying capacity (also adopted by MAP's Priority Actions Programme – PAP) as:

...the maximum number of people that may visit a tourist destination at the same time, without causing destruction of the physical, economic and sociocultural environment and an unacceptable decrease in the quality of visitors' satisfaction (PAP/RAC, 1997).

It is evident that there is a large degree of agreement between all the abovementioned definitions, which proves that the concept itself is being generally accepted. However, there is more disagreement and scepticism regarding the practical application of this idea, in particular with regard to its use as a management tool.

Many authors agree that while carrying out TCCA some of the main elements to be taken in consideration are: environmental situation, cultural heritage, residents' aspirations, and quality of the visitors' experience. Following this argument, the carrying capacity has four major facets: physical, social, economic and psychological carrying capacity. Capacity can also vary according to the time of the year, the characteristics of the site, and the interactions between tourists, residents and their environment. But in practice, most of the attempts aimed at measuring the carrying capacity only took into consideration the physical capacities at a specific location, or the capacities of the facilities available, such as the number of beds, car parking spaces, restaurant capacities and so on. Taking in consideration other dimensions of the carrying capacity was less obvious. Why has TCCA not been used more often, if the concept itself looks so attractive? Some obstacles to the wider application of the carrying capacity analysis may be the following:

- a belief that carrying capacity concept is a complicated and time-consuming academic exercise without clear benefit
- carrying capacity could be a limiting factor for the economic development and job creation
- carrying capacity could be reducing the potential of travel and tourism as growth industries
- carrying capacity could reduce the competitive pressure of the private sector and their desire for short-term profits (Chamberlain, 1997).

Guidelines for Tourism Carrying Capacity Assessment

There are not so many practical approaches aimed at assessing the carrying capacity for tourism. The Priority Actions Programme (PAP) created one a few years ago (PAP/RAC, 1997). The specific focus was on coastal areas. The guidelines were applied in a number of demonstration sites in the Mediterranean (Vis, Rhodes, Brijuni, Fuka-Matrouh, Lalzit Bay, Malta and Rimini). Basic elements of the guidelines will be described below.

The guidelines were conceived as a response to the growing need to assess the carrying capacity for tourism. The document was addressed to decision makers, professionals and the public involved in the tourism planning. They were also addressed to physical planners and coastal managers. Hence the need to integrate this TCCA procedure with the process of Integrated Coastal Areas Management (ICAM).

The TCCA takes in consideration three main groups of parameters: physical-environmental; socio-demographic; and political and economic. The details of each group are given below:

- The *physical and environmental* parameters refer to all components of the natural environment as well as to the infrastructure systems. These components are ecological capacity, the natural heritage capacity, length of the coastline, climate, natural resources, and so on. As these components are easy to measure, their numerical values should be determined. The capacity of the elements of infrastructure systems, such as water supply, sewerage, electricity and gas networks, transportation, as well as public services such as post and telecommunications, health, law and order, banks, shops, and so forth could be calculated only as an orientation. Their physical capacity could be flexible if influenced by political and economic decisions such as investments, tax allowances, subsidies, and so on.

- The *socio-demographic* parameters refer to local communities, tourist population, and their interrelationships. While the demographic parameters are easy to calculate, social ones are more difficult to measure. Political and economic decisions may affect some of the socio-demographic parameters such as, for example, migration policies.

- The *political-economic* parameters primarily refer to the possible investments and other economic measures employed to stimulate tourist development. Although these parameters are somewhat corrective in relation to socio-demographic and physical-environmental ones, sometimes they might have a decisive impact on the actual carrying capacity. If for example a decision is taken by the government to invest in local infrastructure in order to stimulate tourism development, then when carrying capacity is being calculated, the planned infrastructure capacities should be taken in consideration, and not the existing ones. Every attempt should be made towards the quantification of these parameters.

The main common features of the Mediterranean coastal environment which directly affect the process of carrying capacity assessment for tourism are: sensitive ecosystems, specific climate, permeable soils, closeness of the shores of the Mediterranean basin, cultural heritage, local traditions and behaviour of communities. All these specific factors have to be taken in consideration when TCCA is being carried out. Some of the characteristics of these elements and possible consequences if they are being neglected in TCCA are given in Table 10.1.

Table 10.1 Issues for the TCCA in the Mediterranean countries

Issue	Reasons why issue is particularly important	Possible negative consequences if neglected
Eco-system	-increased sensitivity due to the specific climate	-disturbance of the natural balance, disappearance of rare wildlife species
Attractive landscapes	-particular sensitivity of the most attractive areas (islands, protected areas)	-damage to the basis of the economy since tourist arrivals are motivated by the quality of the eco-systems
Water supply	- shortage of water in summer - soil permeability	-threat to the development of tourism -threat to traditional activities, specially agriculture -high prices of water
Waste waters	- dry climate of summers - the Mediterranean basin is closed	-further deterioration of the already high level of pollution of the sea and land waters
Traffic	- exaggerated traffic increase in the summer season - narrow roads, especially in historic settlements - sensitivity of cultural monuments to air and noise pollution	- traffic congestion - high levels of air pollution in tourist settlements - devastation of cultural monuments
Economic issues	-lower degree of economic development than in the countries from which tourists come	- further increase of social inequalities - decline of the traditional Mediterranean economy
Cultural and historic heritage	- exceptionally rich cultural and historic heritage - limited funds for conservation and improvement of the cultural and historic heritage	- devastation of cultural monuments - diminished appeal of tourist areas due to the threatened historic heritage
Socio-cultural issues	- specific traditional culture and norms of behavior - existence of a number of small specific closed communities with preserved local identity	- destruction of local culture - conflicts between local population and tourist - increase in criminal activities

Source: Adapted from PAP/RAC (1997)

The PAP guidelines for TCCA propose that the preparation of study be conducted in five main phases (PAP/RAC, 1997):

1. Collection and analysis of documentation and mapping

    - boundaries of the tourist destination area (region)
    - general characteristics of the tourist destination (region) and its development
    - tourism appeal and attractions
    - tourism, economy and population
    - state of documentation
    - additional collection of data

2. Analysis

    - typology of the tourist destination
    - relationship of the tourist destination to its wider environment
    - stated limitations or controls
    - evaluation of tourism resources, tourism demand and tourist product
    - alternative solutions

3. Preparation of the tourism development options

    - preparation of alternative scenarios
    - analysis of scenarios
    - selection of the most suitable scenario

4. Calculation of TCCA

    - tourism development model design
    - calculation of carrying capacity
    - instructions for the application of CCA5. Application,   monitoring   and evaluation.

TCCA should be a tool of ICAM. The main purpose of TCCA is to provide parameters relative to the development of tourism, which is again one of the major components of coastal area development. The PAP guidelines for TCCA provide two alternatives for the process:

    - the tourism master plan and TCCA, as its integral part, are prepared before the initiation of the ICAM process, but its results should be used subsequently in the ICAM process as an input
    - TCCA is prepared within the ICAM process.

Guidelines provide detailed steps on what needs to be done in either of the above cases. It is important to note here that outputs of the ICAM process, based on TCCA, could be used as valuable inputs for the coastal spatial planning.

Experiences from the Development and Implementation of TCCA

The evidence shows only a limited number of TCCAs being undertaken in the Mediterranean or in other parts of the world. This may be a proof that the concept has not yet become mature enough, or that there are still some methodological problems in its practical implementation.

Clark (1997) cites several examples carried out on small islands or enclosed bays. In *Bermuda*, capacity was established at 1.5 million visitors annually, based on physical carrying capacity levels (not more than 14,500 hotel rooms were allowed). *Barbados* limited the docking space, and at the *U.S. Virgin Islands* a reduced number of commercial tour boats were allowed to visit some of the most important coral reefs. Ecuador set a limit on *Galapagos Island National Park* of 12,000 visitors per year, although this was later raised to 25,000, while 47,000 were actually allowed. However, some sensitive sites are restricted to a maximum of 12 visitors, while more durable ones have a carrying capacity of 90 visitors per day. Some areas are limiting the number of special boat moorings. Costa Rica set a limit of 25 visitors per night to the turtle nesting area of *Nancite Beach* in Santa Rosa National Park. The State of Queensland in Australia limits visitors to a total of 100 per day at *Michelmas Bay* to protect seabirds. These are examples of TCCA being used as a regulatory tool, and in areas (such as national parks and marine protected areas) where it could be implemented relatively easily. Clark also mentions that many carrying capacity limits are never implemented in practice.

'Wise Coastal Practices for Sustainable Development' website (2001) offers several examples of CCA implemented in small tropical island states. A high level of social and environmental vulnerability characterizes these states. It is the result of rapid population growth and coastal development, high human pressures on coastal resources, the fact that tourism is considered as the only viable development option, increasing conflicts between the interests of tourists and residents, and physical constraints. In *La Reunion*, the TCCA methodology consisted of three steps: (1) coastal zoning to define consistent management units, (2) environmental and social studies to determine the carrying capacity of each geographical unit, and (3) development of a general coastal land use plan. Also, environmental and social vulnerability assessments were made. The acceptable level of environmental and social impacts was taken into consideration while determining the carrying capacity. A more specific case was prepared for the *Bird Island in the Seychelles*. It is a small private island of 70 hectares, where the owner wanted to develop a small number of bungalows. The number of tourists was set to no more than 20 per day and accommodation for 48 persons. Socio-economic and environmental evaluations were carried out.

In the Mediterranean, PAP has conducted and/or advised national authorities in several TCCAs. In the early 1990s, these studies were carried out in Croatia (islands of Vis and Brijuni) and in Greece (northeastern part of the island of Rhodes). In the late 1990s, three more studies were prepared or initiated: in Egypt (Fuka-Matrouh area), in Malta and in Albania (Lalzit Bay). Recently, a number of local authorities in the region have also carried out these studies (Calvià in Spain, and Rimini and Elba in Italy, among others).

TCCA in *Fuka-Matrouh* was prepared as part of the larger project: the Coastal Area Management Programme (CAMP) of MAP (PAP/RAC, 1999). Therefore, it was closely related to the ICAM activities in the area. The area is located 210 km west of Alexandria, with the city of Matrouh being the major settlement there. This zone was once highly productive, especially during Roman times when dry land farming practices were used based on development of water resources and storage of rain water in underground reservoirs. The length of the coastline is approximately 100 km. The area is scarcely populated (about 300,000 inhabitants). Trying to avoid mechanical calculation of capacities, the CCA study introduced socio-economic and cultural parameters. It turned out that they were crucial for the definition of the tourism carrying capacity. The existing tourism development patterns, dominated by secondary residence resorts for domestic population, is likely to produce tourist saturation of the area within a relatively short period.

Three possible scenarios of future tourism development were considered: (1) continuation of the existing trend of almost uncontrolled development with short-term benefits and extensive use of resources, (2) an enclave concept of tourism development – tourism oases for foreigners with low contribution for local economic development, and (3) balanced, sustainable tourism development. The sustainable option is based on a tourism product designed to attract domestic as well as international market and, as a result, to extend the tourist season.

Carrying capacity based on the third option was further elaborated using three main categories of parameters. Finally, the maximum accommodation capacity of the entire area was estimated at between 80,000 and 100,000 beds. Bearing in mind the existing accommodation capacities, together with the capacity of the so-called 'tourist resorts', the future commercial tourism development can bring in an additional 40,000 to 50,000 beds. This was an important input for planners in the preparation of the spatial model for the integrated coastal area management plan of the area.

The TCCA for the *Maltese islands* is a comprehensive study undertaken by the National Tourist Organization of Malta with advisory support of PAP. Owing to the multidisciplinary nature of the exercise a team composed of representatives of various bodies was set up including: the Ministry of Tourism, Malta Tourism Authority, the Planning Authority, Air Malta, MHRA, and the University of Malta. Additional contributions were received from the Water Services Corporation, Malta Transport Authority, and the Ministry for the Environment. The main objective of the study was the formulation of the optimal level of future tourism development of the Maltese Islands.

The Maltese Islands have an area of 316 square kilometres; the population is 383,418 inhabitants. Visitor population is about 1.2 million per annum (approximately 11.3 million guest nights). Population density ranges from 166 per sq. km in Mgarr to 21,092 per sq. km in Senglea. Different scenarios were developed:

- free development scenario
- limited growth scenario
- no growth scenario
- up-market scenario.

The TCCA Committee established that the limited growth scenario for the next ten years is the most viable option to follow. Major factors influencing such a decision were the following: prevailing contribution of tourism to the Maltese economy, ideal occupancy rate for the industry's accommodation sector bearing in mind current and planned bed stock characteristics, seasonal spread of tourism demand to Malta, impact of tourist flows on utilities, attractions and facilities and environmental resources, changes in the Maltese demographic profile with the resulting social consequences, local population's perceptions of the tourism industry and their expectations, and visitor satisfaction levels may be reduced as a consequence of saturation, mainly during peak periods and in particular areas.

The directions of the selected scenario are the following: aim at increasing total foreign exchange earnings and tourist per capita expenditure, direct investment to segments crucial for attracting increased earnings, need assessment of which segments have increased investment potential, resource allocation directed to increase employment and value added, and offer opportunities for spending. In terms of accommodation parameters, the directions of the scenario areas follows: stabilize bed stock and not increase supply, improve the quality of service of existing establishments, increase current occupancy rate, eventually be in a position to charge more feasible room rates, and develop specific types of accommodation.

Social implications of the selected scenario are as follows. Firstly in peak summer months arrivals often exceeded 115,000 but never 160,000 per month (indications show that 160,000 per month is past the maximum socially acceptable level due to problems of overcrowding, traffic, urbanization and too many visitors at a very low price). Secondly there is a need to stabilize summer volumes as levels of saturation are being reached and experienced. Thirdly growth is to take place within the winter months but not to repeat summer experiences. Forthly human resources to service both tourism and other industries require forward planning in order for training and recruitment to take place. Fifthly it is necessary improve presentation and build on existing assets which could assist in raising visitor satisfaction, and so on.

The TCCA study for the *Lalzit Bay* in Albania started in 1996. It was the zone in the 'take-off' stage of tourism development. Unfortunately, due to the unsettling political situation in the country, which occurred soon after the work started, the study had to be discontinued. However, it is useful to see what methodology for CCA was then proposed. The following elements were to be taken into consideration: type, size and sensitivity of the elements of tourist offer, national and regional requirements, tourism and environmental policy, type of tourism and level of tourism development in the regional context, all interrelations between the region and the site, and political, cultural and economic preferences of the resident population. The tourism development scenarios proposed were the following:

- large-scale, high-capacity sustainable development
- small-scale, low-capacity, but high-spend sustainable ecotourism
- medium-scale, optimal capacity, limited development.

Unfortunately the current situation in the area is not very encouraging. Because the TCCA was never completed and adopted by the relevant authorities the government has been freely issuing building permits for new tourist development, and today the area is in a serious danger of being saturated by low-quality tourism development.

The TCCA for the *island of Elba* in Italy was carried out within the ISOLE project financed by the EU. Elba is the largest of the Tuscan islands, located 10 km from the mainland and with an area of 224 square km. Its coast stretches for 147 km and it has a population of about 30,000. Elba is relatively accessible resulting in around 500,000 tourist arrivals in 2001. The project had five stages: definition of constraints; scenario definition; assessment of anthropic pressures; a comparison between anthropic pressures and scenarios; and the definition of the critical time periods. After a critical value for each limiting factor (water, waste, beaches, other natural resources, population pressures) were defined, the following scenarios was developed:

- conservation scenario (53,000 tourists per day)
- high sustainability scenario (60,000)
- low sustainability scenario (65,000)
- degenerative scenario (90,000).

Carrying capacities for the four scenarios were calculated and applied during the tourist season of 1998. The first scenario was attained for 11 days, the second for eight, the third for 38 days, and the fourth for 66 days. For the time being, the above scenarios have been used only as a monitoring tool, while the local authority is still expected to take a more decisive action towards preparing action plans aimed at the implementation of the preferred scenario (PAP/RAC, 2003).

Lessons Learned

Experience shows that the concept of carrying capacity for tourism is an attractive one, because it easily catches the attention of major stakeholders and decision makers. However, practical approaches to actually defining it are met with a number of difficulties. On the one hand, there are requests that TCCA's major output be a precise 'number' followed by the strict rules that would regulate the number of tourists in a certain location. On the other hand, more moderate proponents of TCCA state that it should only be a tool that would guide tourist development in a certain area. TCCA should be a guiding tool for implementing the strategy of tourism development, while the quantification should be made wherever possible.

TCCA is particularly important in the coastal areas, because it is the area where most of the tourism development takes place, where development expectations in many countries are at the highest level, but also the area where natural systems are extremely sensitive. TCCA should be closely linked to the Integrated Coastal Area Management.

The recent experiences with the application of TCCA in the Mediterranean region, summarized in a report published by PAP/RAC (2003), show that the following lessons have been learned:

- the decision making process for TCCA can be undertaken using either a 'bottom-up' (better suited for highly developed areas) or a 'top-down' (in less developed tourism areas) approach
- the size of areas for TCCA differs, but the best results are achieved in middle-sized areas (micro-regions or sub-regions within a country) and with precise administrative boundaries
- the utilization of data is more dependent on the political and organizational framework where TCCA are being applied, than on the quality of data used
- use of indicators of sustainable development should be encouraged, particularly for the analysis of tourism development scenarios
- public participation process and public awareness are important for acceptance of the proposed scenarios
- identification and selection of tourism development scenarios are crucial steps in the TCCA process
- carrying capacity should always be based on the selected, presumably sustainable, tourism development option
- the integration of TCCA with other forms of planning, ICAM or structural planning, is necessary because it gives a legal prerequisite to TCCA, although self-standing TCCA studies could also provide valuable input for guiding tourism development
- implementation of TCCA will be more efficient in areas where public participation is more embedded in the resource management process.

References

Blangy, S. (1997), 'A Few Concepts and Definitions', *Naturopa*, No. 84, Council of Europe, Strasbourg.

Chabason, L. (1999), 'Crowded shores', *Our Planet*, Vol. 10, No. 4, UNEP, Nairobi.

Chamberlain, K. (1997), 'Carrying Capacity', *UNEP Industry and Environment*, No. 8, UNEP IE, Paris.

Clark, J. (1997), *Coastal Zone Management Handbook*, Lewis Publishers, Boca Raton.

Committee of Ministers of the Council of Europe (1995), *The Recommendations of the Committee of Ministers of the Environment*, Council of Europe, Strasbourg.

Council of Europe (1997), *Tourism and Environment: Questions and Answers*, Centre Naturopa, Strasbourg.

Grenon, M. and M. Batisse, M. (1989), *The Futures of the Mediterranean Basin*, Oxford, Oxford University Press, Oxford.

Hall, M.C. and Lew, A.A. (eds.) (1998), *Sustainable Tourism: A Geographical Perspective*, Longman, Harlow.

Middleton, V.C. and Hawkins, R. (1998), *Sustainable Tourism: A Marketing Perspective*, Butterworth-Heinemann, Oxford.

Ministry of the Environment, Physical Planning and Public Works of Greece (1994), *Environment and Tourism. Multidimensional Interaction Between Environment and Tourism*, prepared for the Informal Council of Ministers of the Environment held on Santorini, 13-15 May 1994, Ministry of the Environment, Physical Planning and Public Works of Greece, Athens.

PAP/RAC (1997), *Guidelines for Carrying Capacity Assessment for Tourism in Mediterranean Coastal Areas*, Priority Actions Programme Regional Activity Centre (PAP/RAC), Split.

PAP/RAC (1999), *Coastal Area Management Programme Fuka-Matrouh: Carrying Capacity Assessment for Tourism Development*, Priority Actions Programme Regional Activity Centre (PAP/RAC), Split.

PAP/RAC (2003), *Guide to Good Practice in Tourism Carrying Capacity Assessment*, Priority Actions Programme Regional Activity Centre (PAP/RAC), Split.

Rees, J. (1990), *Natural Resources Allocation, Economics and Policy*, Routledge, London.

Saveriades, A. (2000), 'Establishing the Social Tourism Carrying Capacity for the Tourist Resorts of the East Coast of the Republic of Cyprus', *Tourism Management*, Vol. 21, pp. 147-56.

Travis, A.S. (1994), 'Sustainable Tourism Concepts and Innovations in Coastal Areas and Coastal City Tourism' in Z. Klaric (ed), *Proceedings of the International Scientific Round Table 'Towards Sustainable Tourism Development in Croatia'*, Institute of Tourism, Zagreb.

Trumbic, I. (1994), 'Coastal Area Management Programme in Albania', in Council of Europe, *Protection of Coastal Areas in the Adriatic*, Environmental Encounters No. 23, Council of Europe, Strasbourg.

UNEP (1995), *Guidelines for Integrated Management of Coastal and Marine Areas With Special Reference to the Mediterranean Basin*, UNEP Regional Seas Reports and Studies No. 161, PAP/RAC (MAP/UNEP), Split.

UNEP/MAP/Blue Plan (1999), *Report of the Workshop on Tourism and Sustainable Development in the Mediterranean. Antalya, Turkey, 17-19 September 1998*, MAP Technical Report Series No. 126, UNEP/MAP, Athens.

UNEP/MAP/PAP (2001), *White Paper: Coastal Zone Management in the Mediterranean*, Priority Actions Programme, Split.

Wise Coastal Practices for Sustainable Development (2001), available at: www.csiwisepractices.org.

Chapter 11

Tourism Carrying Capacity Assessment in Islands

Apostolos Parpairis

Introduction

In recent years there has been considerable concern about the effectiveness of the available planning and management tools to control and regulate human activities in sensitive environments as in the case of small islands. This contribution examines some of the key problems existing in small islands' ecosystems, the causes leading to conflicts (environmental degradation, intensive pressure on island resources, land use changes, pollution, and so on), and recognizes the necessity for environmental protection and for balancing conflicts between human and natural systems, towards sustainable development.

Within this framework, the concept of carrying capacity is proposed as an alternative methodological tool towards sustainable management of islands, safeguarding resources and surpassing constraints in the process of economic development (including tourism), while protecting the environment of scenic geologically and ecologically vulnerable areas, as often found in islands (Parpairis, 2001a).

Recently the issue of environmental carrying capacity has featured frequently in development plans, strategic development projects and in the wider planning and environmental management literature. This is a manifestation of the increasing emphasis on environmental issues in planning and management studies and practices (Dragicevic, 1990; Costa and van der Borg, 1992; Parpairis, 1993b; UNEP, 1996).

Moreover, the concept of environmental carrying capacity is closely allied to the concept of sustainable development, through the idea that there are identifiable quantitative and qualitative capacity limits which should not be breached, in the interest of both present and future generations. Within this framework, one should consider the particularities of small island environments in relation to one of the human activities: tourism. Tourism, a multifunctional activity, developing with intensity in space and time often leads to environmental degradation in island ecosystems, and coastal areas (Fritz, 1997; Parpairis, 1998 and 2001b).

The relationship between tourism, environment and island development, is important today, perhaps more than ever before. Since the middle of the 20th century, when the phenomenon of mass tourism started, coastal areas and small islands have faced considerable challenges. Their attributes, which make them attractive to residents, visitors and business alike, include heritage features, rural setting and tourist infrastructure (accommodation, leisure, shopping, cultural and transport facilities).

In many islands tourism and recreation co-exist with other activities such as industry, fishing and agriculture (Richez, 1996; Vera and Rippin, 1996; Morris, 1996). Often though, as these develop in an intensive way often concentrated along the island coastlines (Parpairis, 1995), problems arise, because of conflicts between the development of activities and the conservation of the natural and cultural environment (Fritz, 1997).

The strong seasonal variations in tourist activity in combination with the saturation phenomenon further aggravate the pressures on the island's sensitive environment. These problems are likely to become more complex in the near future as a result of further pressures from tourist development and new forms of leisure and recreation (sailing, windsurfing, skiing, and so on) or new types of infrastructure development (marinas for example) with significant impact in the small island environment. Such problems may be further aggravated by ineffective legal and administrative systems which fail to control or regulate activities, as responsibilities are often split between local authorities and central government agencies (for defence, marine, tourism, environment, economic development and so on).

The question is: can such tourism growth destroy the very characteristics which make the small islands attractive?

Several responses have been adopted to face tourism pressures: prohibition of hotel establishment in saturated areas, protection of cultural heritage through restoration and maintenance of historic urban fabric, traffic management to relieve pressures in certain zones, and most recently visitor management (Coccossis and Parpairis, 2000). But there are increasing concerns about the scale and impact of new development (tourism, infrastructure, second houses, and so on) and the capacity of islands to sustain further growth. It is becoming increasingly accepted that effective planning and management of tourism is required and that the development of human activities should be approached through the concept of carrying capacity. Furthermore, the complexity of the problems faced in islands underline the urgent need to replace ad hoc actions with integrated approaches to management.

Methodological Framework of Assessing the Concept of Environmental Carrying Capacity

The concept of environmental carrying capacity has emerged, as a concern for the natural environment, but has been expanded to refer to the environment in general (Parpairis, 1993a) including natural (ecological), cultural, social, economic and built environment.

Environmental carrying capacity expresses the threshold that separates abusive and/or irreversible exploitation and the non-destructive human exploitation of resources (Murphy, 1987). The levels of tolerance vary depending on the type of environment and even depending on the season. When carrying capacity levels are not respected by tourism development levels there is often environmental stress.

Carrying capacity assessment seeks to define the levels of activity (such as tourist development) that can be satisfactorily accommodated without jeopardizing existing or future environmental resources. The basic methodology derives from recreational, tourist and environmental planning and management. In this context, the focus is on how to explore the tensions between place (islands) characteristics and user demands, with a view to conserve the islands' environmental characteristics (Table 11.1).

Table 11.1 Model of polyparametric approach of environmental carrying capacity (C.C.)

MAIN INDICATORS FOR EVALUATION OF ISLAND RESOURCES

C.C. Sector	*Users Space*	*Tourist / Local Space*	*Beds/ Houses*	*Main Beds / Secondary Beds*	*Users/ Resources*	*Land Use Changes*	*Tourist Employment*	*Tourist Income*	*Indicators Average Value*
Ecological C.C.	X				X	X			
Social – Socio/gical C.C.		X			X	X	X	X	
Cultural C.C.		X			X			X	
Economic C.C.				X	X		X	X	
Man-made C.C.	X	X	X	X	X	X			
TOTAL C.C.	X	X	X	X	X	X	X	X	

Table 11.2 Life cycle of tourist product (of a period of 1 to 30 or 40 years or longer)

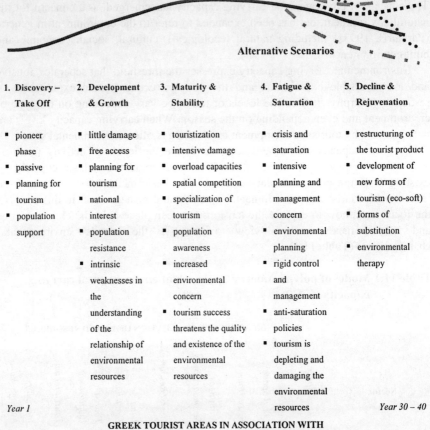

Alternative Scenarios

1. Discovery – Take Off	2. Development & Growth	3. Maturity & Stability	4. Fatigue & Saturation	5. Decline & Rejuvenation
▪ pioneer phase	▪ little damage	▪ touristization	▪ crisis and saturation	▪ restructuring of the tourist product
▪ passive planning for tourism	▪ free access	▪ intensive damage	▪ intensive planning and management concern	▪ development of new forms of tourism (eco-soft)
▪ population support	▪ planning for tourism	▪ overload capacities		▪ forms of substitution
	▪ national interest	▪ spatial competition	▪ environmental planning	▪ environmental therapy
	▪ population resistance	▪ specialization of tourism	▪ rigid control and management	
	▪ intrinsic weaknesses in the understanding of the relationship of environmental resources	▪ population awareness	▪ anti-saturation policies	
		▪ increased environmental concern	▪ tourism is depleting and damaging the environmental resources	
		▪ tourism success threatens the quality and existence of the environmental resources		

Year 1   *Year 30 – 40*

**GREEK TOURIST AREAS IN ASSOCIATION WITH
THE PHASES OF THE LIFE CYCLE OF THE TOURIST PRODUCT**

Lefkada	Samos	Lasithi	Mykonos	Attica (Athens)
Chios	Chania	Magnisia (Volos,	Corfu	Evia
Mani	Syros	Pilion)	Argolida	Korinthia
Samothraki	Kefalonia	Iraklion	Achaia	Thessaloniki
Ikaria	Lesvos	Paros	Dodecanese	Chalkidiki
Alonissos	Naxos	Santorini	(Rhodes, Kos)	Pieria
Skyros	Rethimnon	Zakinthos	Magnisia	
	Messina	Patmos	(Skiathos)	
	Skopelos			

These tensions need to be recognised explicitly in examining future growth in an island in consideration of planning and environmental measures.

The analysis of carrying capacity levels must establish a balance between positive and negative factors and hence the volume of tourism that will bring optimum benefits to the island or region, to the local population, and to tourists themselves in maintaining their satisfaction levels.

The spatial diffusion of tourist pressures can alleviate environmental degradation and reduce congestion in overdeveloped small islands thus affecting carrying capacity in the end.

Carrying capacity can be established for various types of destinations such as islands emerging as tourist destinations, islands already developed and islands reaching or exceeding their carrying capacity levels. However it is often the developed destinations which experience problems of overdevelopment, where capacity levels are of policy concern.

Carrying capacity can be estimated for specific islands or areas on the basis of two aspects:

- The local natural, man-made, cultural and socioeconomic environment (maintaining the proper balance between development and conservation).
- The tourism image and tourist product (the number of tourists in relation to the image of the tourist product and the types of environmental and cultural experiences that the visitors are seeking).

In this approach, optimum capacity levels for each island can be assessed on the basis of the characteristics of the island and the type of tourism it receives. For each case, acceptable levels can be expressed in terms of environmental damage (air, water and noise pollution), conservation needs for wildlife and natural vegetation at land and sea, visual impact levels, congestion levels, employment and income levels, level of tourism activity to maintain cultural monuments, customs, adequate utility services (water supply, electricity, sewage and solid waste system, and so on), tourist attraction features, and acceptable cost of living standards.

Carrying capacity can be introduced in planning, expressed in terms of standards of number of visitors using various tourist attractions, facilities and services, although such standards may vary from island to island, depending on environmental characteristics, and types of tourist product and may include: accessibility, quality of beaches, beach capacity, resort densities, standards for air, water and noise pollution, as well as infrastructure development thresholds.

It is also possible to use indicators (i.e. ratios) of the island's carrying capacity, such as the ratio of tourists to local population, residential built-up areas to tourist built-up areas, historical village stock to new built up areas, changes in land and building uses through time.

In understanding carrying capacity it is also useful to employ general conceptualizations of tourism growth, the process of tourist development, the impacts, and so on. One such model is that of the life cycle of tourist product

(Butler, 1980) which is particularly useful if applied to new areas that emerge as tourist destinations (Table 11.2).

However, information and knowledge which is available regarding patterns and models of tourism development suggest that there are reservations as to the general application of such concepts, particularly the sequence that 'touristization' follows in various stages, and whether these stages or phases are identifiable in the process (Miossec, 1977; Parpairis, 1993b).

Overall there is a growing concern that carrying capacity has been exceeded and that this happening so intensively as to lead to a decline in the tourist product.

In Malta (Young, 1991), levels of saturation were identified as: areas with acceptable levels of saturation, places regarded as 'disaster areas' but with possibility of treatment, and finally disaster areas without possibility of treatment and suitable only for ... bulldozers!

Tourism carrying capacity assessment can be valuable when introduced in the early stages of planning for tourist development, where limits and levels of development are considered. In this context a useful tool may be the Rhombus-mirror (Parpairis, 1993b), which gives an idea of where the tourist system of an island is moving to and which of the main parameters of the system are short of the desirable targets (Figure 11.1).

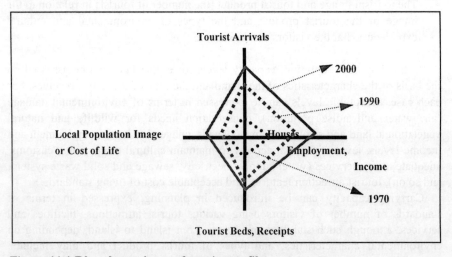

Figure 11.1 Rhombus-mirror of tourist profile

Source: Parpairis, 1993

Although the carrying capacity assessment analysis has become one of the most important methodologies of tourism and recreation planning and management (Dragicevic, 1990; Costa and van der Borg, 1992; Parpairis, 1993b; UNEP, 1996), there are limitations in its application due to the fact that the identification of quantitative and qualitative limits remains a very complex exercise. A central task is to determine the possible upper limits of development, that is the optimal use of tourist resources that will sustain and protect the tourist resources and the tourist market (Figure 11.2). Arriving at absolute figures at the current state of development of evaluation techniques to assess saturation problems of all tourist destinations is a difficult task at an operational level (Figure 11.2). In spite of that, the introduction of this tool within the principles of sustainable tourism development of island and coastal ecosystems properly adapted to the local particularities remains a priority in spite of all possible limitations and obstacles.

The incorporation of the above tool in the island planning and management can be achieved through criteria, parameters and guidelines set for various destinations at various stages of tourist development and in the formulation of tourist policy and plans at various spatial levels.

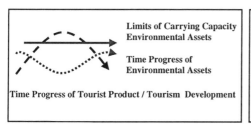

Figure 11.2a Carrying capacity surpasses the environmental resources and the unsustainable tourist development

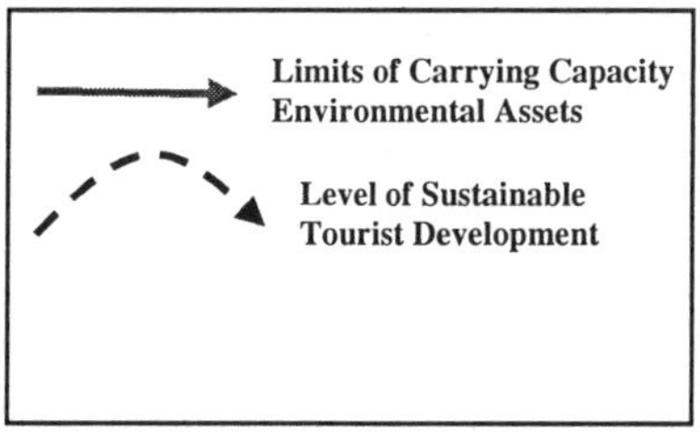

Figure 11.2b Harmonic relation of the environmental assets and sustainable tourism development based on carrying capacity limits

The concept of environmental carrying capacity has already been applied in studies in tourist destinations, like Greece (Parpairis, 1993b), in cities as well as islands and coastal zones such as the coastal zone of Croatia (Dragicevic, 1990), the city of Chester (BDP, 1995), the city of Venice (Costa and van der Borg, 1992), the island of Malta (Young, 1991) and others.

This can assist decision makers to examine alternative policies and strategies to plan and manage tourism more effectively. Within this framework, the application of carrying capacity can be beneficial, in order to identify the levels of permissible capacities regarding the ecological, cultural, economic, social and physical environment of the area, according to certain criteria and guidelines which have already been introduced (UNEP, 1996).

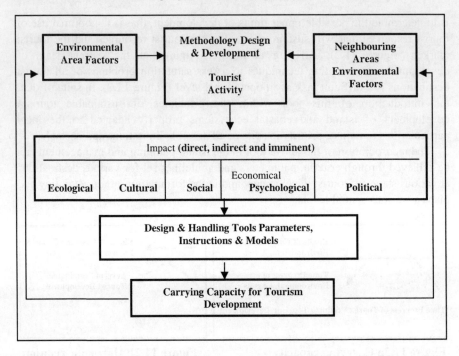

Figure 11.3 Evaluating the environmental system's carrying capacity

The Experience of Tourist Development in the Island of Myconos, Cyclades

It is nowadays widely believed that the majority of tourists not only value environmental quality in tourist resorts, but also become increasingly critical of environmental conditions. This is not surprising considering the great pressure of tourism on sensitive environments such as small islands and coastal ecosystems. The following example of Myconos Island represents such a case, although other islands and Greek tourist destinations can be seen in this perspective.

Myconos, an internationally well-known tourist island, occupying some 103.50 km^2, with a coastline of 81.50 km of which about 16.20 km are sandy beaches, is composed of three islands – Myconos, Rinia and Delos (an archaeological site). It is part of the Cyclades archipelago, a major destination.

The island is home to about 9,800 inhabitants (2001) and more than 120,000 tourists (estimated arrivals in all types of accommodation, 2001), while these figures do not include a number of cruise ships which call at the island on a daily basis. Accommodation capacity jumped from almost 100 hotel beds in 1961 to 8,609 in 2001, while the non-hotel beds reached the level of 16,000 in 2001 (Figure 11.4). The evolution in the demand of tourist services shows a continuous drop in the percentage of visitor arrivals at primary accommodation (hotels) in favour of arrivals in secondary forms of accommodation (rooms to let), a tendency which becomes even more marked in the case of bed-nights.

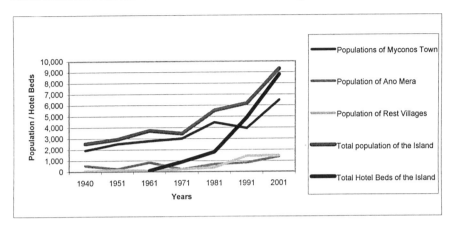

Figure 11.4 Population evolution and hotel beds in Myconos island

It is also worth noting that the rate of growth, in the number of Greek tourists in terms of arrivals and bed-nights, has been several times greater in the last decade than the equivalent of foreigners, while it was the opposite case in the previous decade. Another important evolution regarding the development of tourism and the growth of population is that during the last decade the majority of visitors have been domestic travellers, mostly long weekend visitors (Coccossis and Parpairis, 1996), representing a new form of domestic tourism.

This new development characterizes the present state of tourist services of the island, which moved from the international profile (way prior to 1991) to that of a domestic one. The recent trends in the structure of the tourist sector have direct and indirect impacts on the island's tourist product as well as on the island's scenic natural environment (Parpairis, 2001b).

Changes are evident in terms of construction of holiday villages and summer houses, expansion of infrastructure (port, airports, peripheral roads, parking areas, warehouses, and so on), and investments in environmental management infrastructure to deal with water supply, litter and other waste, and so on.

A large proportion of the island's extremely limited land surface has been absorbed by intensive housing constructions, tourism development and accompanying infrastructure, thus causing widespread loss of agricultural land (Figure 11.5).

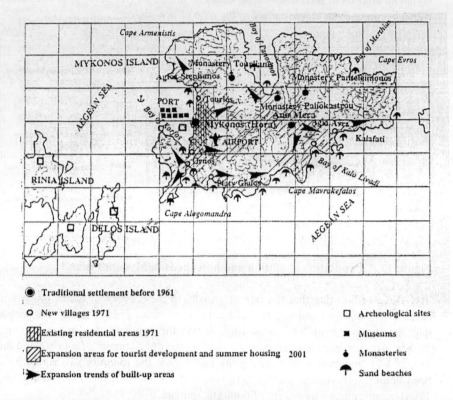

●   Traditional settlement before 1961

○   New villages 1971   □   Archeological sites

▨ Existing residential areas 1971   ■   Museums

▱ Expansion areas for tourist development and summer housing   2001   ♦   Monasteries

➤ Expansion trends of built-up areas   ↑   Sand beaches

Figure 11.5 Cultural resources and development of built-up areas of Myconos island

Symptoms of saturation and undesirable effects on the island's characteristics can already be observed (environmental degradation, congestion in traditional settlements and beaches, traffic congestion, lack of parking spaces, water shortage, noise and air pollution).

The limited natural resources of the island are insufficient to cope with the competing demands placed on these resources as a result of uncontrolled tourism and housing development in the last three decades.

Myconos by all indications has surpassed its carrying capacity level, mainly because it has developed without the benefits of effective planning, something that applies to many other islands and places in the Mediterranean region and elsewhere (Dragicevic, 1990; Costa and van der Borg, 1992; Parpairis, 1993b). As pressures for development are expected to grow, leading to 'saturation', appropriate policies and carrying capacity limits need to be introduced.

Carrying Capacity in Islands: New Prospects

Introducing the concept of carrying capacity could be seen as a preventive, precautionary and anticipatory approach developing in an adaptive way, rather than as a problem solving process at one particular time period and case. This will reduce the risk and prevent long-term or irreversible adverse effects and the degradation of the environment.

The carrying capacity concept needs to be introduced together with strategic environmental impact assessment, standards, limits, and special measures for tourist development, cultural treatment and environmental planning as well as education techniques of all 'actors' involved in the process of development. In this way, an integrated approach to island and coastal planning and management of sustainable tourist development could safeguard and fulfil the present, as well as the future, needs and lead to a balanced environmental protection and tourist development.

Recent trends internationally are likely to positively influence the evolution of the tourism in islands. The increasingly environmentally conscious values of tourists, with environmentally driven actions taken in tourist destinations (environmental protection, controlled development), are likely to lead to an alleviation of saturation, improving the carrying capacity considerations. The introduction of environmental management tools (such as EIA or SEA) and continuous monitoring of tourist and island development are essential elements in contemporary island planning. This can be accompanied by the establishment of governance to avoid conflicts through non-conventional actions and uses of resources, respective environmental boundaries, derived from the natural and cultural characteristics in a region consisting mainly of small islands, the human actions and their effects.

Co-operation, consensus, sustainable development and environmental planning (based on the concept of carrying capacity), integrated island management planning are important tools. In this context tourism could be the common ground for a new take-off of sustainable tourism development for the island tourism activity, and development should respect the scale, nature and character of the island's environment in which it is sited. Harmony must be sought among the tourist needs, the island's environment, and the local population's expectations from the development of tourism.

Tourism development should respect the island's carrying capacity limits and should be guided by the island's environmental requirements. Determining the concept of carrying capacity of an island on the basis of the local environment, as well as on the type of tourist product, should be integrated in the environmental planning process, to manage tourist development at a local and regional level (island group scale).

References

Building Design Partnership (BDP) (1995), *Environmental Capacity: A Methodology for Historic Cities*, Ove Arup, London.

Butler, R.W. (1980), 'The Concept of a Tourist Area Cycle of Evolution: Implications for Management Resources', *Canadian Geographer*, 24(1).

Coccossis, H. and Parpairis, A. (1996), 'Tourism and Carrying Capacity in Coastal Areas', in Priestley, G.K. and Coccossis, H.N. (eds.), *Sustainable Tourism?*, CAB International, pp. 153-175.

Coccossis, H. and Parpairis, A. (2000), 'Tourism and the Environment: Some Observations of the Concept of Carrying Capacity', in Briassoulis, H. and Straaten, J. van der (eds.), *Tourism and Environment: Regional, Economic and Policy Issues*, Kluwer Academic Publ., Dordrecht, pp. 23-33.

Costa, P. and Borg, J. van der (1992), 'Managing Mass Tourism in Vulnerable Art Cities Venice and 19 other European Destinations', *6th Workshop of the RRS in Southern Europe*, Nafplion.

Dragicevic, M. (1990), *Methodological Framework of Assessing Tourist Carrying Capacity in Mediterranean Coastal Zones*, PAP Zagreb.

Fritz, G. (1997), *Biodiversity and Tourism*, GRANC, Bonn.

Miossec, J.M. (1977), 'Un Modele de l'Espace Touristique', *L'Espace Geographique* (1), pp. 41-48.

Morris, A. (1996), 'Tourism and Local Awareness: Costa Brava, Spain', in Priestley, G.K. and Coccossis, H.N. (eds.), *Sustainable Tourism?*, CAB International.

Murphy, P.E. (1987), *Tourism. A Community Approach*, London, Methuen, New York.

Parpairis, A. (1993a), 'The Evolution of the Life Cycle of a Tourist Product', in Proceedings of the *3rd International Conference on Environmental Science and Technology*, University of the Aegean, Lesvos, Vol. B, pp. 673-689.

Parpairis, A. (1993b), *The Concept of Carrying Capacity*, Ph.D. Dissertation, Department of Environmental Studies, University of the Aegean, Mytiliny.

Parpairis, A. (1995), *Evaluation of the Myconos Tourist Product*, Modern Issues, Athens.

Parpairis, A. (1998), 'The Concept of Carrying Capacity of Tourism Development in Coastal Ecosystems', in Proceedings of the *Kriton Con International Symposium on Environment Management in the Mediterranean Region*, Bogazici University, Antalya, Turkey, June 18-20.

Parpairis, A. (2001a), *Environmental Planning of Special Projects*, Educational material for the Hellenic Open University, Greece.

Parpairis, A. (2001b), *Protection and Restoration of Coastal Areas and Landscapes*, Educational material for the Hellenic Open University, Greece.

Richez, G. (1996), 'Sustaining Local Culture Identity: Social Unrest and Tourism in Corsica', in Priestley, G.K. and Coccossis, H. (eds.), *Sustainable Tourism?*, CAB International.

UNEP (1996), *Guidelines for Carrying Capacity Assessment for Tourism in Mediterranean Coastal Areas*, Priority Action Programme, Regional Activity Centre, Split.

Vera, F. and Rippin, R. (1996), 'Decline of a Mediterranean Tourist Area and Restructuring Strategies: the Valencian Region', in Priestley, G.K. and Coccossis, H. (eds.), *Sustainable Tourism?*, CAB International.

Young, B. (1991), *At Risk – The Mediterranean, the Mediterranean Way, and Mediterranean Tourism: Perspective on Change,* International Symposium on Architecture of Tourism in the Mediterranean, Istanbul.

Chapter 12

Tourism Carrying Capacity and Public Participation: The Methodology Used in the Case of the Island of Rhodes, Greece

Michael Scoullos

Introduction

Tourism is one of the most important economic sectors of our era, particularly for regions with limited industrial or agricultural development options, where comparative traditional development disadvantages, such as small-scale economies or lack of complex infrastructures and so on, may be turned into comparative advantages for quality tourism. Many Mediterranean tourist destinations could be considered as typical examples of such a case. Experience shows that although tourism is, in principle, one of the activities which could be adaptable to sustainability criteria, in the vast majority of cases it 'consumes' the natural and cultural capital on which it is based. This happens whenever tourist activities exceed the *carrying capacity* of the system. To adequately address the sustainability planning of a region or city where tourism constitutes a major activity it is of utmost importance that *carrying capacity* is properly assessed.

This work derives from a part of a major research project supported by the European Commission under the title *Sustainable Development in European Cities and Regions* (SUDECIR) carried out in Rhodes, Greece, by one of the participating institutions, namely the Mediterranean Information Office for Environment, Culture and Sustainable Development (MIO-ECSDE) under the direction and management of the author. Further analysis and description of the project have been given in the book entitled *Sustainable Development of European Cities and Regions* (SUDECIR), edited by G.H. Vonkeman (2000) (see relevant chapter by Kontostanou-Karalivanou et al.).

According to a WTO definition, the *carrying capacity* of a tourist resort may be defined as the maximum number of people that may visit a tourist destination at the same time, without causing destruction of the physical, economic and socio-cultural environment and an unacceptable decrease in the quality of visitor satisfaction. This definition was developed long before the adoption of the notion of sustainable development but it refers to all three dimensions of sustainability: environment, economy and society.

The most common approach for a *Carrying Capacity Assessment* (CCA) is the determination of the desirable upper limit of economic development which is in correlation with the optimal use of tourism resources / tourism capital. The main practice in CCA is first to define an appropriate development scenario for the site under examination and then, accordingly, the carrying capacity of the site. One of the main components is the identification of the limiting factors. In doing so, the various stakeholders and the general public have to be properly informed and involved in the process at the right time. Achieving the widest possible consensus is a basic prerequisite for the smooth implementation of a sustainable development plan on the CCA in a tourist destination and for its future monitoring.

It should be kept in mind that the carrying capacity approach is not universally accepted. It has been subject to criticism as a largely mechanistic analysis based on imprecise notions of *vital space*, qualitative and inadequate methods for measurement of perceptions. Some consider the CCA as a useful tool mainly when the capacity of the site presents obvious indications of decline and in this case the results of this technique can provide powerful arguments for withholding further deterioration. Until now, the ability to quantify carrying capacity has been limited and planners usually determine this on the basis of qualitative details, which may change with time and/or prevailing lifestyles.

Despite the various arguments, a CCA based both on data analysis and expert judgment could be considered as a very useful tool in the hands of development planners and decision makers. Setting a carrying capacity for a tourist destination is not only helpful in comprehensive planning and defining the role and the contribution of the tourism sector in sustainable development, but also secures a positive feed-back effect on the tourist market itself.

Elaborating on the Notion of Carrying Capacity and its Limitations

Carrying capacity is in fact a 'metaphor'. Humans, for example, can carry a wide range of loads of different weight and volume. However, there is an average and a maximum load that cannot be surpassed, and some individuals have a carrying capacity much smaller than the average. If they are forced to carry more they will collapse.

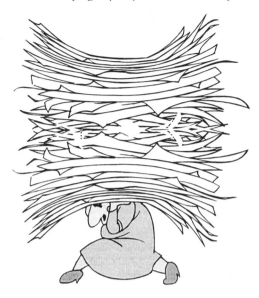

Figure 12.1 Carrying capacity

Similarly, any vehicle has a given carrying capacity that cannot be surpassed for a number of reasons (weight, volume, geometry, construction, safety, performance, comfort). In a common small car, designed for 4 - 5 persons, the margins between securing comfort (4 persons) and compromising safety (6 persons) are rather narrow, clearly understandable and therefore subject even to strict regulations. The larger the system becomes (for example, in the case of vehicles, a bus) the wider the margins are. Using advanced technology perhaps the same 'geometry' would be able to carry more. Therefore we have a readily understandable 'technological enlargement' of carrying capacity.

Apparently the carrying capacity concept for human systems is more complex than the ecological carrying capacity in nature that is closely linked with the notions of vital space and the 'stenoec' or 'euryec' character of the members of the bio-community of an ecosystem (their ability to tolerate a certain set of physicochemical conditions), although the frequently used definition seems to be quite simplistic: *a measure of the amount of renewable resources in the environment in units of the number of organisms these resources support* (Roughgarden, 1979).

For human societies, there are substantial individual differences in types and quantities of resources consumed and rapid cultural (including technological) evolution of the types and quantities of resources supplying each unit of consumption. Thus, carrying capacity varies markedly with culture and level of economic and social development (Daily et al., 1991). There is a clear distinction between the 'ecological carrying capacity' and the 'social carrying capacity' (the maxima that could be sustained under various social systems and especially the associated patterns of resource consumption). Hardin (1986) suggests that at any level of technological development, social carrying capacities are necessarily less than biophysical carrying capacities. It is more likely that they are different but not necessarily less, since technology and human resources play a complementary role in the biophysical carrying capacity ('natural space' and 'natural resources').

According to many analysts technology and trade can expand ecological carrying capacity, asserting that technological advances will sufficiently lower impacts *per capita*. Technology can lead to efficiency improvements, resource substitutions and other innovations. However, others claim that even under the best circumstances, technological innovation may increase the 'vital space' but does not increase carrying capacity *per se*. In fact, it only increases the efficiency of the resource use. In theory, shifting to more energy-and material-efficient technologies should enable a defined environment to support a larger population at the same or higher material standard, which amounts to increasing carrying capacity.

At a more general level, Hannon (1975) argues that in practice technology induced energy, material and, in the end, money savings by individuals are usually redirected to alternative forms of investment and consumption, cancelling some or all of the initial potential benefits to the environment. To this extent such mechanisms contribute to increased aggregate material consumption and accelerated stock depletion and indirectly they reduce carrying capacity.

On the other hand, the carrying capacity gains from trade are also questionable. While some claim that commodity trade may release a local population from carrying capacity constraints in its own home territory, others argue that this merely displaces some fraction of that population's environmental load to distant exporting regions. In effect, local populations import others' 'surplus' carrying capacity. This is a typical problem for tourist-overpopulated areas. The temporary increase in population and resource use (especially during peak periods) increases the aggregate human load on the ecosphere. In this way there is no net gain in carrying capacity, since trade reduces the load-bearing capacity if access to cheap imports (for example food) lowers the incentive for people of the host areas to conserve their local natural capital stocks (for example agricultural land), while simultaneously leading to the accelerated depletion of natural capital in distant export regions ('environmental footprint'). In such a case we usually have a double displacement of the 'load'. If a tourist from a north European country comes to Rhodes, for example, he or she dislocates carrying capacity from Rhodes to his place of origin for the time of his absence from his country. At the same time he or she will consume material and fuel for energy not produced in Rhodes but at a third place from where carrying capacity is displaced to Rhodes. If now the whole package is paid in north Europe and the main part of the profit is invested elsewhere, then the effects are spread even further. If this view, that is in essence correct, is adopted, it is unlikely that any major tourist area (or even a wider region) could ever have a truly sustainable development, unless major changes are made at a global level. The SUDECIR starting point was that sustainability should start at the local and regional level and move up to the maximum feasible level.

Furthermore, tourism cannot be reduced to flows of material units alone. It is primarily connected to consumption and use of 'unusual' (if not necessarily 'quality') material flows and also of immaterial goods. Cultural (in the widest context) considerations are very important. There is a certain distinction between mere existence, or mere supply of necessary goods for survival, and the quality of life connected with vacations and tourism. It is obvious that such a quality must include a reasonable (though undefined) amount of 'luxury' food (fresh vegetables, quality meats, fish and sea-food, refreshing drinks, and so on), clothing (beyond that needed for mere cover and conservation of body heat), comfortable accommodation (eventually space heating or air conditioning), adequate transportation, electronic equipment, and so on (Hardin, 1986). Humans also need books, paintings, music, theatre, TV, sports, museums, exhibitions, art in general, action and inspiration, which are vital for the well-being and balanced development of the society and every individual. The immaterial 'goods' are needed by tourists even more than the material ones in order to be attracted to a destination.

Many real components of this quality of life are left out of any energy or natural resource measure (litres of water or kilograms of coal equivalent per capita per annum), particularly the aesthetic values, the inter-personal goods and even the spiritual goods or the cultural heritage. The maximum that could be achieved with calculations is for material and energy sources to be inter-converted into 'facilitators' of immaterial goods.

Though it is recognized that the enjoyment of non-material goods requires a minimum of material well-being and *vice versa*, it is unlikely that a distinction between energy and material directly consumed, on one hand, and indirectly 'facilitating', on the other, will be of any practical significance in assessing carrying capacity.

Earlier Attempts at Carrying Capacity Assessment (CCA)

The various standards and indicators related to CCA are quite diverse. They may be divided into the following basic groups:

- Standards related to the capacity of the physical environment;
- Standards related to the construction of tourist accommodation establishments and facilities;
- Standards related to the protection against various forms of pollution;
- Infrastructure and transportation standards;
- Standards related to sociocultural, demographic and economic issues.

The difficulty lies in the fact that frequently standards are different or interpreted in different ways on a case-by-case basis. The 1997 review of such standards by the Priority Action Plan/Regional Activity Centre (PAP/RAC) of the UNEP Mediterranean Action Plan revealed that some of the applied parameters differ considerably from one country to another, and in some cases vary by as much as 100 per cent, making most comparisons meaningless. Furthermore, standards related to CCA vary with the location that is being assessed, its physical characteristics, planned characteristics of the 'tourist experience' (degree of satisfaction) to be offered, and so on. Even the minimum required bathing area per user might vary widely within a range from $6m^2$, for intensively used sandy beaches, to $25m^2$ in specific cases.

A Combined Set of Indicators for Assessing Carrying Capacity

According to the approach developed in the SUDECIR programme the carrying capacity for tourism cannot be based on spatial considerations alone, on the available local natural resources, or on technological infrastructure considerations. The calculation of carrying capacity for sustainable tourism also needs to seriously take into account ecological, socio-economic and cultural parameters that are very well understood by all concerned parties, but are rarely quantifiable in a scientifically sound way with reasonable accuracy.

The indicators that may be used are sometimes totally different in nature and in suitability to be quantified, but all of them are important. Within the context of SUDECIR four sets of indicators (spatial, natural, infrastructure and socio-economic/cultural) had been proposed to be used. A selection of these is given in Table 12.1.

Table 12.1 Selection of indicators for carrying capacity assessment clustered in four thematic sets

SPATIAL PARAMETERS	INFRASTRUCTURE AND TECHNOLOGICAL PARAMETERS
Tourists per km²or beds per km²	Length of roads (in km) per passenger and per car
Tourists per surface unit of coast	Percentage of hotels serviced by biological sewage treatment plants. Number of tourists per recreational area
Tourists per metre of coastline front	Existence and capacity of solid waste collection and disposal systems (in tonnes, m³, or person equivalent)
m³ of coastal seawater (depths up to 10m) per bather	Transportation networks/ connections/ average distance and/or time per tourist to reach the destination (this may be transcribed also as fuel per tourist to reach the destination, pressure parameters)
Ratio of built space to green space	Communication networks, telephone lines per user
Ratio of artificial coastline to natural coastline	Number of pleasure boats (yachts, etc.) and so on serviced by marinas per km of coastline

NATURAL RESOURCES PARAMETERS	SOCIO-ECONOMIC AND CULTURAL PARAMETERS
m³ of freshwater per tourist	Percentage contribution of tourism to GDP of the region
Percentage of water consumed by tourism to available (exploitable) natural water reserves of the area	Tourism receipts (in absolute terms)
Energy consumed per capita	Percentage of active working population employed directly or indirectly in the tourism sector
Percentage of energy contributed by local and renewable sources	Average annual employment (days/year) in tourism vs. total employment in all sectors
Percentage of food (in value or tonnage) produced locally to total food consumed	Ratio of tourists to permanent inhabitants in peak periods and throughout the year
Percentage of local wines/spirits, light drinks etc. to the total consumed	Migrant labour (absolute number per year)
Contribution of local building material for construction of buildings and infrastructures	Migrant / local labour
	Average daily expenditure per capita 'in situ' (for tourists)
	Distribution of tourists in expenditure 'classes'
	Distribution of tourists in groups of countries of origin
	Percentage of tourists understanding/using language of the destination
	Length of stay / acquaintance with culture of the destination

Rhodes as a Tourist Destination

A. In order to test the suggested methodology for sustainable tourism development, a case study was conducted on a typical Mediterranean coastal region, the island of Rhodes, located in the south-eastern Aegean Sea, in the Dodecanese. Its development is dominated by tourism (see Table 12.2).

Table 12.2 Tourism statistics on Rhodes island

Overall surface of Rhodes	1,398 sq.km
Population (2001)	117,007 inhabitants
Total tourist arrivals (1999)	1,254,751 tourists
Greek tourist arrivals (1999)	154,555 tourists
Tourists from abroad (1999)	1,100,196 tourists
Nights spent by tourists (1999)	10,811,354 nights
Tourist arrivals by charter flights (1997)	652,000 tourists
Number of hotel beds (2000)	66, 501 beds
Average length of stay (1995 – 1997)	9 – 10 days

Share of tourism in the GDP of the Dodecanese Prefecture was 70.1% vs. the average Greek 56.9% (1997)

62% of all kinds of co-financed investments (private sector and public including EU subsidies) in the Dodecanese were hotels (up to 1997)

83% of all new jobs in the Dodecanese were in the tourism sector (1997)

24% of all Greek hotel-bed capacity occurred in Rhodes (1997)

B. From Table 12.2 it is apparent that tourism and related activities contribute by approximately 70 per cent to the region's GDP. The island is not developed evenly in all its areas. The northern and to a less extent the eastern part of the island are the tourist-developed and rich areas, while the west and south of the island are almost virgin to tourism and therefore substantially poorer.

C. However, in the developed area more negative environmental impacts can be witnessed such as: loss of biodiversity, increase in pollution and forest fire incidents, soil and sealing erosion, rapid degradation by the great number of visitors, increase of noise, decrease and/or degradation of water resources and so forth, unequal distribution of profit in the various parts of the island, inadequate use of incentives, inadequate development plans especially with regard to their supervision, inefficient collaboration between various stakeholders.

The MIO-ECSDE Model of Carrying Capacity

The model of carrying capacity used in the analysis of Rhodes resembles a system of connected reservoirs which was inspired by ideas borrowed from hydraulic and ecotoxicological experiments (see Figure 12.2). As already stated, we recognize that carrying capacity for tourism cannot be based only on spatial considerations, but it should also consider a series of other parameters, which are, however, linked with the spatial ones.

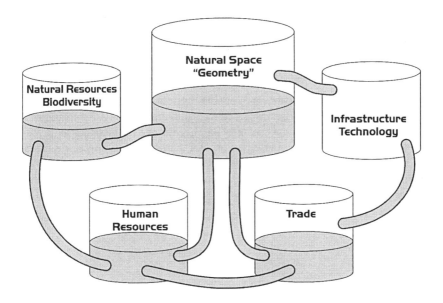

Figure 12.2 The model of carrying capacity used in the analysis of Rhodes

It is assumed that the natural space, geometry and geomorphology could be enlarged, provided that adequate natural resources exist, including a rich biodiversity, and provided that technology and trade are employed in an appropriate way. Finally, if suitable human resources exist for services and ingenuity and creativity, which is a fundamental dynamic component of carrying capacity, a certain limited number of other component-tanks may be added to the system. To better reflect the critical interconnections dominating it the result might be viewed as a system of 'tanks' of various volumes, which represent each one of the parameters (the natural space, the natural resources and so on). The tanks are connected at different depths, so that for each 'resource' to contribute in the overall carrying capacity, a certain 'critical mass' or 'background level' is necessary. It is also important that the sequence of filling the tanks is critical. For example if one starts filling with liquid the 'natural space' reservoir at a given moment very soon the excess liquid added will be directed to the 'natural resources', the 'human resources' and trade tanks but it will take some time for liquid to reach the 'infrastructure' tank. The level of the surface of the natural space tank for some time will remain unaltered and the system appears to be 'absorbing' the added liquid, but in fact it is filling up the connected tanks. After some time the infrastructure technology tank will start to fill through the trade tank. After a certain load of liquid the system reacts as a single reservoir where any new addition is reflected in all and each of the connected tanks. If we block the connection between 'trade' and 'infrastructure' and we start filling the system through the 'infrastructure' tank the distribution of pressures absorbed by the various tanks/components of the system will be different. This signifies that appropriate mixtures of natural, human/socio-cultural and technological characteristics and the history of their involvement could result in different 'carrying capacities'.

In fact the model becomes more realistic and interesting when 'pressure' is exerted on the 'carrying capacity' of the system described. This could be schematically understood by pouring a certain amount of a toxic for example, (for the purposes of demonstration a coloured liquid) into one of the tanks in the centre of the system. After a given time diffusion will distribute the 'poison' in all tanks in an uneven but still largely predictable and visible way (see Figure 12.3). We may also consider in the model the introduction of thorough mixing or even the addition, in cases of emergency, of a limited number of new tanks in order to obtain more efficient dilution by enlarging the overall volume.

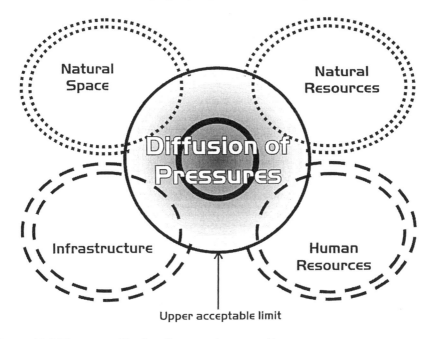

Figure 12.3 Elements affecting the carrying capacity

In order not to exceed the carrying capacity of the system the different groups of 'aquatic organisms' (representing indicators) placed randomly in the various tanks should not exceed at any point a certain level of risk, which might be defined by consensus (for example the 'non-effect' level or the LD_{50}[1] and so on, but in any case the lethal dose for the specific organisms kept in each one of the tanks should not be exceeded).

That means that while the connection of more tanks in the system might enlarge the carrying capacity and the volume (and therefore dilute the toxic substance added and decrease its concentration), at the same time we add a new possibility for vulnerability. The new organisms contained in the newly added tanks might be the most sensitive. The toxic effect might be stronger on them either for short periods, when the initial peak values in part of the system are high, or for longer periods when the effect is connected mainly to the final, homogenized 'sub-lethal' concentrations.

Of course, the model in its present form is qualitative and suitable to demonstrate carrying capacity with the help of hydraulic/chemical and biological-ecotoxicological interactions. In this way, in the phase of its development and by its nature, the model served primarily as an educational tool for decision makers and for demonstration to stakeholders and the public.

---

[1] LD_{50} : *'Lethal Dose', Concentration of a toxic substance that kills 50% of the experiment population of animals in laboratory tests*

In this model sustainable development – and more specifically sustainable tourism – corresponds to 'no effect' concentrations for all organisms present in all and each one of the tanks at any moment of development, including the 'enlargement' and filling processes (the latter correspond to periods of construction of major infrastructures and so on in tourist destinations).

The model indicates that not only the total and 'final' concentrations matter but also the peak concentrations and the length of the peak periods. Relatively high sub-lethal doses might become equally or more ecotoxic (at least for some organisms) than very brief exposures to higher concentrations.

To interpret the model for tourism we need to consider 'tanks' for space, infrastructure and technological parameters, natural resources as well as socio-economic and cultural parameters and indicators.

The parameters which may be used are sometimes totally different in nature and in suitability and difficult to quantify, but all of them are important. Some examples are given in Table 12.1.

The CCA in the Overall Scheme of Sustainable Development Planning of Rhodes and its Connection to Public Involvement

The CCA was introduced as an integral part of the Advanced Regional and Urban Analysis of Rhodes which followed the identification of the key economic sector of the region (tourism). The analysis included understanding the evolution of the activity, relationship of tourism with other sectors such as agriculture, manufacturing industry, handicrafts, characteristics and the results of an audit based on statistics from data gathered by the statistical office, other authorities or locally (from the Chamber of Hoteliers) using questionnaires and interviews and so on. This part of the analysis is indicated in the overall SUDECIR process diagram (see Figure 12.4) as step-box C.

The arrow 3a indicates the flow of data from the audit into this box while the outcome of the analysis becomes the major, more technical input to the Draft Sustainability Plan and it is indicated by arrow 3b.

Although reaching a consensus on the draft Sustainability Plan was obviously the major objective of the public participation component of the whole project the methodology placed emphasis on public involvement in the entire process from the very early steps including; (i) the cultivation, formulation and consolidation of a common vision for the future of the destination and the overall region, (ii) the comparison of the 'vision' with the subjective assessment of the prevailing situation, (iii) the identification and agreement on the root causes of current problems and any eventual deviation from the 'vision', and (iv) the development and adoption of the objectives and criteria of sustainable development and the role of tourism within it. Keep in mind, however, that the process is long and that a step-by-step familiarization with new directives and improvement is more likely than an 'ideal total transformation' of unsustainable practices into sustainable ones.

Therefore the innovative element in the followed approach is the extensive involvement of the public in the entire process from the early stages and with a decisive role. This aspect is crucial for the whole process and is, therefore described and analysed below. A more extensive description of the modes of public participation and partnership, the nature of the groups involved and so on, has been published elsewhere (Scoullos et al., 1999).

Securing Input from Public Participation

The public participation was secured by contacting first the widest possible list of representative relevant stakeholders taking care to explain to them in depth and from the very beginning the purpose of this exercise, its objective, its limitations and the methodology of the process seeking first their interest in it and their active involvement. The stakeholders involved included authorities and bodies active at national, regional and local level are listed in Table 12.3.

Table 12.3 The stakeholders involved in the Rhodes case study

National level: Several agencies and organizations have been contacted

Governmental: Ministry of Development; Greek National Tourism Organization; Ministry of the Environment Physical Planning; Ministry of Agriculture; Ministry of Mercantile Marine; Ministry of Interior; Ministry of National Economy; Ministry of Commerce.

Tourism: Greek Hotels Association; Greek Chamber of Hotels; Yacht Owners Association; a private air-carrier enterprise; two major Greek tour-operators; a major hotel chain; Association of Rooms for Rent (bed & breakfast); Association of Greek Restaurants.

Environmental: Two Greek national environmental associations also active in Rhodes; two consulting firms specialized in the environment and tourism.

Socio-cultural and Academic: a consumer association; two expert researchers; three universities involved in sustainable tourism projects or surveys.

Regional level: Collaboration with the Ministry of the Aegean, and authorities at Prefecture level had been promoted.

Local level: Of the authorities and bodies on the island of Rhodes the following had been contacted; the local private tourist sector (hotels, restaurants, yachts, and so on); local authorities at city and municipal level (Mayors and town councils); communities of towns and villages; the local environmental groups of citizens (NGOs).

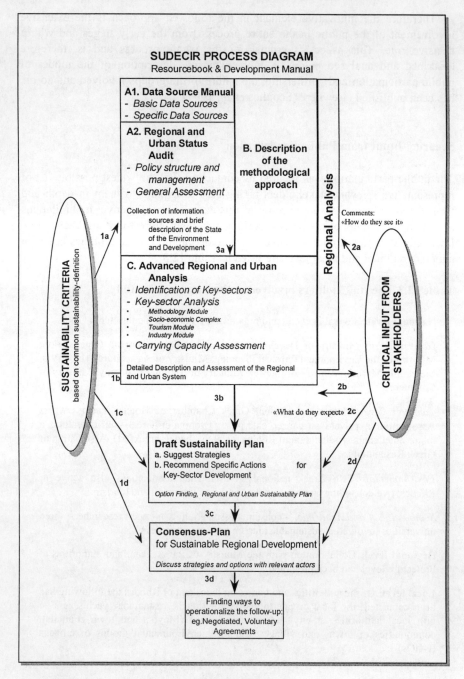

Figure 12.4 The overall scheme of SUDECIR

The involvement of the public included several actions in various forms producing different outputs. It contained a series of preliminary interviews with 'focus groups' followed by an extensive 'survey' based on one-to-one interviews. It also included collection of written comments at various phases of the development of the plan. Two workshops were organized in Rhodes as public debates for the discussion of the criteria, outcomes of the audit and the regional analysis and recommendations.

A Closer Look at the Participation Methodologies

I. Preliminary Interviews – Focus Groups

Preliminary interviews with key figures and discussions with small 'focus groups' of academics, researchers and politicians were held to provide experiences of good and/or bad strategic interventions in tourism development during the past years, as well as useful feedback, that can help in the eligibility of alternative policies and tools for the near future.

Discussions were held in focus groups and with individual residents of Rhodes, the latter chosen arbitrarily on the streets or in public places, thus giving people the chance to express informally, and often critically, their opinions about the current problems of the island, relating them to the governmental decisions, the tourists' behavior and the policies or tools preferred to promote sustainable practices.

II. The Survey

A detailed questionnaire (given in Annex) was carefully drafted and circulated personally to 70 key players in the fields of tourism and the environment in Greece and major stakeholders, at national, regional and local level.

The interviewers, on the basis of the answers given by the various stakeholders, filled in most questionnaires. The 'face to face' interviews allowed for all questionnaires to be fully answered. The response rate was thus excellent. A very small number of questionnaires were filled in by the stakeholders themselves and returned by post, also with an excellent response rate. The reason for the high response may be the very good pre-information about the project and the careful selection of representative stakeholders: decision makers and others with keen interest for the tourism sector. Most of them (40 per cent) had a background in tourism, covering the whole range of sub-sectors. The rest were distributed as follows: 22 per cent economics or business, 12 per cent science, 10 per cent environment, 5 per cent marketing, 3 per cent sociology, 8 per cent various. Most of the people interviewed had a long professional experience (95 per cent more than 10 and 47 per cent more than 20 years).

III. Written Comments

Several stakeholders (authorities), the Chamber of Tourism and Industry submitted written comments at various stages of the process.

The results of *I*, *II* and *III* were grouped and processed in several ways, producing very interesting input about the perception, identification of problems, aspirations ('vision') and suggestions. The aforementioned interviews and the results of the survey and written comments were integral parts of the overall methodological scheme of the SUDECIR Process Diagram, presented in Figure 12.4 and corresponding to 'group 2' of arrows.

IV. Workshops – Public Debate

Two workshops were organized with all key actors and regional stakeholders.

The first workshop (24/1/1998, Rhodes) was dedicated to remind or familiarize all actors with the project and the steps of its methodology. It was also intended to inform them of the set of sustainability criteria, the carrying capacity approach and the qualitative use of the model. The criteria were accepted, in principle, by the participants, as were the first results of the audit and scientific regional analysis and everybody agreed that specific actions had to be initiated in order to reorient tourism towards more sustainable patterns. A step towards building consensus was accomplished.

The second meeting (2/5/1998, Rhodes) with the stakeholders was devoted to the presentation of a more concrete set of recommendations for the Sustainability Plan and of triggering actions, many of which derived from the first workshop. The second meeting accepted the Sustainability Plan and endorsed its recommendations including the key points deriving from the debates on the carrying capacity and for the formulation of a draft sustainability plan.

Brief Account of the Results

The direct outcome of the survey produced a large series of very interesting results. Among them there was a wide consensus (78 per cent) accepting that tourism and the environment could and should secure mutual benefit and a further 10 per cent who agreed at least on the possibility of co-existence (see Figure 12.5).

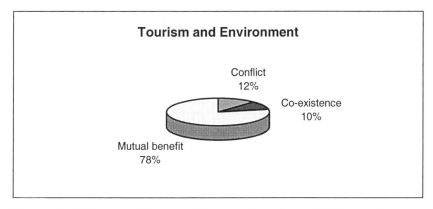

Figure 12.5 The reconciliation and expectation of the relationship between tourism and environmental integrity

A sector of 12 per cent retained its reservations and views tourism as incompatible to any kind of support to the environment. Approaching the needed means and tools to obtain sustainable tourism the people interviewed consider 'long-term planning' and 'education and training' as the most important prerequisites for efficient and proper implementation of measures (see Figure 12.6).

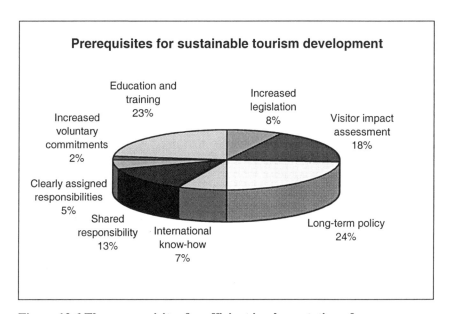

Figure 12.6 The prerequisites for efficient implementation of measures

The carrying capacity assessment introduced as part of the visitors' impact assessment ranks third in order, higher than the 'shared responsibilities', 'increase of legislation', 'international know-how' and so on.

A noteworthy result of the survey is that from all policy instruments proposed 'planning' was by far the preferred option followed by public awareness and participation ahead of technological and economic instruments. Legislation was the least preferred tool indicating people's mistrust in the ability or willingness of the authorities to propose and implement just, sound and efficient legislation (see Figure 12.7).

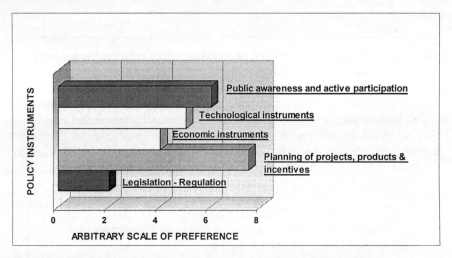

Figure 12.7 Acceptance of policy instruments by main stakeholders

Public discussions provided us with several important inputs. Key points, deriving from the discussions on the formulation of a draft sustainability plan focusing on tourism, are classified into two sets; (A) the agreement on the operation of the dialogue itself for the development of the strategy, (B) guiding principles to be followed for the drafting of the plan:

A. The Operational Protocol: Step-by-Step Analysis for the Development of the Strategy

1. Community groups of stakeholders to be mobilized for consultation and 'Action'.
2. Priority to be given to the decision on the guiding principles for sustainability, based on certain indicators.
3. Establishment of a working process to be followed without change for at least one year.

4.   Setting up of a Steering Committee and Working Groups of the existing stakeholders, open also to dedicated locals and invited experts.
5.   Review and/or proposals for establishment of the basic legal framework with the associated priorities (in parallel to paragraphs 4, 6 and 7).
6.   The implementation phase should go further than 5 based on drafting of 'negotiated', voluntary agreements, in coordination with consultations about new legislation, introduction of ISO 14000 and EMAS in the hotel industry, and so on.
7.   Distribution of responsibilities throughout the process.

Steering Committee and its Administrative framework: this should include the representatives of the main stakeholders.

Terms of reference had not yet been decided, but the main focus was the creation of a partnership that would bring all together by promoting smooth negotiations. The group requested the assistance of MIO-ECSDE as facilitator/coordinator of the group. Funds were going to be raised by national and local authorities.

B. Decisions for the Agreed Guiding Principles of the Sustainability Draft Plan

1.   Rhodes as an island should be considered as tourist 'saturated'.
2.   Although the over-construction of the hotels took place in the northern part, the island should be taken as a whole. Respect for the island's carrying capacity is strongly needed.
3.   A shift from the 'quantitative' to more 'qualitative' criteria must take place.
4.   A wide agreement on the type of tourism–culture relationship, is needed: Tourism should respect the genuine local cultural character of the island, its local natural resources and the island's eco-systems.
5.   No 'monoculture' of tourism is desired.
6.   Creation and promotion of a more sustainable tourism business environment. ISO 9000, ISO 14000 and EMAS should be implemented.
7.   Eco-efficient changes in production and consumption processes related to tourism are needed.
8.   Sustainable employment opportunities for the tourist and rural areas should be increased by promoting alternative and additional traditional jobs.
9.   Part-time or seasonal employment is not a negative situation if it is combined with other profitable local production activities.

The aforementioned principles were agreed upon by the stakeholders after having considered the regional analysis including the CCA, the main results of which are given below.

Results Related to Carrying Capacity Based on the Preliminary Application of our Model

The deliverables of the analysis differentiated the results from those of a previous assessment of carrying capacity carried out in the framework of a Coastal Area Management Programme (CAMP) coordinated by the MAP/UNEP (UNEP/MAP, 1996). A detailed presentation of our results is given in G.H. Vonkeman (ed.) (2000), Scoullos M.J. et al. (1999), Scoullos M.J. et al. (1998), indicating the role of factors other than economic parameters including demographic and cultural.

For instance the previous assessment considered demographic and cultural parameters were not critical as limiting factors 'because the adaptability of the inhabitants to tourists is very high'. This is true only for a major part of the economically active population, particularly in the northern part and not for all groups of people. Similarly the 'acceptance' and tolerance of migrant labour force is a factor changing rapidly, diminishing in the last few years.

The preliminary application of the model to Rhodes suggests that in principle there is an agreement about the (over) 'saturated' zones as well as on those of relatively intensive development, but there is a different understanding of the role of 'hinterland' and its 'capacity'.

According to the CAMP Assessment, the maximum carrying capacity of the central-eastern part of Rhodes during the peak period for the projected year 2010 is 30,000 tourist beds (tourists). This value was considered as below the physical carrying capacity, which in the case of the beach area of the central-eastern zone of Rhodes amounts to 73,400 beach users. The projected value is also smaller than the ecological carrying capacity which was calculated by CAMP at 57,000 visitors, in peak periods.

As a result it is recommended that in the near future a total of 16,000 beds could be added to the already existing 14,000 beds in the central-eastern part of the island. The final suggestion, by CAMP, was based on economic indicators (for example the fall of prices in tourism due to a reduction of the neighbouring northern zone) and the degradation of the environment by, among others, inappropriate new buildings and numerous forest fires which had disastrous effects. The CAMP CCA considered both the northern part of the island as well as a zone around Lindos as 'saturated' and calculated the carrying capacity for the central and eastern part independently of the state of the other two zones. In this respect the assessment in fact neglected the beneficial 'diluting' and 'buffering' effect of the less developed parts of the island in the overall present degree of economic development and state of the environment of the island of Rhodes. In fact the 'empty' 'hinterland' space according to our approach effectively increases the carrying capacity of the presently 'saturated' northern section allowing for more acceptable higher tourist satisfaction and socio-cultural resilience of the local population. It represents in our model the part of the tanks, for example part of the 'natural space' and part of the 'natural resources-biodiversity', which have not yet been 'polluted' by diffusion.

According to the point of view we have developed within the SUDECIR approach, we have suggested that the island (the region in this case) should be considered as a whole and therefore it is likely that we are already near saturation level, if all other parameters are taken into account. For instance, applying the same indicators as CAMP for the beach areas of the northern and the central-eastern zones taken together the calculated physical carrying capacity to the order of $15-18 \times 10^4$ beach users. However applying other preliminary indicators, for example beach users per coastline front, the above mentioned corresponds to nearly 3 persons per meter of front all along the coast considered! There are not enough references for valid comparisons from other regions and the use of several of the indicators suggested may result in figures with one or even two orders of magnitude difference. Considering that the present over-saturated tourist and urban areas already 'consume' space of the hinterland, roads and so on, it was concluded that the carrying capacity of the island is 18×10^4 out of which 10×10^4 is the resident population at any time: if the current bed capacity is 7.5×10^4 there is a margin of approximately 0.5×10^4 for additional beds. This corresponds to a small increase of 5 to 10 per cent in tourism which may be allowed for the next 10 years. However, this may take place not necessarily only in the central and eastern part (where concentrations are low) and it should be combined with improvements of eco-efficiency and restructuring of tourist service to a more qualitative (not necessarily more expensive) product.

Another basic difference between previous CCA suggestions and the present one is the distribution of tourist load over time. The 'panacea' suggested by nearly all similar studies, expansion of the tourism season, is not in fact supported by the approach described. In fact this corresponds to MIO-ECSDE's model to a longer exposure to 'sub-lethal' low concentrations which, however, are always above the no-effect levels.

There is, indeed, a small margin for increase of tourist load during the rest of the year which could keep some permanent residents employed in the tourism sector and increase specialization and professionalism. However this should not altogether destroy other activities and sectors which 'resist' the tourism 'monoculture'. Moreover the relatively long 'quiet' (tourist-free) intervals are absolutely necessary for local natural and socio-cultural systems and mechanisms 'to recover' in a smooth, natural way.

Maintenance of extremely low concentrations of pollutants and absence of pressures on biotopes for certain months is very critical for the survival of certain ecosystems. The same is true for the society which needs to satisfy some of the socio-cultural sustainability indicators at least for a reasonable part of the year. These goals cannot be obtained if the tourism period is expanded, even if the annual tourist load is kept approximately at the same levels. For instance the early cleaning-up of a site (road, archaeological site, coast) from vegetation in order to receive even a few tourists, or even simply walking on it in early spring, may decrease its biodiversity by destroying plants before they produce seeds necessary for their reproduction. This is a direct and severe degradation which could be avoided if the same activities took place a few weeks later. Moreover the expansion of the tourist period will inevitably increase the number of tourists visiting the island but not necessarily in a proportional way the income, while consuming the same or more natural and human resources.

Culturally this is even more obvious. Islanders during the 'low season' of autumn, winter and spring, devote much more time to traditional occupations, farming, construction, handicrafts and, naturally to their children and family in general. This is fundamental for the well-being and structure of the local society.

An additional element supporting the view for the need of 'intervals' was provided by the case of water. The previous CAMP study (UNEP/MAP, 1996) considered water as a limiting factor for the carrying capacity of the island and also identified pressures among which were certain cases of salinization of ground water. From the results of original measurements and analyses we have conducted at the Chemistry Department of the University of Athens we have confirmed the intrusion of saline water during the summer months. What was an interesting surprise, however, was the reversibility of the phenomenon after the autumn-winter rains. This was possible only because of the existence of a relatively long 'recovery' period.

Finally the 'consensus' point which is so important for the decision of the 'development' level in our case was quite different than that described by previous CCAs. In fact the vast majority of stakeholders including all hoteliers' organizations and the National Tourism Organization agreed that the present level corresponds to saturation for the entire island, while the pressure for expanding tourism, deriving perhaps from some local interests, was neutralized and not recorded as a major tendency or decisive factor.

In conclusion, the CCA in the case of the island of Rhodes indicated that the final outcome could be affected considerably by the involvement of the various stakeholders and the public at large.

The nature of CCA requires technical and scientific background and skills for the identification of the most relevant indicators and limiting factors. However, even for the ranking of indicators and the definition of acceptable levels and thresholds the local public opinion is of utmost importance. Through a well organized programmed and transparent public participation scheme established from the very beginning of the process many misunderstandings could be avoided, common public vision could be formulated about the desired and unwanted characteristics of future tourism development and impacts of small but powerful lobbies of particular local interest could be neutralized. Experience has shown, however, that even the best designed processes where consensus has been established cannot deliver automatically by themselves if the necessary funds and provisions are not secured from the authorities for the implementation phase.

References

Daily, G.C., Ehrlich, P.R., Mooney, H.A., Ehrlich A.H. (1991), 'Greenhouse Economics: Learn Before you Leap', *Ecol. Econ.* Vol.4, pp. 1-10.

Hannon, B. (1975), 'Energy Conservation and the Consumer', *Science*, 189, pp. 95-102.

Hardin, G. (1986), 'Cultural Carrying Capacity: A Biological Approach to Human Problems, *BioScience* Vol. 36, pp. 599-600.

Kontostanou-Karalivanou, O., Maxson, P.A., Sauerborn, K., Scoullos, M., Tischer, M., Vonkeman, G.H., Wallner, H.P. (2000), 'Sustainable Development of European Cities and Regions (SUDECIR)', edited by Vonkeman, G.H., Kluwer Academic Publishers, p. 300.

MAP/UNEP (1996), *The Island of Rhodes – Integrated Planning Study for the Island of Rhodes, Final Report*, MAP Coastal Area Management Program, CAMP, Activity No 13, UNEP/METAP.

PAP/RAC (1997), *Guidelines for Carrying Capacity Assessment for Tourism in Mediterranean Coastal Areas*, PAP-9/1997/G.1, Priority Actions Programme Regional Centre, Split.

Roughgarden, J. (1979), *Theory of Population Genetics and Evolutionary Ecology: An Introduction*, Macmillan, New York.

Scoullos, M., Kontostanou, O., Andronikidou, D. (1998), 'Public Awareness and Participation on Sustainable Tourism Development in Rhodes Island-Greece', *International Conference on Communication, Public Participation and Education*, Rhodes.

Scoullos, M., Kontostanou-Karalivanou, O., Andronikidou, D., Constantianos, V. (1999), *Planning Sustainable Regional Development. Principles, Tools and Practices. The Case Study of Rhodes Island-Greece*, MIO-ECSDE Publication, Athens, p. 64.

ANNEX
SURVEY QUESTIONNAIRE
General Information about the Interviewed Person

In which specific field are you specialized?
- Tourism
- Economics
- Marketing
- Natural sciences
- Environment
- Sociology
- Other

How many years have you in this field?
- 1-10 years
- 10-20 years
- More

Age:
- 20-30
- 30-40
- 40-50
- 50-60
- More

Please use the following ranking for your answers:
I fully agree
I agree
Neutral
I disagree
I completely disagree

Questions on Tourism/General

(In this part of the questionnaire you will be requested to state your opinion on general themes concerning tourism)
Ranking: 1 2 3 4 5

1. According to your opinion tourism contributes to the:
   - Development and aesthetic improvement of a region
   - Destruction of a region
   - Creation and solving of problems in regions
   - Other...
2. Which is (are) the main goal(s) of tourism (primarily):
   - Increase of monetary exchange to the benefit of the region
   - Upgrading of standards of services
   - Higher category of tourists
   - Decrease of the number of incomers
   - None of the aforementioned
   - Other...
3. In your opinion, which are the main beneficial consequences of tourism economy-wise:
   - Creation of employment opportunities (jobs)
   - Contribution to the GDP and the balance of payment
   - Improvement of infrastructure

- Diversification and development of the local societies, especially in remote areas
- Other (s)...

4. In your opinion, which are the most negative consequences of tourism economy-wise:
    - Creation of unbalanced economical situation
    - Change of the traditional pattern of land-use, leading to uncontrolled consequences concerned with economical planning
    - Creation of inflation stress
    - Increase of land cost
    - Few benefits for the local society

5. In your opinion, which are the main beneficial consequences of tourism, socially-wise:
    - Reinforces exchanges of social character between various groups of people
    - It can serve to increase mutual understanding on the international level
    - Contributes to international peace
    - Increases peoples'(of countries) knowledge and experiences of one another
    - Other(s)...

6. In your opinion, which are the most negative consequences of tourism socially-wise:
    - Creates tension and conflict amongst the main parties involved
    - Causes a high burden on sites and sights, due to the number of visitors
    - Creates problems to the social coherence, due to the interference with tourists
    - Leads to involuntary movement of local residents
    - Contributes to the increase of criminality
    - Contributes to the change of morals and traditions, non-beneficially
    - Other(s)...

7. In your opinion, which are the main beneficial consequences of tourism, environmentally-wise:
    - Helps preserve the natural environment, through special programmes of preservation and rehabilitation
    - Provides financing incentives for the private sector, for environmentally-friendly actions and special measures
    - By the interchange of international experience, it promotes opportunities for the creation of protected areas and the exchange of know-how for their management
    - Healthy competition among countries that are touristic, eventually leads to the proper estimation of natural (and at the same time touristic) resources' degradation hazards
    - Contributes to the increase of tourists' and local residents' awareness on hazards concerning environmental degradation and loss of species

- Other(s)...

8. In your opinion, which are the most negative consequences of tourism, environmentally-wise?
   - Leads to permanent loss of natural open spaces
   - Leads to environmental pollution (air, water, soil, aesthetic pollution, noise pollution)
   - Creates traffic problems
   - Increases waste loads
   - Leads to the overexploitation of natural resources
   - Disturbs natural ecosystems and contributes to the loss of species
   - Destroys the aesthetic of landscapes
   - Contributes to urban anarchy
   - Other(s)...

9. In your opinion, which are the main beneficial consequences of tourism concerning the cultural heritage:
   - Contributes to the revitalization of local culture, to the revival of traditional customs and arts
   - Motivates local cultural pride
   - Preserves historical and cultural sites and sustains the awareness about them
   - Contributes to the European and, in general, international integration
   - Promotes inter-cultural exchange of habitudes and understanding between peoples of various countries
   - Other(s)...

10. In your opinion, which are the most negative consequences of tourism concerning the cultural heritage:
    - Destroys peoples' cultural heritage
    - Leads to the loss of national identity
    - Disorients local societies regarding traditional morals and customs
    - Other(s)...

11. Do you think that the relationship between tourism and environment is based on:
    - Conflict   yes   no
    - Co-existence   yes   no
    - Mutual benefit   yes   no
    - Other...

12. In your opinion, which are the most rational ways to promote/reinforce long-term policies for the development of tourism, taking into consideration the protection of the environment:
    - New legislative framework
    - Consensus of all involved parties
    - Creation of a consultative body comprising of representatives of all the involved parties

- Long-term policy planning, based on goals of sustainable development of the tourism sector, as they are formulated in the 5th Framework Action Programme of the European Union
- Exchange of experiences and know-how by countries who have successfully confronted relevant problems
- Configuration of new terms in the credit system, with special provision of benefits to healthy enterprises, e.g. possibility of their entrance on the Stock Market and their financing, large-scale privatizations, bank loans from specific 'green accounts' of banks, which promote and subsidize private programmes or projects aiming at environmental protection, environmental management, sustainable development, etc.
- Clarify completely the role of each participant, with key-roles
- Special measures such as:
  Management of tourist flow
  Large-scale voluntary agreements of the private sector on issues related to environmentally-friendly management
  Educational and awareness initiatives, focusing on local residents, tourists and employees of the tourism sector, informing on the environment, the preservation of biodiversity and sustainable development
  Increase of use and application of new technologies, of know-how on environmental issues, of specific management achievements in the tourism sector and dissemination of knowledge concerning direct and indirect consequences of tourism in the various destinations
- Other(s)...

13. If you were to choose between 'unconditional' development of the tourism sector and environment, what would you choose:
    - Tourism
    - Environment
14. Which aspects do you consider negative in the tourist destination under consideration:
    - Infrastructure
    - Tourists
    - Policy
    - Environment
    - Other...
15. Which of the following would take TOP priority:
    - Infrastructure
    - Tourists
    - Policy
    - Environment
    - Other...
16. How do you apprehend the term 'Sustainable Development of Tourism':
    ....
    ....

The Development of Tourism in Rhodes

(In this part of the questionnaire you are asked for your opinion on the development of tourism in Rhodes and the specific problems of the region. Rationality in managing the future tourist flux has direct impact on the island's economy, biodiversity, and sustainable development.)

Please express your opinion freely, ranking your answers according to:
1 = I fully agree
2 = I agree
3 = neutral
4 = I disagree
5 = I entirely disagree

1. According to your opinion which are the main negative aspects characterizing Rhodes's present tourism development:
   - Lack of basic infrastructure
   - Urban anarchy
   - Over-burden of tourists, geographically and during peak period
   - Environmental pollution
   - Destruction of ecosystems
   - Depletion of non-renewable energy resources
   - Low category of tourists
   - Negative image in the international tourism market
   - Unsatisfactory urban planning / lack of open space
   - Noise pollution or aesthetic pollution
   - Low quality of the provided services
   - Lack of efficient marketing and of advertising means
   - Lack of experienced personnel
   - Non-competitive enterprises regarding international standards
   - Other(s) ...
2. In your opinion, which are the main positive aspects of Rhodes, which should be further promoted by a strategy of long-term planning:
   - Uniqueness of landscapes
   - Revitalization of customs
   - Rare ecosystems (Butterflies' Valley)
   - Potential of development of special types of tourism (health, eco-, agro-tourism, yachting etc.)
   - Cultural heritage, architectural monuments
   - Touristic enterprises, which implement total quality systems in their management or systems of environmental control
3. Who do you think is most competent to set a long-term policy for tourism which, along with the sustainable development of all the economical potentials, will aim at solving the region's problems and to redetermine Rhodes's status in the international market?

- The Government
- Local Authorities
- Non-Governmental Organizations
- The private sector
- The scientific community, the experts
- The tourists
- All together
- Other…

4. Which do you consider the most helpful tools for the establishment of an efficient framework for sustainable development in Rhodes?
   - Long-term planning
   - Participation of all involved parties in the formulation of the basic points of the strategic planning
   - Consensus
   - Paying special attention to the protection of the environment, by promoting Environmental Impact Assessments for all works and Environmental Management Systems in all tourists' habitations (EMAS, ISO 14001, BS7750)
   - Dissemination of know-how on recycling, on materials' re-use, on the use of environmentally friendly materials
   - Awareness on the rational use of non-renewable energy resources
   - Programmes which aim to inform and promote practical aspects of using solar or wind energy
   - Use of environmental measurements in order to set policies
   - Education of all personnel employed in the sector on environmental issues
   - Collaboration with EU countries experienced in appropriate environmental management
   - Constant rewarding of pioneer initiatives concerning tourism and the environment
   - New types of space and urban planning, taking into consideration:
   - Changes in patterns of land-use
   - Zoning
   - Cost-benefit analysis, in cases of conflicts in land-use
   - More free space and expansion of pedestrian zones
   - Creation of parks
   - Systems of tourists' influx management, together with exclusion of cars from the city centre, promotion of public transportation means, creation of parkings, street signs etc.
   - Reformation and updating of Development Law(s) by introducing new criteria for financing enterprises
   - Increase of financing possibilities for tourism business, by their introduction to the Stock Market
   - Promotion of Total Quality Management in all tourism businesses, as well as in services

- Broad information campaigns aiming to increase the awareness of involved parties on the efforts made to accomplish the newly set goals
- New modern and dynamic marketing and communication campaigns (green marketing)
- Reformation of the public sector, promote employment of experts to ensure qualified staff, further education of employees for new practices on the tourism sector, exchange of know-how between countries, promote trans-national programmes concerning tourism and new trends, operation of the public sector under realistic private-economic criteria
- Promotion of new technologies and scientific applications in tourism (multimedia, cd-rom, GIS etc.)
- Other(s)…

Chapter 13

Managing the Impacts of Tourism in European Destinations: Using Carrying Capacity

Alexandra Mexa and Anna Collovini

Introduction

In this chapter the main characteristics of tourism development (for example economic aspects of tourism development, impacts due to tourism development, main types of tourist destinations) as appearing in European countries (mainly members of the European Union) are discussed.

Furthermore the application of tourism carrying capacity assessment (TCCA) in European tourist destinations on the basis of theory and case studies review (the main sources of information included review of published material – papers in journals, books, other reports – and internet survey) is presented. It is quite probable that there may be more cases where TCCA has been utilized, which are however not published or available through the aforementioned sources, indicating the need to promote dissemination of information so as to facilitate exchange of experience.

Current presentation includes a few case studies where the approach of TCCA is *explicitly* utilized but also a selected number of case studies where the concept of tourism carrying capacity assessment is *implicitly* applied, suggesting that the various approaches adopted (such as policy measures to control visitor flows and zoning) reflect the basic concept of tourism carrying capacity: the need to impose some kind of limits on the number of visitors, the various uses, etc. In this latter case the majority of the case studies presented concern areas of significant ecological value, indicating not only that the need to manage tourism flows in these cases is essential but perhaps more attainable due to existing institutional provisions and respective status for protection.

Evidence from literature and practice indicates that managers as well as decision-makers are still reluctant to apply more integrated approaches for managing tourism growth and related impacts, or are simply not aware of the necessity and the opportunities arising from the adoption of such approaches.

The analysis of the lessons learnt from the implementation of both TCCA and of other management approaches is particularly difficult since to a certain extent it requires the consideration of local and national particularities in respect to institutional aspects, planning procedures, cultural issues, decision-making process, etc. Furthermore in each case study/project the outcome is often shaped by several 'internal' factors (for example composition of the study team, time or budget constraints). As the case studies examined in this chapter are spread among various European countries, furthermore information was not always available (in several cases information existed only for the phase of the design of the various activities and not so much for their implementation, rendering assessment almost impossible), the consideration of all aforementioned factors was not possible within the time limits of the study *Defining, Measuring and Evaluating Carrying Capacity in European Tourism Destinations* (EC, 2002a), of which some findings are presented here. Therefore the discussion consists of a first approach in assessing the implementation of TCCA in European destinations.

Tourism Development in the Countries of the European Union

Key Characteristics

Tourism and recreation has become one of the world's leading economic activities. In many regions it represents the single largest source of investment and employment. In the European Union it is recognized as one of the strongest economic sectors. For years European countries have been the primary destinations for tourists, receiving almost 60 per cent of all international arrivals and earning almost half of the world's tourism receipts. France, Spain, Italy, United Kingdom and Austria are placed among the ten most popular world tourism destinations (WTO, 2002) – see Table 13.1.

Europe, rich in natural and cultural resources, possesses a leading place in the world tourism market, despite the emergence of new destinations. Its diversity from an environmental but also sociocultural point of view, presents a major asset; each European country, not to say each region, independently of size, exhibits its own unique characteristics. This coupled with the relatively high level of technical and tourist infrastructure and the long tradition in services provision renders Europe a rather popular destination.

Tourism activities in all Member States involve around 2 million businesses (mostly small and medium-sized enterprises), which generated in 1998 up to 12 per cent of GDP (directly or indirectly), 6 per cent of employment (directly) and 30 per cent of external trade. All these figures are expected to increase as tourism demand and capital investments are expected to grow (EEA, 2001).

In 2001, tourism in EU countries generated US$ 931.93 billion of GDP (directly and indirectly), with the share in the total ranging from 7.58 per cent in Sweden to 18.96 per cent in Spain. It is also a strong employment generator with a total of 21.17 million jobs (direct and indirect employment) with the share in total employment ranging from 7.27 per cent in Sweden to 20.72 per cent in Spain

(WTTC, 2003). However, there are significant regional differences in European countries in respect to tourism development. Mallorca for example is one of the well-known tourist resorts where the prosperity of local society is attributed to tourism development, which contributes 70 per cent to GDP (EEA, 2001).

Prospects for tourism development are promising. Household expenditure on recreational, entertainment, educational, and cultural services, including tourism, increased in Europe by 16 per cent between 1990 and 1997. As leisure time grows and relative holiday costs fall, tourism is taking a larger share of household expenditure. This share is expected to grow as the EU's retired population both grows in number and, thanks to medical advances, remains healthy and active (ibid 2001).

Tourism is not only growing in terms of numbers. It has slowly transformed into a diversified and complex economic activity. Although mass coastal tourism remains the predominant type of tourism, other types of tourism related to culture, nature, business, education, health, religion, etc. have emerged. Demand will become increasingly specialized (German Federal Agency for Nature Conservation, 1997).

Table 13.1 The world's top 15 tourist destinations

Rank	Country	International Tourist Arrivals (millions)		Market share (%)
		2000	2001[*]	2001[*]
1	France	75.6	76.5	11.0
2	Spain	47.9	49.5	7.1
3	United States	50.9	45.5	6.6
4	Italy	41.2	39.0	5.6
5	China	31.2	33.2	4.8
6	United Kingdom	25.2	23.4	3.4
7	Russian Federation	21.2	-	-
8	Mexico	20.6	19.8	2.9
9	Canada	19.7	19.7	2.8
10	Austria	18.0	18.2	2.6
11	Germany	19.0	17.9	2.6
12	Hungary	15.6	15.3	2.2
13	Poland	17.4	15.0	2.2
14	Hong Kong (China)	13.1	13.7	2.0
15	Greece	13.1	-	-

*Data as collected by WTO in June 2002

Source: World Tourism Organization (WTO)

Some of these new forms of tourism reflect among others preferences for environmental quality and a more active and adventurous form of recreation. Skiing, hiking, cycling, climbing, canoeing, etc. are attracting more 'fans' than ever, satisfying the need to be close to nature, exercise, explore and learn. These new activities are also responsible for environmental degradation since they are often dispersed in areas with no proper infrastructure development or capacity to handle tourism. Furthermore higher environmental awareness on the part of tourists, besides its positive impacts, may also impose threat on relatively untouched nature areas, which are becoming popular destinations.

Types of Tourist Destination

The vast majority of European tourists (91 per cent) choose to visit a location in Europe (EEA, 2001). The majority of European holiday makers (63 per cent) choose the sea as the first destination, while 25 per cent prefer the cities and 23 per cent the countryside. Furthermore the high peak of tourism is concentrated in the summer season, while a lower peak is recorded in the winter months, mainly for winter sports (EC, 1998). The above suggests that to a great extent the internal market supports tourism development in Europe. Furthermore it indicates that 'traditional' types of holidays, related to sun, sea and sand, are still dominant. Due to this, tourism development in certain European countries remains to a great extent seasonal in character.

Within this context it is possible to identify the following types of tourist destinations, also examined in this paper:

Coastal areas: They are considered as the most valuable parts of many countries' territories, from both an ecological and socioeconomic perspective. Recently the significance of these areas and the need to promote their integrated management at European level has been acknowledged (EC, 1999; EC, 2000).

Coastal zones occupy less than 15 per cent of the earth's land surface, yet they accommodate more than 60 per cent of world population. In EU about one-third of the population is concentrated near coastal areas (EEA, 1999). Many human activities are developed along the coastline as well (agriculture, fishing and aquaculture, mining, trade, etc.), with tourism and recreation appearing quite often as the dominant ones. Activities compete with each other for land and other limited coastal resources, resulting in conflicts and over-exploitation of coastal resources.

The Mediterranean countries are major destinations. Tourism in the Mediterranean region accounts for 30 per cent of international arrivals and 25 per cent of receipts from international tourism. The number of tourists in Mediterranean countries is expected to increase from 260 million in 1990 (with 135 million in the coastal regions) to 440 to 655 million in 2025 (with 235 to 355 in the coastal regions) (EEA, 2001). EU Mediterranean countries (France, Spain, Italy and Greece) remain by far the main destinations for international tourism.

Table 13.2 Contribution of tourism to economic development

Countries	Contribution of Tourism to GDP (direct impact only)				Employment (direct employment only)			
	2001		2013 (foreseen)		2001		2013 (foreseen)	
	EUR Bn.	% of total GDP	EUR Bn.	% of total GDP	Jobs (000's)	% of total employment	Jobs (000's)	% of total employment
Austria	11.08	5.27	17.86	4.94	245.49	6.03	277.75	6.36
Belgium	9.17	3.57	15.36	3.64	157.45	3.92	168.57	4.09
Denmark DKK Bn	42.75	3.18	66.24	2.95	68.47	3.08	66.80	2.90
Finland	4.94	3.63	9.00	3.62	86.89	3.67	99.25	3.86
France	71.90	4.91	121.73	5.06	1,369.22	5.67	1,555.74	6.09
Germany	63.58	3.07	89.93	3.09	1,265.79	3.25	1,199.17	3.09
Greece	6.56	5.04	13.22	5.08	227.37	5.62	253.08	5.80
Iceland ISK Bn	50.01	6.64	101.16	7.13	10.64	6.82	12.56	7.42
Ireland	2.60	2.25	5.65	2.11	38.28	2.20	50.95	2.21
Italy	60.22	4.95	104.06	4.93	1,102.70	5.12	1,175.51	5.34
Luxembourg	0.66	3.89	1.35	4.22	8.09	4.38	10.59	4.97
Netherlands	14.38	3.38	24.21	3.38	257.28	3.42	259.13	3.40
Norway NOK Bn	39.01	2.58	68.96	2.71	74.65	3.28	80.07	3.11
Portugal	7.69	6.25	14.11	6.56	335.96	6.85	372.98	7.39
Spain	48.97	7.51	94.05	8.02	1,333.12	8.36	1,697.33	9.22
Sweden SEK Bn	56.72	2.62	95.86	2.98	99.29	2.34	112.83	2.50
UK GBP Bn	40.13	4.06	65.93	3.79	1,090.18	3.70	1,056.42	3.35
EU US$ Bn	**338.68**	**4.29**	**660.57**	**4.37**	**7,685.60**	**4.65**	**8,356.10**	**4.81**
World US$ Bn	**1,201.29**	**3.81**	**2,279.20**	**3.82**	**69,212.00**	**2.76**	**83,893.60**	**2.85**

Source: World Travel and Tourism Council, 2003

They attract the majority of tourists visiting the region benefiting with almost 80 per cent of the total tourism income generated in the Mediterranean region. Tourism development is often concentrated in the already densely populated coast:

> ... in the northern Mediterranean tourism development is regarded to be amongst the most extensive and intensive in the world. It is estimated that by the year 2050, 95 per cent of that coastline will be urbanized. The Mediterranean basin may have to support more than 500 million inhabitants and 200 million tourists with 150 million cars (Williams, 1992).

In Greece for example, the country with the most extended coastline among all other Mediterranean countries, almost 90 per cent of tourism and leisure activities are located along the coast both of the mainland and the islands, leading to an increased urbanization of the coast (Coccossis and Mexa, 2002a; Coccossis and Mexa, 1997).

This concentration is leading to major conflicts. The Mediterranean countries, characterized by high biodiversity, have the greatest potential conflict in comparison to the countries of Northern Europe and Western Europe (with a relatively low and medium conflict potential respectively, with the exception of the Great Britain and Netherlands which have a high potential) (German Federal Agency for Nature Conservation, 1997). In southern and western Europe mass tourism on urbanized coasts with high-rise buildings is a common type of development.

In the future increased pressure is expected to be exerted in the marine part of the coastal areas due to a significant growth in cruises (ibid).

Islands: They constitute important tourist destinations. Small islands present a particular case of interest due to their limited resources and the fragile relationship between economy, society and the environment (Coccossis, 1998). Small islands are particularly susceptible to the negative impacts of intensive tourism development. Although there are great differences in terms of characteristics and context of development, there are certain common issues and problems to be considered related to the relationships between economic growth, social coherence and viability and environmental management, in terms of dependence, self-sufficiency, isolation, diversity, risks and fragility. In particular the limited natural and human resources impede the development of several activities (Coccossis and Mexa, 2002b).

During the past decades several islands revealed signs of abandonment leading to economic recession and population decline. Recently, tourism development served as a means for regional development, providing opportunities for employment and local income. The rich cultural heritage, the natural and built environment of unique value, their geographical particularity (insularity), attract a significant number of tourists every year. However inefficiency of planning, along with weak implementation has resulted in a rather unorganized type of tourism development, in several cases altering irreversible, local identity (ibid).

Mountain resorts: In several European countries tourism has been promoted as an ideal means to combat economic decline and reverse the loss of population in mountain areas. In several cases tourism has succeeded in becoming either the only or the primary economic activity, often resulting in economic monoculture. In such cases, tourism has contributed to the development of a strong, dynamic but also vulnerable local economy while it has generated pressures on the environment.

The majority of tourism and recreation in European mountain areas is concentrated in the Alps, which have the second highest tourism intensity in Europe, with 59.8 million arrivals and a total of 370 million bed nights per year. The total added value deriving from visitors in commercial accommodation in the Alpine region is about 24 billion EUR per year (EEA, 2001). The characteristics of tourism development in the mountains vary considerably. In the case of the Alps, only 10 per cent of all alpine communities host large tourist infrastructures while some 40 per cent do not host tourism at all (EEA, 1999). This type of concentration raises many issues in respect to socioeconomic equity but also in respect to the opportunities for environmental conservation. Countries traditionally hosting summer tourism activities are recently facing increased demand for winter tourism and specifically mountain tourism (for example Greece). In the former case, the number of visitors during the summer has stayed roughly constant over the last twenty years, while winter visitors have increased considerably (EEA, 1995). In the latter, increased demand has led to the development of infrastructure. Efforts are being concentrated on the development of a tourism that will be adjusted to local particularities (scale of infrastructure, etc.) and will be integrated into local economy.

Tourism in these areas encompasses a variety of activities such as nature and adventure tourism (hiking, trekking, rock and mountain climbing, etc.), winter sports (skiing) but also summer holidays. Trends indicate a stabilization of downhill skiing and an increase in activities such as hiking, cross-country skiing and snowmobiling (Fredman and Heberlein, 2003). This may have environmental implications as downhill skiing is concentrated in certain areas contrary to other activities, rendering the management of environmental impacts more difficult, while increasing the possibilities of user conflicts (ibid).

Mountain adventure tourism, 'accused' for encouraging the transformation of mountains into commodities, is expected to increase further (Beedie and Hudson, 2003).

Heritage sites and cities: History, culture and religion constitute significant elements of tourism. A visit to famous historic centres, temples and places of a unique cultural value is a desire for millions of people. Many of these major tourist attractions of Europe are often located in proximity to large urban centres or are part of them. Heritage cities host a large proportion of the world's tourists; many argue that the heritage tourism segment offers even better growth than any other (Borg et al., 1996).

Protected areas: By April 2002 2,827 sites, covering 222,480 km^2, had been designated as special protection areas under the birds directive, while 14,901 sites, covering 436,456 km^2, had been proposed as sites of community interest under the habitat directive, in all up to 16 per cent of the territory of the European Union. In addition to the national and European designations, the member countries have also designated sites under other international and regional conventions and programmes (Ramsar convention, World Heritage sites, etc.) (EEA, 2003). Protected areas constitute important tourist destinations. The number of visitors to environmentally sensitive areas is increasing, due to a growing interest in nature all over Europe. Activities (for example bird watching) related to scientific and educational purposes along with other recreational activities are often developed in protected areas, like wetlands. According to 1994 statistical data 40 to 60 per cent of tourists, at the international level, had nature as their final destination, accounting for 211 to 317 million, out of which 106 to 211 million are tourists who have wild nature as their destination (Ministry for Development and Greek National Tourism Organization, 2000). Domestic tourists are not included in the above figures, indicating that the actual number of tourists visiting natural areas is even higher. WTO notes that tourism, which has nature as a destination, corresponds to 7 per cent of the international tourism expenditures. Tourist agencies report that the demand for tourism in nature increases every year by 10-25 per cent (ibid). However, national parks and protected areas are inherently vulnerable to environmental degradation and the development of any recreational activity requires careful environmental management.

Rural areas: Rural areas are popular tourist destinations throughout Europe. Rural tourism, which is one of the emerging and expanding forms of tourism in Europe, contributes to the diversification, enrichment and strengthening of rural economy, which faces severe problems due to the declining role of agriculture. Rural tourism contains a great range of activities provided on the basis of natural, social and cultural elements. In principle, this type of tourism is integrated into the local community and the local environment since it is being developed in a complementary way to the other economic activities in the area. Furthermore, it utilizes local resources, promotes the consumption of local products and last but not least encourages the participation of tourists in local (traditional) activities (for example open-air activities, local cuisine, etc.).

More and more countries are marketing nature as an additional attraction. Spain for example is enriching its tourist product by developing tourism in localities of natural beauty and rural areas (German Federal Agency for Nature Conservation, 1997).

The richness and diversity of environments and landscapes make Europe widely attractive for tourism activity. However tourism is concentrated mainly in specific areas, primarily coastal regions and islands, the alpine region and urban centres. In most cases the increasing concentration of tourists, in time and space, is the main cause of problems. The study of impacts from tourism development requires a careful consideration of local particularities. Nevertheless it is possible to identify common impacts in most tourist resorts and organize them in three distinct groups: physical-ecological impacts, sociocultural impacts and economic-political impacts, which are briefly described below. Furthermore some of the major impacts (both ecological and socioeconomic) are presented in the following section for each type of tourist destination identified previously.

The description should not be regarded as exhaustive since several other problems may arise as a result of the specific conditions of both the locality and the type of tourism development (for example mass tourism vis à vis selective types of tourism development, seasonality, concentration of excursionists and tourists in time and space, average length of stay, kind of activities exercised by tourists, socioeconomic characteristics and behaviour of tourists, degree of use of tourist infrastructure).

Physical-Ecological Impacts

This group involves impacts on the environment, like pollution phenomena, loss of biodiversity and impacts on the ecological equilibrium, loss of landscape as well as impacts related to facilities, accommodation and infrastructure, like traffic and congestion problems and overburdened infrastructure system.

Tourism is responsible for a large share of the air and road traffic and consumption of energy. In France for example, 5-7 per cent of greenhouse gas emissions are due to tourism, mainly because 80 per cent of domestic tourist travel is by private car (EEA, 2001). Increased consumption of fossil fuels (for travelling, heating, air-conditioning, etc.) contributes to increased emissions of greenhouse gases and acidifying substances, the former responsible for the problem of global climate change and the latter for acid rain.

Furthermore tourism is a large consumer of natural resources, and a producer of a significant load of waste, often exceeding the capacity of the ecosystems. Tourists consume not only energy but also several other local, non-renewable resources like water. The construction of hotels, swimming pools, golf courses, etc., exerts significant pressure on water resources, particularly in regions such as the Mediterranean where resources are scarce. Tourists typically consume around 300 litres of water and generate 180 litres of wastewater per day while in most cases tourists consume more compared to local population. In Mallorca, water consumption in rural areas is 140 litres per person per day, in urban areas 250 litres per person per day, while the average tourist consumption is 440 litres per person per day, or even 880 litres per person per day in the case of a luxury establishment (EEA, 2001). Waste production and sewage output increase notably during the tourist season leading to increased water pollution. Environmental hazards such as erosion, land slippage, flooding, etc. and land-use conflicts resulting from poor planning, sitting and inappropriate construction of tourist facilities may become major issues.

Many tourist localities often suffer from increased traffic, congestion of the city centre and parking problems during the tourist season due to the huge number of tourists reaching the destination using private cars or buses. Noise pollution from tourist activities and vehicles also need to be considered. Furthermore the infrastructure systems, like water supply, telecommunications and energy supply, become overburdened.

Uncontrolled tourism development leads to over-urbanization, which may cause the alteration of historic settlements and landscape, and create conflicts with other land uses.

Many types of physical-ecological impacts may be generated by tourism development; however if tourism is well planned, developed and managed it may also generate positive impacts. Appropriate tourism development leads to major investments for conservation of important natural areas and wildlife, archaeological and historic sites, since they represent major tourist attractions, actions for the improvement of the overall environmental quality of tourist areas, to keep them more attractive for tourists, and improvements of tourism infrastructure contributing to better quality of life for the local communities.

Sociocultural Impacts

As far as sociocultural impacts are concerned the main issues involved are those of employment, quality of life, cost of living, etc., while cultural conflicts between visitors and host communities are more rarely reported. Negative sociocultural impacts have a stronger effect especially in small and traditional communities. Although, sociocultural impacts are generally of lesser importance in the case of European destinations compared to the physical-ecological ones, there are still some cases where small local communities may be negatively influenced by tourism like in the case of small islands, rural and mountain communities. Tourist colonization provokes the adjustment of residents to tourist life styles, leading to the gradual loss of the local sociocultural identity. Tourism may alter life styles, values, customs and traditions, belief systems, family structures, community organization. This may happen in cases where tourists are economically and culturally 'stronger' than hosting communities since they tend to impose their needs and preferences. However in all cases one should carefully consider the influence of other factors (for example the Internet, media), which may be the main causes for the impacts observed.

In historical cities tourism may dominate urban societies pushing out other activities or functions from the centre to the suburbs. This is the so-called crowding-out phenomenon, which may lead to tourism monoculture.

Conflicts with the local population may arise over the use of basic services (public transport, water supply, etc.), enjoyment of attractions (museums, urban parks, etc.) and amenity features (pubs, theatres, restaurants, and such like). Cases with overcrowding of local attractions and amenity features as well as occasional irritation of local population may appear. Over-commercialization of the arts may lead to the loss of authenticity of dance, music, drama and crafts.

However since cultural heritage is part of the tourist attraction, it is possible that tourism may provide the justification for their conservation. In addition tourism supports museums, theatres and other cultural facilities that are used by both residents and tourists. Tourism may contribute to the strengthening of feelings of pride of the local community towards their cultural heritage.

Tourism also may be seen as an opportunity for cross-cultural exchanges. Both tourists and residents can learn about one another's culture, which can lead to mutual understanding and acceptance and peaceful relationships among people of different cultural backgrounds.

Economic-Political Impacts

Tourism has a generally positive impact on the economy of a destination since it increases direct (hotels, restaurants, tour and travel operations and retail shops) and indirect (supplying sectors such as agriculture, fisheries, craft production, manufacturing and construction) benefits for employment and income. It contributes to government revenues at all levels including the local level through local taxes for tourism, which can be used to improve community facilities and services and local infrastructure. Furthermore the multiplier effect of tourism serves as a catalyst for the expansion of other local economic activities such as agriculture, fisheries, crafts, and acts as a stimulator for local entrepreneurship through the creation of local tourism enterprises and development of skills.

However tourism may also have negative impacts on local society due to the uneven distribution of economic benefits. Higher cost of living for residents, increased public costs and expenses for infrastructure, management, intervention against pollution, etc., which are not adequately shared by tourists, are only some of the costs undertaken by local population. The needs of tourism activity may create conflicts with other activities for example concerning land-use allocation and land prices. Seasonality of employment and income, along with increased rate of withdrawal from education (a phenomenon witnessed in several famous tourist destinations in Greece, such as the island complex of Cyclades) also need to be carefully considered.

A major risk is represented by the over-dependence of the local economy on tourism activity in some destinations, since changes in tourism flows may lead to the loss of the main source of local income, causing an economic crisis.

Impacts of Tourism on Various Destinations

Impacts are largely dependent on the specific setting, type and scale of activity. Although in all cases management of tourism growth is necessary, the focus of policy measures in each case may be different. This underlines the need to consider a different emphasis – or significance – in carrying capacity considerations in each type of tourist destination.

The presentation should not be regarded as exhaustive since several other problems may arise as a result of the specific conditions of both the locality and the type of tourism development.

Impacts of Tourism in Coastal Areas

Local coastal communities benefit significantly from tourism through relatively higher income, higher employment rate and investments, infrastructure development, etc. However many negative impacts of tourism development are evident in coastal areas.

Some coastal areas are undergoing high pressure from large numbers of tourists. The greatest pressures are still exerted in the Mediterranean.

Deterioration of limited water resources and urbanization along the coast are some of the major impacts of tourism development. Lack of sewage treatment leads to marine and freshwater pollution from tourist establishments. Marine pollution may also result from the discharges from tourist vessels (yachts, speed boats, excursion boats), passenger liners and car-ferries. Unsustainable exploitation of natural resources, including excessive abstraction of drinking water and exploitation of fisheries' resources, represents a serious problem in coastal areas. During the summer months in some localities, especially in the Mediterranean region, water supplies are exacerbated by tourist flows for use in hotels, swimming pools and golf courses leading to water shortages, over-extraction and salinization.

Unplanned growth of hotels and tourism facilities with little regard to visual impacts or local architecture has led to visual degradation over vast areas and to the artificialization of coastal environment. Ribbon development is a common phenomenon on the east coast of Spain, on the north coast of Crete, in the northwest part of the Peloponnese and in several parts of the south coast of France and is one of the main reasons for the decrease of the attractiveness of these areas.

Most sensitive European areas are located in coastal areas. Important and sensitive habitats (sand dunes, coastal wetlands, sand beaches) are deteriorated or destroyed due to uncontrolled tourism development or high tourist pressure, in this way threatening the existence of endangered species (German Federal Agency for Nature Conservation, 1997). Vegetation loss or alteration, destruction of coastal forests due to fires, coastal erosion due to improper sitting of structures, soil erosion leading to desertification are also some of the problems often caused by improper tourist development.

During past decades, efforts have been concentrated on the development of other types of tourism (for example health, congress, ecotourism, cultural tourism), complementary to the predominant type of mass 3s (sea, sand and sun) tourism. In spite of these efforts tourism development is still seasonal in character. Seasonal over-concentration leads to increased pressure on environmental and cultural resources.

Impacts of Tourism in Islands

The limited natural resources coupled with intense pressures often leads to the over-exploitation of resources or to their abandonment. The exhaustion and degradation (salinization) of water resources due to the increasing demands for agriculture and mainly tourism is a typical example of over-exploitation.

In most of the islands, tourism development confronts significant problems in respect to seasonality, limited diversification of the tourism product, inadequate transport services, arbitrary development of tourism facilities, etc. During summer population concentration in many islands is high often exceeding the carrying capacity of the natural ecosystems, the organizational capacity, etc., causing severe impacts, often irreversible (reduction of agricultural land, exhaustion of water resources, and deterioration of landscape). This over-concentration calls for investments for the provision of required infrastructure which ameliorates the situation further enhancing the attraction of the destination, often leading to another cycle of new investments, urbanization, congestion, degradation, and so on.

Management of waste, both solid and liquid, remains one of the most critical problems for all islands, often leading to pollution incidents. Increased demand for energy resources, rather limited in several islands, is also a critical problem.

In many islands, the landscape and coastline are being visibly affected by widespread urbanization and the intrusive impacts of hotel, marina, air and road construction. The sprawling and continuous urban development along the coast has caused losses of agricultural land and open spaces, which could also serve as habitat areas and sites for recreation. Land speculation due to prospects for tourism development is a rather acute problem.

There is an increased concern regarding the impacts on local identity (architecture and landscape), local resources, services and infrastructure from tourism development, which does not always respect the scale and the capacity of small islands.

The contribution of tourism in island development can also be very positive (retention of population, particularly of the younger, opportunities for employment and increased income) under the condition that local particularities are carefully assessed and that development takes into account both comparative advantages and constraints (for example availability of natural resources). It should be noted though that the narrow economic base provides limited opportunities for local employment, while the dependence of local economy exclusively on a single economic activity (for example tourism) may result in major problems, when this activity is proved economically unprofitable, resulting in severe impacts on economic and social structure.

Thus it is of great importance to ensure that any further development maintains the unique sense of historic, cultural and community identity present in the islands.

Impacts of Tourism on Mountain Resorts

The growing number of winter tourists has resulted in an inappropriate and uncontrolled development of ski-centres. Environmental consequences are reported where the main cause is the use of heavy machinery for lift construction: hill tracks being cut into the mountainside, vegetation loss leading to subsequent loss of soil stabilization and flash floods, threats to the fauna of the area, deterioration of aesthetic value and naturalness of the area are some of the impacts observed (Holden, 1998). Natural forest barriers may be replaced with unsightly concrete, plastic and wooden barriers causing visual degradation and impacts on landscape. Furthermore ski activities often need artificial snow leading to an unsustainable use of water for snow cannons. By 1992, 4000 snow cannons were producing artificial snow to lengthen the ski season in the Alps, using 28 million litres of water per kilometre of ski slope and competing with other uses. In Le Meunieres (France) 185 cannons installed for the 1992 Olympics were supplied by drinking water sources (EEA, 1995). Finally ski lifts consume a significant amount of electric energy, equivalent in the French Alps to one-third of the annual production of a nuclear plant (EEA, 2003).

The Winter Olympic games of Albertville in 1992 were spread throughout 13 villages in the Savoy, with a total population of 340,000 inhabitants. In the past few decades, accommodation for 340,000 visitors was built in the Savoy region, doubling the population during the peak ski season. During the Olympics, the region accommodated 1,500 athletes, 7,000 journalists and around one million spectators. The games left behind substantial environmental impacts and economic bankruptcy for 4 out of the 13 Olympic villages. Although the residents of the villages benefited in terms of improved infrastructure, the large amounts invested by local governments have not been recouped due to the tourism rates being lower than expected (Arrol, 1997).

In addition to the environmental impacts from skiing activities, many other impacts have appeared as a result of the decision to diversify the tourism product, through the development of additional activities attracting visitors during the summer months. Mountain biking, trekking, canyoning and hiking are only some of these activities affecting undisturbed areas such as gorges or rock faces.

Tourism also results in sewage and waste disposal difficulties leading to water pollution. In the French Pyrenees the sewage from summer tourist resorts discharges directly to streams leading to water pollution. In the Alps it has been reported that the use of chemicals to prepare 36 glaciers for skiing led to the increase of nitrogen and phosphorus levels in drinking water (EEA, 1995).

Finally the exhausts from cars and coaches are believed to trigger acid rain and tree damage, leading to loss of habitats and disturbance of endangered species. The loss of plant life leads to increased erosion rates and landslide risk.

However tourism helps to revitalize local economy and change population trends (Holden, 1998). In Greece, tourism development has contributed to the regeneration of several rural and mountain areas. Pilio, Metsovo, Kerkini and Papigo are rural, mountain areas where proper tourism development had significant positive impacts on the socioeconomic development while environmental impacts are still considered limited (Ministry for Development and Greek National Tourism Organization, 2000).

Impacts of Tourism on Heritage Sites and Cities

In the case of heritage cities socioeconomic implications of tourism are as important as environmental ones.

It should be noted that there is considerable difference between the type and the intensity of impacts due to tourism in a major city (for example London, Paris, Vienna) in comparison to a smaller historic city. In the first case the large host population and the adequate infrastructures can accommodate high-volume tourism flows more easily (Curtis, 1998). On the contrary in smaller and confined areas such as walled towns or historic sites the concentration of tourists produces serious environmental management problems since small towns have greater difficulty in coping with the congestion, noise, pollution and other problems that accompany tourism. Furthermore in cities with high tourist flows, tourism may produce irritation for the local population, crowding-out of normal economic activities from the town centre and increased prices, leading to a higher cost of living for residents, pressure on local services, an increase in crime, etc. (Glasson et al., 1995). In Bruges (Belgium) the city centre has been gradually abandoned by the resident-oriented shops and businesses while the streets have been swamped by souvenir and speciality shops, leading to an excessive simplification of the economic structure in some parts of the city centre. The local population has mainly moved to the suburbs and beyond (Curtis, 1998).

The problem most frequently confronted in heritage cities is traffic and parking. The high number of tourist buses delivering excursionists, especially during weekends and holidays, creates congestion and serious traffic problems, with associated pollution from exhausts, noise and disturbance to the local population.

Important heritage sites are threatened by huge visitor flows causing wear and tear phenomena. Litter is a particular concern in some places while there may also be minor acts of vandalism.

However tourism may act as an incentive for urban redevelopment, create employment opportunities and contribute to the maintenance overheads and to income.

Impacts of Tourism on Protected Areas

The main problems are caused by the excessive use of passenger cars, overcrowding during peak periods, particularly at sites that are close to urban centres. For example in Hohe Tauner, Austria, visitors are concentrated in a period of six months and most of them (over 90 per cent) are day trippers reaching the locality by private car increasing the traffic and causing congestion of car parking space and litter problems (EEA, 1995).

Nature and national parks are already under extreme pressure from the increased number of visitors, the demand for outdoor activities and the development of tourism facilities. Path erosion and wear and tear arise from walking or mountain biking. Visitor intrusion may disturb wildlife, especially during breeding periods.

Conflicts arise among tourism and nature conservation, traditional hunting and agriculture. For example the Coto Doñana National Park located in the southwest of Spain is an important breeding site for many of Europe's birds, and home of endangered species like the imperial eagle (*Aquila heliaca*), and Spanish lynx (*Lynx pardina*), but it is now threatened by water extraction from tourism and local agriculture (ibid, 1995).

Tourism development in such areas may involve several socioeconomic implications as well. In cases where local communities are being excluded from the management and exploitation of natural resources, they may express discontent and even hostility towards efforts for protection and management of natural areas. During the establishment of a protection regime in the forest of Dadia-Leukimi-Soufli in Greece, there were several oppositions from the local community. The main reason was the prohibition of woodcutting, which represented the main economic activity in the areas of absolute protection. Compensation for the losses of income was not easy and in any case cannot always be sufficient. Within this context, it was necessary to develop alternative types of economic activities such as tourism and recreation, in accordance to the environmental particularities of the area (Ministry for Development and Greek National Tourism Organization, 2000). Increased tourism and recreation may also contribute to improved resource management as a result of higher incomes for local communities.

Impacts of Tourism on Rural Areas

Tourism, in rural areas, is emerging as an alternative economic activity that could provide income and employment opportunities to local communities, but tourism development may also have significant impacts on the continuation of traditional farming practices, which contribute to nature conservation and landscape management. In certain cases rural tourism activities can take the form of ecotourism in the sense that they are developed on the basis of natural characteristics. Such kinds of activities may involve lower environmental impacts and are becoming increasingly popular.

In spite of the socioeconomic benefits of rural tourism one should not overlook the costs related to the development of required infrastructure (road network, water supply, waste disposal). In addition, rural tourism does not necessarily imply an environmental friendly type of tourism development. There is always the possibility of damages particularly in the case of environmentally sensitive areas. The main reason for this is the significant number of visitors often throughout the year.

Special attention is needed in the case of particular recreational activities such as golf and hunting that represent an environmental threat. It should be noted though that these activities can be hosted in rural areas, they cause problems in respect to the availability and quality of water resources, loss of biodiversity, etc., requiring careful planning and management. An 18-hole golf course for example requires an average 48.2 hectares of land.

Noise and fragmentation of habitats could also be some of the impacts of tourism development. Wildlife species in riparian habitats could be affected if a large number of tourists are concentrated near rivers. The combined impacts of tourism and recreation, including transport, waste production, noise, water extraction, etc., could be relevant in certain areas. In Loch Lomond in the southern Scottish Highlands, although recreation is an important activity in the area, environmental impacts are not only due to recreation and tourism but also due to changes in other types of land use and to variations in natural environmental conditions. For this it has been recognized that management for tourism and outdoor recreation must take place within an integrated framework (Dickinson, 1996).

Experiences from the Implementation of Tourism Carrying Capacity

Given the growing concern about the negative implications of tourism activity on natural and man-made environments and the recognition of the threat that these impacts may impose on future tourism development, some destinations are implementing policies and measures for managing tourism. However examples of implementation of tourism carrying capacity assessment are still limited in Europe. In the following paragraphs some aspects of selected case studies, those of Rhodes in Greece, Calvià and Lanzarote in Spain, and Elba island and Rimini in Italy are discussed.

Key Characteristics of the Area

TCC can be implemented in areas with different levels of tourism development including mature destinations as well as developing tourist resorts. The majority of the cases described belong in the first case. The pressing environmental problems, which have resulted in a deterioration of both the natural and the built environment, have triggered the exploration of some limits in an effort to safeguard economic development and confront rising competition from emerging tourist destinations.

Most of these resorts are characterized by tourism growth accompanied by urbanization, sprawling of development along the coasts, threatening the natural environment and cultural heritage; increasing dependence on tourism (monoculture), while the predominant tourism development model experiences a crisis suggesting the need to broaden the tourist product. Among the most significant environmental problems are waste management, water and energy supply. However pre-growth attitudes often prevail.

The *Province of Rimini* (Italy), the *island of Rhodes* (Greece) and *Calvià* (Spain) are typical mature destinations. The Province of Rimini is the most famous tourist coastal destination in Italy, a mature tourism area, saturated from the point of view of land use and the pressures exerted on natural resources (Conte., 2001). Rhodes is among the most important tourist destinations in Greece. It is characterized by a high concentration of population and economic activities in the northern part of the island, close to the town of Rhodes, increased development along the coast, economic monoculture, etc. (Coccossis et al., 2002). Calvià, is a known mass tourist destination as well. Over recent decades accelerated building development has exceeded the carrying capacity of the coastal ecosystems, producing impacts on the island's natural environment, as well as excessive use of basic imported resources such as water, energy and materials. The emissions of carbon dioxide into the atmosphere are heavy, 58 per cent of which are from transporting tourists in and out of Mallorca. Underground water is also being over-exploited while 60 per cent of the territory is affected by soil erosion. Overall human pressure on Calvià's territory has increased significantly. The pressure has been distributed unevenly: the coastline of over 2,000 hectares has densely populated areas (3,000 inhabitants per sq. km in the high season), while the remaining two-thirds of the island territory have a significantly lower density (Ajuntament de Calvià Mallorca, 1999).

The Context

Carrying capacity assessment can be a demanding, long-term process, demanding significant resources not always available at the local level. Broader initiatives such as the Coastal Area Management Program can secure partial financing, along with scientific and technical guidance.

In the case of *Rimini* as well as that of the island of *Rhodes* the application of TCCA had been part of respective Coastal Area Management Programs utilized with the cooperation of local authorities with the Priority Actions Program (PAP/RAC, 1997; PAP/RAC, 2003), while in *Calvià* carrying capacity considerations have been addressed as part of a broader project that of Local Agenda 21.

Principal Goals for Undertaking a Tourism Carrying Capacity Study

The principal goals for undertaking a carrying capacity assessment usually relate to the anticipation of environmental pressure, the enhancement of visitor satisfaction, while securing long-term economic viability of tourism activities.

In the case of *Rimini* it was acknowledged that planning for future development should aim at the reduction of the pressure on the environment, the promotion of sustainable policies and the encouragement of the participation of the private sector in the above actions as a way to assure effective implementation of foreseen initiatives (Conte, 2001). In the case of *Lanzarote* island (Spain) goals included the maintenance of the ecological equilibrium and the improvement of the quality of life of both residents and visitors. In the case of *Elba* island (Italy) goals included the maintenance of the quality of the tourist experience and the safeguarding of the conservation of natural resources. In the case of *Rhodes* (Greece) the analysis of TCC had as an objective to provide decision-makers with a framework for planning and management for sustainable tourism (PAP/RAC, 1993).

Objectives of the Tourism Carrying Capacity Study

The Carrying Capacity Study in *Rimini* (Conte, 2001) aimed at the assessment of the socioeconomic and environmental impacts of tourism. In the case of *Lanzarote* and in order to achieve the aforementioned goals, it was recognized as necessary to reduce human pressure on the system, suggesting a reduction of tourist flows to rates compatible with the assimilation capacity of the island, and the reorientation of development policy on the basis of sustainability criteria.

Methodological Issues

Carrying capacity assessment does not follow a unique approach. On the contrary there may be several ways to define limits. Some of the aspects of the approaches adopted in each one of the cases described above will be highlighted. No doubt there are some common issues, including among others the use of indicators, standards, the exploration of the future through the elaboration of alternative scenarios/options, the selection of some critical factors/problems for further study and for the definition of capacity limits, the consideration of environmental, physical, sociocultural and economic aspects in the area, the correlation of limits with goals and management objectives, the consideration of ecological limits and of visitor satisfaction, etc. Differences may evolve in respect to participation of key stakeholders and local community, integration of TCCA into existing planning schemes, and such like.

In the case of *Rimini* a selected group of various indicators, evolving around either some key variables/driving forces of the system (for example tourist flows) or around some key issues and problems (for example employment, water consumption), had been used as a means to monitor problems and therefore access the success of the various policies promoted but also as a means of identifying the capacity limits of the system, suggesting more or less in this case that there is a direct relationship between the problems – and therefore of the capacity of the system – and the number of visitors.

The indicators selected for the evaluation of the carrying capacity described both the socioeconomic and the environmental sector. For each sector key thematic areas (nine overall), representing more or less critical issues for tourism management were defined:

- Type of tourist system (tourist flows, tourist density, etc.)
- Employment and income (employment, GDP from tourism activities, etc.)
- Energy consumption and CO_2 emissions
- Waste production and management
- Water (water consumption, water quality sampling, etc.)
- Natural environment, territory and biodiversity (land use, urbanised areas, etc.)
- Transport and mobility (daily traffic, number of accidents, etc.)
- Air quality
- Noise.

For each thematic area some indicators have been selected in order to monitor the effectiveness of the policies implemented. The final decision for the indicators to be used will be taken in consultation with the various stakeholders (public administration, tourist operators, environmental associations, citizens, etc.).

The above analysis is expected to allow for the identification of critical social or environmental problems. Until the final calculation of carrying capacity, limits are being defined taking into account one of the most critical problems of the area, that of waste management (Conte, 2001).

In case of *Calvià,* emphasis has been placed on defining and implementing limits on land development and respectively on the growth of the number of tourist beds. This has encouraged the revision of the 1991 General Town Planning Regulation (GTPR). Although the 1991 GTPR restricted building in comparison with the previous situation, it still allowed for the construction of 250,000 tourist and residential units, 65 per cent more than those existing. The revision contributed to a progressive reduction in the theoretical population ceiling: from 400,000 units allowed in the 1982 Plan to 250,000 in the 1991 Plan and to 215,000 in the 1998 Plan. Furthermore, initiatives in respect to key environmental sectors, which are characterized by unsustainable uses like local mobility, water, energy consumption and urban waste, have been undertaken. Within this context the Building Clearance Plan has been implemented, as part of the Tourist Excellence Plan, resulting in the demolition of 12 buildings in areas with mass development, which have then been replaced by green spaces or leisure facilities (Ajuntament de Calvià, 1999).

In *Lanzarote* an exploration of the future opportunities and threats had been promoted, based on the analysis of the system (state of development and environment, analysis of trends and of risk factors). The analysis has been enriched with the results of a wide survey (conducted mainly through interviews) regarding population opinions and aspirations. Two alternative development scenarios have been elaborated: the 'Risk Scenario', reflecting prevailing development trends, and the 'Biosphere Strategy', based on sustainability criteria.

The scenarios described the future of the area vis à vis some key dimensions organized in seven thematic areas (population, cultural identity and heritage, economy and tourism, the urban system, island ecology, key environmental sectors). Indicators were also used.

Evaluation indicated that the Risk Scenario is not a desirable option since the costs will overpass enormously the benefits, suggesting that the ecological, social and economic carrying capacity of the island has reached its limits.

For the Biosphere Strategy scenario eight axes for actions and twenty-eight programmes were defined, among them the limitation of the tourist flows to a scale and rate compatible to the sustainability limits of the island. A limit has been suggested for the creation of new tourist establishments (8,000 instead of the 200,000 previously foreseen) for the following ten years, while the replacement of outdated tourist units has been promoted. Additional programmes for the sustainable development of the island would be also required (Estrategia Lanzarote en la Biosfera, 1998).

In the case of *Elba Island* (Italy) a mathematical model has been used. The analysis focused on the physical-ecological and sociocultural aspects of TCC, starting with the identification of the measurable limiting factors, such as the water supply capacity, the waste treatment capacity, the utilization of basic resources (expressed as beach surface per person) and the pressure on local population (expressed as a tourist to inhabitants ratio). Following this four sustainability scenarios were defined: conservative, high sustainability, low sustainability and degenerative, each one correlated with one of the previous limiting factors. Exceeding the critical value of a limiting factor (for example water treatment capacity per day) caused the shift from one scenario to the other. The most critical factor proved to be water supply. Finally the number of tourists correlated to each scenario is calculated. The utilization of the above model allows the monitoring of tourism flows on a daily basis and the identification of critical areas and periods of the year where the island exceeds its tourism carrying capacity (Quintè, 2001).

In the case of the island of *Rhodes* the maximum level of tourism usage took into consideration tourism business intensity, tolerance of tourists and constraints related to economic and sociocultural aspects. The process followed included: *identification of key problems* (for example limited availability of local labour force for employment in tourism), *identification of constraints, definition of qualitative determinants* (for example decrease in the long run of the dependence of island's economy on tourism, demand for more specialized tourist products), *definition of quantitative determinants* (for example one employee per two tourist beds), *identification of key constraint* (migrant labour), *formulation of alternative hypothesis* for population growth for the years 2000 and 2010, *elaboration of two scenarios for the migrant labour* for the years 2000 and 2010 on the basis of the above hypotheses, calculation of selected *indicators* (number of beds, overnight stays, arrivals, receipts, ratio of tourists to local population and average tourist expenditure) for each scenario, *selection of desirable option* and finally *calculation of the total carrying capacity* on the basis of the real key constraint (migrant labour) for the whole area taking into account a desired upper limit of the tourist expenditure (PAP/RAC, 1993).

Incorporating Tourism Carrying Capacity Assessment in Tourism Planning Process

In some cases the integration of tourism carrying capacity assessment into physical planning or tourism planning is pursued. This may secure the implementation (even partially) of the recommendations of TCCA.

The most well-known case of incorporation of carrying capacity studies in tourism development plans is the implementation of the Local Agenda 21 in *Calvià* (Spain). Carrying capacity is a concept intrinsic in all Local Agenda 21 projects. In the case of Calvià, the concept of absorption capacity or desirable limits for change has been incorporated within a broader framework of planning for sustainable development, including an overall vision and a statement of solidarity against global environmental problems.

In the case of *Rhodes* the carrying capacity study has provided input for an Integrated Planning Study for the island of Rhodes, which then formed the basis for the conduction of a Special Spatial Development Study for the island of Rhodes, which aimed at the identification of priorities for action and zones of land uses and building regulations. Its proposals are expected to be implemented (Coccossis et al., 2002).

Experiences from the Implementation of Various Other Management Approaches

In the following paragraphs selected cases are presented where tourism carrying capacity is in a way implicitly followed, suggesting more or less that the basic principle, that of imposing some kind of limits on numbers or activities, is applied.

Most examples concern natural areas and in general areas with high ecological significance. Zoning and management of visitor flows are among the most commonly applied management practices. Some initiatives refer to heritage sites and cities as well. The following case studies are only a few from a larger number of initiatives. Some more cases have been described in previous chapters of this volume.

Abruzzo National Park (Italy)

Zoning is a quite common approach used for managing tourism flows, particularly in areas with significant ecological value. The Abruzzo National Park (Italy) is internationally considered as a good example in nature conservation, succeeding in demonstrating that the protection of the environment can provide positive impacts and economic advantages such as higher income and employment opportunities. A zoning system has been implemented while a special agreement with local Communities exists in order to overcome conflicts related to urban planning provisions (Caruso and Maugeri, 1995). In particular the *Wilderness Area* is the most sensitive part of the Park, which requires absolute conservation. Access to visitors is only allowed on foot. Visitors can walk along restricted footpaths usually accompanied by the Park's guides. The *Nature Reserve* consists of an extensive 'green area' that needs to be conserved but where some human activities take place. Traditional activities like agriculture, forestry and sheep farming are allowed under the control of the Park authorities. Visitors can walk or ride along specific routes; motor vehicles are allowed only on roads authorized for circulation. A *Protected Area* consists of a typical rural environment in which agricultural and pastoral activities dominate. The practice of these activities is encouraged, along with the respect of local traditions. Access to this area is unrestricted. Finally the *Development Area* is an area with villages whose historical centres are being restored and revitalized. There are also picnic areas, animal reserves, visitor centres and nature trails. This zone allows for the development of cultural and recreational activities for local communities and visitors (ibid).

Protected Forest of Dadia (Greece)

Zoning has proved to be an effective measure in several other cases such as the protected forest of Dadia in Northern Greece. Two cores of absolute protection with a total surface of 72.5 sq. km have been identified along with a buffer zone with a total surface of 357.1 sq. km. It should be noted that there would be no particular zones for tourism development but *conditions* for the practice of various tourism activities for each one of these zones (Ministry for Development and Greek National Tourism Organization, 2000).

A monitoring system is also being implemented in order to acquire information about the conditions and the changes incurring in the protected area. This application allows the identification of the parameters and issues that would render the conversion of the existing system of zoning necessary so as to assure the protection of the area (the zoning system could be extended so as to ensure protection). Monitoring is significant for the development of ecotourism since it allows early identification of impacts. It can be also useful for the management of visitor flows.

Medes Archipelago (Spain)

The marine reserve in the Medes Archipelago is formed by seven small islets and numerous reefs. The area is extremely rich in marine life, an ideal place for underwater activities. Since 1990 the marine area around the islets has been protected. In the first zone regulation of water and underwater activities is foreseen while in the second zone all activities are prohibited (Oficina de Turisme de l'Estartit).

Steinhuder Meer Nature Park (Germany)

The Steinhuder Meer Nature Park is an important bird habitat (Ramsar area, EU Bird Protection Directive area) but also the most attractive recreational area for the conurbation of Hanover, in the north of Germany, where several recreational activities take place including water-sports, biking and hiking. The Lake Steinhuder Meer constitutes the core area of the park. A zoning system has been introduced, in close cooperation between the park authorities with the local and regional authorities, in an attempt to protect habitats and wildlife. Facilities for tourism and recreation are concentrated in two areas while all other areas along the lake are strictly protected. A circular path around the lake used for hiking and biking concentrates visitors in certain areas, avoiding dispersion. Water-sports are allowed now only from the 1st April till the 31st October in order to avoid disturbance of the birds. Furthermore, certain parts of the lake have been designated as nature protection areas, and access to them is prohibited. Information is provided regarding the various restrictions and in general, visitors have accepted the restrictions introduced, with the exception of the water-sports limitations (Société d'Eco-Aménagement, 2001).

Tammisaari National Park (Finland)

The Tammisaari National Park is made up of a group of islands, which are part of the archipelago of Uusimaa Province in Finland. The site is under pressure from various users: the large number of boats sailing between Helsinki and Hanko, visitors and owners of second houses who visit the island in the summer and land-owners with building rights.

In order to regulate future development in the site and minimize impacts, a master plan has been prepared. On the basis of research and existing inventories on habitat and species, the most fragile zones of the park have been identified and restrictions on the various uses have been imposed. Water traffic has also been restricted in the most fragile areas.

Facilities for tourism and recreation are provided in the less sensitive areas, while strictly protected areas do not host any facilities in order to discourage visitors and minimize the possibility of environmental destruction. Access to the marine zone is prohibited during spring and summer to avoid disturbance of the many rare and endangered bird species present in the area. Access is permitted in the terrestrial part of the park always with the presence of a guide. The Park visitor centre is located in the mainland in order to discourage boat traffic (Société d'Eco-Aménagement, 2001).

Island of Terschelling (Netherlands)

On the small island of Terschelling (Netherlands) the number of tourists have recently increased to over 350,000 a year, but yet the island's natural values are still in good condition due to careful planning and visitor management. In 1974 the Municipality in co-operation with the National Forest Service drew up a long-term Plan, integrating policies for agriculture, nature protection and tourism development plans. This plan is coherent with the policies and management plans of the National Forest Service, which owns and manages 80 per cent of the island.

A limit to the number of beds in the tourist sector had been set (20,000). The economy of Terschelling depends on tourism while nature provides the basis for it. Approximately 80 per cent of the inhabitants are employed directly or indirectly in the tourism sector. Tourism management aims at the maintenance of the quality of nature and landscape and at the maximization of tourist satisfaction. The management has resulted in a zoning scheme based on the segmentation of the main categories of visitors (conservationists, nature-lovers and pleasure seekers), providing different facilities for each category and taking into account the vulnerability of the area:

- Facilities for *conservationists* have the lowest possible impact (for example paths and tracks are not paved)
- Facilities for *nature lovers* (marked trails for walking, cycling and horse-riding) are concentrated in the central part of the island and are supported by informative and educational facilities, with the purpose of guiding the large number of visitors
- A zone for *pleasure seekers* has been created in one part of the beach with a small dune lake, parking area, and a path connecting the beach and the campsites. Facilities for recreation are provided. Safety issues and prevention of damages or nuisance are properly taken care of.

Although the number of tourists has increased in the last twenty years, the number of birds and species has increased too. Monitoring of tourism is essential so as to prevent negative impacts (Société d'Eco-Aménagement, 2001 and Seidenstücker, 2000).

Oulanka National Park (Finland)

The Oulanka National Park in the Kuusamo region (Finland) has instigated a number of measures to protect the natural environment from tourism activities. The first is related to routing of the nature trails in order to avoid sensitive or fragile areas. In this way tourists are channelled through a very small portion of the park, instead of having 150 kilometres of trails available. The provision of various facilities along the trails encourages visitors to follow the suggested route. Furthermore wardens regularly monitor visitor use for damage signs or lower visitor satisfaction levels, which can be addressed before they become serious problems. Overcrowding and damaged facilities may have negative impacts on people's enjoyment and safety even on their expectations in terms of scenery, tranquillity, adventure and sense of wilderness. (EC, 2002b).

The French Alps

The French government has attempted to control development in mountain areas through the prohibition of the development of new ski resorts in the French Alps since 1997 and for a period of five years. The French decision responded to the demand of the regional governments as well as to the pressures from the European Parliament (Arrol, 1997).

Canterbury (UK)

Canterbury (UK) has elaborated over the last 15 years a visitor management strategy, on the basis of a long-term plan for sustainable tourism set up in 1985. The objectives included confrontation of the physical impacts of tourism, anticipating growth in visitor pressure, channelling part of the profits from tourism for preservation projects and protection of the quality of life of local population. Within this context six strategic themes have been developed (Curtis, 1998):

- *Control of traffic.* A program of pedestrianization has reduced the volume of traffic from the city centre. A parking strategy (price and provision of park and ride facilities) discouraged parking in the city centre.
- *Conservation.* Imposition of a strict design control on commercial development with the scope to control modifications of old buildings.
- *Dispersal through product development.* Introducing new attractions in restored historic buildings so as to disperse visitors around the city. This policy has produced benefits for retail and catering business located outside the tourist core.
- *Providing for groups.* Creation of new park site for coaches in proximity to the city centre, providing facilities for tourists and drivers. This policy allows for a greater degree of control over the coach trade.
- *Price Policy.* The cost for parking in the city centre is higher than parking at the park and ride facilities. An entrance fee has also been introduced to the cathedral.
- *Involving the host community.* Creation of a public/private organization (Canterbury City Centre Initiative) aiming at involving the resident and business community in the decisions affecting the city centre.

Canterbury has made great progress in coping with its growing popularity as a tourist destination, however the adoption of management measures have encouraged further growth in visitor flows to the point where the city's carrying capacity is frequently exceeded (ibid).

Oxford (UK)

Visitor management initiatives can be pursued under a variety of policy frameworks. The Oxford Local Plan Review (1999-2001) included policies on transport and tourism, accommodation and information of tourists.

The establishment of the Oxford Tourism Forum represents an important contribution towards policy implementation. The Forum has already been a catalyst for public and private sector coordination and joint funding. Recent initiatives include a more coordinated approach to central coach parking, visitor dispersal via new walking trails and an extension of bus routes and the development of an 'Oxford Package' of linked activities with joint ticketing. Implementation depends on the attitudes of the key actors involved and their willingness or otherwise to accept the implications of a management approach (Glasson et al., 1995).

Bruges (Belgium)

Bruges authorities have encouraged concentration of tourism development in the city centre discouraging tourists from visiting residential suburbs. The policy was designed primarily to protect sensitive residential areas from hotel development. It has not been possible to avoid the gradual disappearance of resident-oriented shops and business from the city centre. The main disadvantage of the policy adopted was the loss of variety. Tourists occasionally found themselves in areas resembling virtual theme parks, surrounded only by other tourists (Curtis, 1998).

Hadrian's Wall (UK)

Tourism pressure on a site may be reduced with the use of dispersion strategies. Tourists tend to visit the most famous and advertised sites, during specific periods of time. The result is a high concentration in time and space in some sites, while other are totally ignored. English Heritage has implemented several policies to spread the tourist load and diminish wear and tear phenomena in several sites, for example through limited publicity of an overcrowded site. In the case of the Hadrian's Wall information for a popular site has been removed from the maps that visitors use, in order to reduce the annual number of visitors (500,000) and prevent irreparable damage (Butler, 1997).

Heidelberg (Germany)

The city of Heidelberg provides an interesting example of a community's response to visitor management. The approach adopted is set out in *Guidelines on Tourism Heidelberg* which is structured around three dimensions, economic, sociocultural and ecological, each one containing main and secondary objectives such as securing present and future jobs in tourism on a seasonal and long-term basis, preserving the distinctive character of Heidelberg and promoting an ecologically acceptable type of tourism. The above had several positive implications including retargeting towards overnight tourism and towards particular groups, strategic shift towards seasonal working to capacity by transferring visitor potential into the low season, safeguarding of the identity and attraction of the city for local residents by providing a programme of cultural events, etc., encouraging environmentally friendly travel by visitors to the town, etc. (Glasson et al., 1995, p.94-95).

Conclusions

In spite of much literature and apparent wide acceptance among planners and decision-makers on carrying capacity, there is limited evidence of its application in practice. In general there is limited experience with the application of carrying capacity in the management of tourist destinations across European countries. This probably reflects the ambiguities involved with the concept and/or the difficulties in its operationalization. Another reason could be that overall there is little experience on the ground of managing tourist destinations therefore with the use of tools and methods for that purpose.

However, the basic element of the concept: the need for a limit – a threshold – in the tourist activity is present in one way or another in the concerns and priorities of local managers and planners. Tourism creates pressures on the natural and cultural environment affecting resources, social structures, cultural patterns, economic activities and land uses in local communities. To the extent that such pressures are felt to create problems on tourism or significantly alter the functioning of nature and the local community, taking special measures to mitigate such impacts can be a viable option. These concerns increase and dominate public policy agendas as modern societies give increasing consideration to issues such as environmental conservation, quality of life and sustainable development. The issue of tourism development is increasingly sought within a local strategy for sustainable development in which case determining the capacity of local systems to sustain tourism becomes a central issue.

Most of the existing experience refers to coastal areas and islands. Protected areas represent preferable cases for the application of carrying capacity assessment and in general of other management approaches. They are well defined and benefit from a special status, which make it easy to apply limits and prohibitions. In these cases zoning is a rather useful tool: it is simple to understand and to apply.

In the case of heritage sites and cities tourism carrying capacity considerations are addressed mainly through a visitor management strategy.

The adoption of an integrated approach to tourism carrying capacity assessment does not imply the inclusion, at least in the final stage of assessment, of all the factors influencing the tourism system. A selection of key themes and key issues would be necessary. Furthermore the participation of key stakeholders from the early stages of planning is essential. Participation may take various forms (for example consultation, selection and agreement on final option, active participation from the early steps of the process). What is the most appropriate form of participation will be decided given local particularities, as well as other factors (for example time and budget constraints). Effective participation of the private sector is recognized as being of fundamental importance. Indicators can assist the assessment and the implementation of tourism carrying capacity.

The implementation of the carrying capacity approach often depends on the political will to control access to a destination in order to protect it. If political support is lacking the carrying capacity assessment remains just a scientific tool with no real application.

References

Ajuntament de Calvià Mallorca, (1999), *Calvià Agenda 21. The Sustainability of a Tourist Municipality. Plan of Action. 10 Strategic Lines of Action and 40 Initiatives*, Calvià.

Arrol, J. (1992), 'French Alps Ski Bans', *Ted Case Studies*, Vol. 1, No. 1, case number 27, available at www.american.edu/ted/FRANCE.HTM

Beedie, P. and Hudson S. (2003), 'Emergence of Mountain-Based Adventure Tourism', *Annals of Tourism Research*, Vol. 30, No. 3, pp. 625-643.

Borg, J. van der, Costa, P., Gotti, G. (1996), 'Tourism in European Heritage Cities' *Annals of Tourism Research*, Vol. 23, No. 2, pp. 306-321.

Butler R. (1997), 'The Concept of Carrying Capacity for Tourism Destinations: Dead or Merely Buried?', in Cooper C. and Wanhill S. (eds), *Tourism Development, Environmental and Community Issues*, Wiley, England.

Caruso, F. and Maugeri, S. (1995), *Nel Parco Nazionale d'Abruzzo*, ATS, Roma.

Coccossis, H. (1998) 'Integrated Island Management in Greece', *Naturopa*, Council of Europe No. 88, p. 25.

Coccossis, H. and Mexa, A. (1997), *Coastal Management in Greece*, Hellenic Ministry for the Environment, Physical Planning and Public Works, Athens.

Coccossis, H. and Mexa, A. (2002a), 'The Coastal Zone', in Coccossis, H., (ed), *Man and the Environment in Greece*, Hellenic Ministry for the Environment, Spatial Planning and Public Works, Athens, pp. 74-80.

Coccossis, H. and Mexa, A. (2002b), 'The Islands', in Coccossis, H. (ed), *Man and the Environment in Greece*, Hellenic Ministry for the Environment, Spatial Planning and Public Works, Athens, pp. 82-89.

Coccossis, H., Collovini, A., Mexa, A. (2002), 'CAMP "Rhodes", Greece', *Coastal Area*

Management Programes: Improving the Implementation. Report and Proceedings of the MAP/PAP/METAP Workshop (Malta, January 17-19, 2002), Priority Actions Programme, Regional Activity Centre (PAP/RAC), Split, pp. 95-108.

Conte, G. (2001), 'Adapting the UNEP Approach to Rimini: a Methodological Proposal', *Proceedings of the International Conference on Sustainable Tourism of Rimini*, 28-30/6/01.

Curtis, S. (1998), 'Visitor Management in Small Historic Cities', *Travel and Tourism Analyst*, No. 3, pp. 75-89.

Dickinson G. (1996), 'Environmental Degradation in the Countryside: Loch Lomond, Scotland' in Priestley G.K., Edwards J.A., Coccossis H. (eds), *Sustainable Tourism? European Experiences*, CAB International, Wallingford, UK, pp. 22-34.

Estrategia Lanzarote en la Biosfera (1998) available at:
www.cabildodelanzarote.com/areas/presidencia/biosfera/biosfera/biosfera.htm

European Commission (EC) (1998), *Facts and Figures on the Europeans on Holiday 1997-1998 - Executive summary*, Brussels European Environmental Agency (EEA) (1999), *Environment in the European Union at the Turn of the Century*, OPOCE, Copenhagen.

European Commission (EC) (1999), *Towards a European Integrated Coastal Zone Management Strategy: General Principles and Policy Options*, Luxembourg.

European Commission (EC) (2000), *Communication from the Commission to the Council and the European Parliament on Integrated Coastal Zone Management: a Strategy for Europe* (COM/2000/547), Brussels.

European Commission (EC) (2002a), *Defining, Measuring and Evaluating Carrying Capacity in European Tourism Destinations. Material for a Document.* Prepared by Coccossis, H., Mexa, A. and Collovini, A., University of the Aegean, Department of Environmental Studies, Laboratory of Environmental Planning, Greece. http://europa.eu.int/comm./environment/iczm/tcca_material.pdf

European Commission (EC) (2002b), *Using Natural and Cultural Heritage for the Development of Sustainable Tourism in Non-Traditional Tourism Destinations* available at:
http://europa.eu.int/comm/enterprise/services/tourism/studies/ecosystems/heritage.htm

European Environmental Agency (EEA) (1995), *Europe's Environment. The Dobris Assessment*, OPOCE, Copenhagen.

European Environmental Agency (EEA) (2001), *Environmental Signals 2001*, OPOCE, Copenhagen.

European Environmental Agency (EEA) (2003), *Europe's Environment: the Third Assessment*, OPOCE, Copenhagen.

Fredman, P. and Heberlein, T. (2003), 'Changes in Skiing and Snowmobiling in Swedish Mountains', *Annals of Tourism Research*, Vol. 30, No. 2, pp. 485-488.

German Federal Agency for Nature Conservation (ed), (1997), *Biodiversity and Tourism. Conflicts on the World's Seacoasts and Strategies for their Solution*, Springer-Verlag, Berlin.

Glasson, J., Godfrey, K., Goodey, B., Absalom, H., Borg, J. van der (1995), *Towards Visitor Impact Management: Visitors Impacts*, Avebury, Aldershot.

Holden A. (1998), 'The Use of Visitor Understanding in Skiing Management and Development Decisions at the Cairngorm Mountains, Scotland', *Tourism Management*. Vol. 19, No 2, pp. 145-152.

Ministry for Development and Greek National Tourism Organization, (2000), *Planning, Actions with Pilot Character for the Development of Ecotourism* (in Greek), prepared by WWF Hellas, Athens.

Oficina de Turisme de l'Estartit, *Medes Islands L'estartit Costa Brava* available at www.ddgi.es/tdm/medes/e1.htm

PAP/RAC (1993), 'Carrying Capacity Assessment of the Central-Eastern Part of the Island Rhodes', Priority Actions Program Regional Activity Centre, Split.

PAP/RAC (1997), *Guidelines for Carrying Capacity Assessment for Tourism in Mediterranean Coastal Areas*, Priority Actions Progamme, Regional Activity Centre, Split.

PAP/RAC (2003), *Guide to Good Practice in Tourism Carrying Capacity Assessment*, Priority Actions Programme, Regional Activity Centre, Split.

Quintè, E. (2001), 'La Capacità di Carico di un'area: Il caso dell'Elba', *Proceedings of the International Conference on Sustainable Tourism of Rimini*, 28-30 June.

Seidenstücker, C. (2000), 'Recreation Management by Zoning on Terschelling, Dutch Wadden Sea', European Union for Coastal Conservation (EUCC), available at www.coastalguide.org/dune/tersche3.html

Société d'Eco-Aménagement (2001), *Sustainable Tourism and Nature 2000. Guideline, initiatives and good practices in Europe*, European Communities, Belgium.

Williams, P.W., (1992), 'Tourism and the Environment: No Place to Hide', *World Leisure and Recreation*, Vol. 34, No. 2, pp. 13-17.

World Tourism Organization (WTO) (2002), *Tourism Highlights 2002*, World Tourism Organisation, Madrid.

World Travel and Tourism Council (WTTC) (2003), *TSA Research Summary and Highlights*, WTTC, Brussels.

Chapter 14

Tourism Carrying Capacity: Future Issues and Policy Considerations

Harry Coccossis and Alexandra Mexa

Benefits and Difficulties in Tourism Carrying Capacity Assessment

Sustainable tourism is at the forefront of contemporary policy agendas and in spite of fuzziness in its interpretation (Coccossis, 1996) there are a few key principles, which are widely accepted. One of these is that tourism growth should be based on carrying capacity in the sense that tourism should be developed in respect to natural resources and ecosystems, community values and lifestyles while ensuring opportunities for social and economic development (EC, 2003). In spite of the wide appeal of the concept at a political level (WTO, 1998; WSSD, 2002) its application has been rather limited in practice (EC, 2002). At this stage it would be interesting to examine some of the policy issues involved in operationalizing tourism carrying capacity assessment into practice, that is, the opportunities and difficulties involved, the types of decisions which have to be made, as well as the risks that could be encountered once a decision is made to proceed with the idea of limiting tourism growth on the basis of carrying capacity.

Tourism carrying capacity assessment entails a challenge for local communities to seek tourism development in an 'acceptable' manner (WTO, 1998 p.172). In that respect tourism carrying capacity provides the opportunity to structure public dialogue about 'desirable' and 'acceptable' change and the role of tourism in this context. In addition tourism carrying capacity assessment provides an integrating framework to examine tourism impacts from multidimensional perspectives thus providing the opportunity to coordinate tourism related policies better. It has a forward-looking perspective, which can help communities and major stakeholders in tourism development to 'envisage' desirable futures. In that sense it can facilitate a process of specifying and structuring goals and objectives. Furthermore tourism carrying capacity assessment can provide a basis for strategic orientation for the tourist product thus assisting destinations to chart feasible options. In a vast increasingly competitive world, tourism carrying capacity assessment may provide an opportunity for upgrading the destination's profile. As a powerful tool at a conceptual level tourism carrying capacity can provide a platform for seeking dialogue and eventually consensus on actions to be taken vis-à-vis tourism development and growth. It can assist tourism managers and entrepreneurs, local and regional administrators, NGOs and the civic society to identify their own roles and ways to incorporate their actions into a broader pattern which could eventually lead to a strategy for tourism. In addition tourism carrying capacity assessment can easily be integrated into a tourism planning process thus facilitating coordination and decision-making.

The above outline some of the advantages offered by employing tourism carrying capacity in tourism planning. However, as already noted, implementation meets with considerable difficulties as well, beyond the methodological issues identified earlier in this volume.

Carrying capacity is about limits but modern societies, in spite of political language and international agreements, are not always comfortable with the idea of limits (Daly, 1999). This is particularly so after a long period of optimism due to technological and organizational innovations which have expanded societal horizons, including leisure and tourism. The imposition of limits may also provoke negative 'feelings' among the key tourism based stakeholders. Furthermore, the requirements for implementing tourism carrying capacity impose a heavy organizational burden on local community structures, which might not have the capacity to face such a challenge. Defining and implementing tourism carrying capacity is information driven and entails an on-going process for collection and storage of data concerning the various components and dimensions of tourism carrying capacity. In addition launching a process of tourism carrying capacity assessment requires the mobilization of stakeholders in a long-term process. A number of communities do not have the capacity or political basis to sustain such a process, resolve conflicts, accommodate various interests and concerns, particularly since some of the key actors might be outside the local system (for example the tour operators). At a destination level often responsibilities are fragmented and shared among a number of actors rendering coordination rather difficult. Furthermore, this might require that communities transcend internal social inertia, which prevents them from developing a 'vision' about their future (and strategic planning). These difficulties are exacerbated in the case of tourist destinations as a result of changes in social structure and cohesion (no permanent population, secondary houses, seasonal employment, and so on). This is often expressed through diverging interests in priorities and futures in the area. Another constraint is also overcoming the perception according to which carrying capacity (imposition of some kind of limits) is an obstacle, even a threat to the 'bonanza' seen in tourism, particularly in contemporary times during which there is a competitive environment and a priority for short-term profits over long-term costs. The imposition of limits may be desirable but also entails the dangers of marginalization of the destination due to competition, unless it is used as part of a broader strategy to upgrade and/or differentiate the tourist product.

Positive Developments and Threats for Tourism Carrying Capacity Assessment

The existence of obstacles does not necessarily imply that applying tourism carrying capacity is an impossibility. Some positive developments may facilitate the implementation of tourism carrying capacity, such as for example broader changes mainly regarding policy (at the European level) in respect to tourism development, environmental protection and management, sustainable development and integration of environmental concerns into specific sectorial policies (discussed earlier in this volume), revival of strategic spatial planning, and so on. Other factors and changes that may give impetus to the application of tourism carrying capacity relate to an expected wider acceptance on the part of modern societies for limits to growth and changes of dominant production and consumption patterns (WSSD, 2002). A number of initiatives towards sustainable tourism and sustainable development confirm such shifts in societal priorities creating various policy platforms for introducing concepts such as tourism carrying capacity assessment. Evidence of this is a proliferation of local and regional strategies which include tourism and adopt such approaches (as for example in the context of the Agenda 21, etc.). Other opportunities are offered by the so-called new policies which are under development for special types of areas such as integrated coastal zone management, rural policy, water framework Directive, and so on which have a spatial dimension and an environmental component favouring the introduction of principles and actions using the logic of tourism carrying capacity assessment, to the extent that tourism is one of the activities considered. Of particular significance are also the initiatives undertaken by various other major actors, such as the private sector, reflecting market tendencies towards the provision of products and services of high quality in accordance with some environmental, ecological and social standards (as for example the tour operators initiative with the support of UNEP, UNESCO and WTO, 2001; WTTC, 1995). These often provide opportunities for businesses to cooperate with others who share the same values, following commonly accepted principles, creating thus *networks* of business with activities, which contribute to fulfilling tourism sustainability goals. In parallel NGOs and various types of institutions (WWF, 2001) focus on raising awareness which contributes to building up a 'culture' of carrying capacity issues by providing guidance to tourists, encouraging them to care for local environmental and cultural resources, to avoid increased consumption of limited resources (for example water resources) and respect local values (culture, customs, and so forth). The rise of new types of tourism (selective types) with an unequivocal preference for environmental quality may also assist the implementation of tourism carrying capacity. The new profile of tourists can have an instrumental role in any attempt to implement limits. Tourists may assume a central role in promoting sustainable tourism development, possibly acting as *'regulators'* in the relationship between the localities and the intermediaries (for example tour operators), in pursuing various goals (economic efficiency versus environmental protection). This may be more effective in the case of new types of tourism, where price is not the only or the most important factor for selecting the final destination (Middleton and Hawkins, 1998). Other developments may further strengthen the tourists' awareness and intermediating role; increased accessibility to information, through the Internet for example, allows tourists to 'interact' with the destinations and proceed directly towards more informed decisions. Tourists may gradually play a central role in implementing or managing limits. Informed and well-educated tourists may also ask for some kinds of limits not only so as to protect their 'satisfaction level' but also for the sake of environmental protection.

Although the application of tourism carrying capacity, encouraged by some broader developments, suggests some benefits for tourist destinations, there are some threats that need to be carefully considered. The possibility of an economic recession remains a major threat for most destinations. On this occasion efforts to upgrade quality of provided services, to secure and enhance quality of environmental and cultural resources can either act in a positive way enhancing a thrust for sustainable development strategies or in a negative way sacrificing long-term perspectives on benefits for the cause of economic stability. Increased competition among the various economic actors (for example tour operators) or the various destinations in an effort to secure and further increase their profits may wipe out some businesses as well as entire destinations. Increased accessibility to information, mainly through the Internet may assist both businesses and destinations to decrease dependence on 'traditional' means (for example promotional campaigns undertaken at a national or regional level) or economic actors. Threats on the implementation of tourism carrying capacity do not only stem from the external environment; ambitious expectations in applying tourism carrying capacity, unrealistic goals and excessive complexity need to be avoided. If the process appears too complex, controversial, often expensive, decision-makers will hesitate to proceed. Political, economic and social realities need to be carefully considered when applying tourism carrying capacity. Within this context realism may suggest proceeding with a flexible, encouraging 'step-by-step' approach instead of full-scale implementation. The incorporation of managing pressing and immediate problems and pressures in tourism carrying capacity assessment may contribute towards this direction. The underestimation of economic aspects may also be a crucial pitfall. Implementing tourism carrying capacity should not be perceived as a threat to economic development but instead as an attempt to secure long term economic stability, possibly increasing profits through a re-orientation of tourism development. Failing to embrace such concerns, failure to incorporate them at an early stage in defining tourism carrying capacity will no doubt inhibit any attempt to implement tourism carrying capacity. Benefits arising from an optimal long-term use of resources and sustainable tourism development may be hard to estimate in quantitative terms, however they need to be as explicit as possible in decision-making.

Future Policy Issues and Research Questions

The above suggest that there are key factors and contexts, which are expected to have significant repercussions in policy-making towards adopting a sustainable tourism strategy within which tourism carrying capacity can have a central role. However they involve important questions which have to be addressed in regard to the political acceptability (or reluctance) and active role (or inertia) of local communities towards their future, the role of key stakeholders, the existence or lack of appropriate mechanisms for concerted action, the effectiveness of policy tools employed, etc. (Simpson, 2001). To some extent they also reflect questions about the values of residents and tourists, their stance on economic development and competitiveness, social equity and environmental conservation, sustainable development, their readiness to comply with restrictions and rules, etc.

Most of these questions though reflect broader uncertainties about society at present and in the future. Coping with uncertainty requires a proactive stance towards policy-making, that is, taking early action in anticipation of change. So should a tourist destination decide to pursue such an approach and use tourism carrying capacity as an integrating concept towards sustainable tourism, there are several steps which can be taken and along each step there are key policy issues to be addressed and some of these are highlighted below:

(A) Initiation: Initiating tourism carrying capacity assessment: what are the bases or driving forces for undertaking tourism carrying capacity assessment?
(B) Definition: Defining goals, expectations for tourism carrying capacity assessment.
(C) Integration: Integrating tourism carrying capacity assessment into broader planning processes and strategies.
(D) Organization: Organizing and structuring tourism carrying capacity process.
(E) Implementation: Implementing tourism carrying capacity assessment, utilizing various tools.

(A) Initiating tourism carrying capacity assessment: What are the bases and driving forces for undertaking tourism carrying capacity assessment?

1. What conditions drive a tourist destination to decide to adopt tourism carrying capacity assessment?

a. Is it the severity of the *problems* encountered? Are mature destinations the ones most likely to adopt such courses of reflection? Do mature, saturated, often heavily degraded resorts (winter resorts, coastal areas and islands) better fulfil some of the preconditions described above (for example political willingness, technological and organizational capacity) and are therefore more capable of undertaking such a task? How easy is it to apply tourism carrying capacity in emerging destinations, where limits and excess of limits are not yet evident?

These questions bring up several policy issues: Is the scope of tourism carrying capacity assessment expected to be different in the case of a mature destination in comparison to an emerging one striving to enter the tourist market? In the first case carrying capacity assessment is expected to serve both *reactive/remedial* and *proactive* needs, while in the latter tourism carrying capacity is expected to adopt a more proactive approach. One of the key policy issues is whether there are *early warning systems* in place that could help tourist destinations to identify the emergence of problems but also assess their underlying causes, the origins and which capacity limits are most relevant or 'convincing' to take action on. Within this context the use of *indicators* can be valuable (Groupe Developpement, 2000).

b.   Is it the *crisis* of the tourist sector or product? Are losers the likely candidates?

Mature destinations, which are also likely to possess the appropriate management means (for example technological, organizational, and so on) may be the ones to undertake the initiative of implementing tourism carrying capacity assessment. In the case where such destinations face fatigue and/or serious degradation the attempt to impose some limits in an effort to upgrade and enrich the tourist product may act as a catalyst to mobilize the local community to safeguard the long-term benefits from tourism development. Within this context *'environmental'* (system-wide) *scanning* will be necessary, as the sustainability of tourism development is subject not only to internal but also external factors. Changes in preferences, oncoming crises of some types of tourist products and activities might erode economic and social prosperity, even threaten environmental quality. Scanning of broader 'environmental' changes would be necessary so as to provide decision makers and managers with the critical information regarding significant changes, trends, and so on. The private sector has assumed this role so far. Nevertheless the public sector needs to incorporate this exploration in its management and planning process so as to minimize risks while maximizing future gains. *Scenarios* can be useful tools towards that direction.

(B) Defining goals, expectations for tourism carrying capacity assessment

2.   What is the policy focus? Increasing competitiveness? How about sustainable development?

Decision-makers and managers need to provide opportunities for economic development and anticipate related impacts for both the short- to medium-term and the long-term future. In doing this they have to secure the equity issue in the sense that the imposition of limits will not result in benefiting only those who went into business at an early stage and at the expense of those who would wish to do so at some point in the future. Imposition of limits needs to take into consideration the principle of distribution of the costs arising from the implementation of tourism carrying capacity but also of the anticipated benefits. Tourism carrying capacity should take into account both future concerns (needs, expectations), of tourists (of future generations as well) and of the local community. These relate not only to the protection of local natural and cultural resources but also of development opportunities but safeguarding the potential (and options) for development for *future generations* as well. *Mechanisms to assure the incorporation of the various interests (present as well as future)* would be necessary. Furthermore a balance needs to be kept between long-term and short-term considerations so as to secure the competitiveness of the tourist product. Efforts to ensure increased competitiveness do not necessarily have to be at the expense of quality either of environmental or of services provided. *Strategic decisions* regarding penetration of new markets (products, tourists, etc.) may secure both competitiveness as well as long-term considerations, evading thus any kind of dilemma.

(C) Integrating tourism carrying capacity assessment into broader planning processes and strategies

3. What is the relationship between tourism planning and destination management? Could the implementation of tourism carrying capacity be easier in certain cases like historic towns which are part of the structure and the functions of broader well-developed systems (urban centres) as it may be easier to assimilate and implement approaches targeted at imposing some kinds of limits, incorporating them into usually more 'mature' planning systems?

Tourism carrying capacity assessment may serve as a bond, linking tourism planning (concerns for future development; broader perspective) with destination management (concerns for pressing, daily problems; focus on specific issues and problems). Caring for the future should not ignore present limits or obstacles and managing critical problems requires input with respect to future decisions, goals, trends, and so on. In this context the role of *visioning* may be critical. However there is a need to overcome and manage methodological and other limitations in visioning. Furthermore the existence or establishment of *integration mechanisms* would be of critical significance. In some cases (for example historic towns, protected areas, etc.) the implementation of tourism carrying capacity assessment may be 'secured' through its better integration into general policy and spatial planning schemes.

4. What are the boundaries of the system? What are the implications of the spatial scale?

Implementing tourism carrying capacity in well-defined systems (for example heritage sites, protected areas) may be relatively easier in comparison to other types of destinations such as coastal and rural areas. However even in these cases a *systemic approach* needs to be adopted as social, economic and ecological processes 'escape' the boundaries of the systems under study. What would be the impacts on neighbouring communities? Do profits from tourism and recreational activities contribute to a balanced regional development or do they encourage polarization, abandonment or concentration, posing threats to the sustainability of other communities or ecosystems (abandonment like overexploitation may also have detrimental effects) by violating their capacity (in this case possibly the *minimum size of activity required*)?

5. Are there 'appropriate' planning frameworks that could facilitate the implementation of tourism carrying capacity assessment?

Taking advantage of approaches such as integrated coastal area management, integrated river basin and coastal area management, and so on in order to integrate capacity concerns regarding tourism development into the development of the broader area could be helpful.

(D) Organizing and structuring the tourism carrying capacity process

6. What is the driving 'actor' or 'force' for undertaking tourism carrying capacity? Are there key stakeholders? Are mature (northern or developed) societies more ready to capture the trend?

As already discussed there are several reasons that may encourage the implementation of tourism carrying capacity. 'Mature' societies (in terms of institutions, organizational and technological capacity) are probably more ready to implement tourism carrying capacity assessment (due to instituted public participation; new types of governance and decision-making, need to 'officially' accommodate market concerns which assume a leading role not only in tourism development but also in environmental protection, and so on). In such case adopting tourism carrying capacity may require a longer, far more (resource) demanding process but it certainly leads to more effective and sustainable – in the literary sense – implementation, as it provides a solid basis (consensus achieved among stakeholders) for future action. One of the key policy issues remains the establishment of *appropriate mechanisms so as to incorporate market concerns into management of tourism destinations as well as to secure shared responsibility* among all stakeholders (including tourists).

7. What is, or what may be the *political focus* in implementing tourism carrying capacity? Is it significant and necessary?

Some limits may be hard to be implemented or less preferable, rendering political decisions difficult. Within this context *communicative issues* may be of particular concern. The *symbolic* character of tourism carrying capacity (similitude to other fundamental concepts such as sustainable development) and its potential in mobilizing society for action should not be neglected.

(E) Implementing tourism carrying capacity assessment, utilizing various tools

8. Should limits be strict vs. flexible in the search for acceptability? What may be the implications of perceiving tourism carrying capacity assessment as a static (inhibiting) vs. a dynamic (enabling) concept?

The acceptance of limits as tourism growth constraints is tightly interrelated to enforcement capabilities which depend on organizational and legal or institutional enabling conditions. The operational and symbolic values of carrying capacity should be considered. However the imposition of limits that are easily 'adapted' (and frequently revised) may provoke confusion, encourage mistrust, and so on. A balanced and cautious approach should be followed. A clear and transparent process of *reviewing tourism carrying capacity* needs to be established at an early stage (design of a programme for defining and implementing tourism carrying capacity).

9. What is the basis for limits? Are there critical factors? How about if there is no evidence on constraints? What is the role of weaknesses and threats in visioning? How convincing can a tourism product re-orientation be to adopt carrying capacity assessment?

In cases of scarcity (land, water, energy, and so forth) the acceptance of carrying capacity assessment is in relative terms easier than in many instances where tangible limits are not evident. In some cases the perception of limits might be an adequate condition to mobilize a tourist destination to pursue tourism carrying capacity assessment and act on the basis of that, limiting tourism growth or re-orienting the tourist product. It is not only limits which can assume such a role but eventually weaknesses or threats in an analysis of existing and future developments in key factors. Tourism carrying capacity can serve as a platform for developing 'visions' for tourism in that respect. In addition, a similar role can be seen in the options considered, in the sense that carrying capacity can offer a platform (or framework) for a definition of alternative new tourist products.

10. Hard limits vs. technological and organizational solutions

The existence of both approaches has been discussed extensively in a previous chapter of this volume. However, organizational and technological innovation is at the basis of modern living and influences decisions with an aura of 'magic solutions' to present future problems. Therefore such approaches are likely to continue to have an appeal for modern society vis-à-vis imposing limits on human activities. Tourism carrying capacity assessment can incorporate such solutions but it is questionable whether it can rely only on this type of interventions, particularly if tourism is considered in a context of sustainable development. In that respect policy and research can focus on the *integration of tools* (serving hard and soft approaches to visitor and development management). As systems change, tourists adapt to some kinds of limits, it would be appropriate to re-examine not only the limits themselves but also the practices and tools applied for that purpose. *Reviewing* the effectiveness of applied tools would be necessary.

...As a Final Note

The above discussion highlights some of the difficulties and issues encountered in policy and research agendas when adopting tourism carrying capacity. It is certain that as a concept tourism carrying capacity assessment is powerful and can be used to mobilize tourist destinations to review the course of development pursued and attempt to steer it towards desirable patterns. There are still many questions which arise when one moves from concept to action. These relate to the conditions of success, that is, the capacity of modern societies to cope with complex problems, the openness to a dialogue about goals and values, the existence of mechanisms to assess conditions and anticipate the future problems, the capacity for visioning, to identify desirable futures, the ability to chart courses of action towards desirable ends. All this is about change and mechanisms to cope with change. No single concept exists which can satisfy all the necessary conditions to succeed in such a task: coping with the future of tourism and its impacts. The future is not necessarily predictable and modern societies are still far from devising effective ways to plan for sustainable tourism. What is essential is to develop mechanisms to monitor and evaluate change in order to take early action. To that end tourism carrying capacity can be a tool which might prove useful. There is probably no better way to proceed.

References

Coccossis, H. (1996), 'Tourism and Sustainability: Perspectives and Implications', in Priestley, G., Edwards, A. and Coccossis, H. (eds.), *Sustainable Tourism? European Experiences*, CAB International, Wallingford, pp. 1-21.

Daly, H.E. (1999), *Ecological Economics and the Ecology of Economics: Essays in Criticism*, Edward Elgar, Northampton, Mass.

European Commission (EC) (2002), *Defining, Measuring and Evaluating Carrying Capacity in European Tourism Destinations. Material for a Document*. Prepared by Coccossis H., Mexa A. and Collovini A., University of the Aegean, Department of Environmental Studies, Laboratory of Environmental Planning, Greece. http://europa.eu.int/comm./environment/iczm/tcca_material.pdf

European Commission (EC) (2003), *Basic Orientations for the Sustainability of European Tourism*, Consultation Document CEC Brussels.

Groupe Developpement (2000), *Checklist for Tourist Projects Based on Indicators of Sustainable Development*, Groupe Developpement.

Middleton, V. and Hawkins, R. (1998), *Sustainable Tourism: a Marketing Perspective*, Butterworth, Oxford.

Simpson, K. (2001), 'Strategic Planning and Community Involvement as Contributors to Sustainable Tourism Development', *Current Issues in Tourism*, 4(1), pp. 3-41.

UNEP-UNESCO and World Tourism Organization (WTO) (2001), *Tour Operators Initiative for Sustainable Tourist Development*, UNEP, Paris.

World Summit for Sustainable Development (WSSD) (2002), *The Johannesburg Plan of Implementation*, Johannesburg.

World Tourism Organization (WTO) (1998), *Guide for Local Authorities on Developing Sustainable Tourism*, WTO, Madrid.

World Travel and Tourism Council (WTTC) (1995), *Agenda 21 for the Travel and Tourism Industry: Towards Environmentally Sustainable Development*, WTTC-WTO-Earth Council, London.

World Wildlife Fund (WWF) (2001), *Holiday Footprinting: A Practical Tool for Responsible Tourism*, WWF-UK Godalming, Surrey, UK.

Place Index

Subject Index